POWER THROUGH PEOPLE AND PRINCIPLES

not Puppets and Prejudices

POWER THROUGH PEOPLE AND PRINCIPLES
not Puppets and Prejudices

VIPEN KAPUR

McGRAW-HILL BOOK CO
Singapore   Malaysia   Thailand   Korea
Taiwan   Hong Kong   Philippines   Indonesia
New York   Auckland   Bogotá   Caracas   Lisbon   London
Madrid   Mexico   Milan   Montreal   New Delhi   Paris
San Juan   San Francisco   St. Louis   Sydney   Toronto

McGraw-Hill

A Division of The McGraw-Hill Companies

POWER THROUGH PEOPLE AND PRINCIPLES
not Puppet and Prejudices

2 3 4 5 6 7 8 9 0 TOM UPE 2 0 9 9

When ordering this title, use ISBN 0-07-116443-X

Printed in Malaysia

FOREWORD 1

We are living in a world of change, of rapid change. Changes are accompanied by economic and political upwings, downwings, disruptions and crises. Changes with a speed which is even higher than it has been. The speed is caused by technological progress, especially by improved telecommunication and traffic opportunities.

Companies are linked to local customers and suppliers via global networks. Here people are needed who can work through regional and cultural differences, people who are able to enjoy cross-cultural fertilization of ideas, values and management style. This is what this book is about. It is real fun to read this book, to reflect the ideas and to practice the results. I have met Vipen Kapur in the course of many meetings, and I know this book is based on deeply reflected personal experiences.

Of atmost importance is that leaders are capable of leading international teams. Leadership is based on an indepth understanding of values and principles for motivating and guiding people.

Power, people and principles or eagle/dove/owl is seen by me as a sum of experiences lived through in an international environment.

I have known Vipen Kapur as somebody who lived upto these principles and contributed to solving problems based on his broad global experience and exposure.

I trust that this very open book, which is based on and describes broad international and local Indonesian experience, will contribute to a better understanding of doing a business globally.

This is a really enjoyable book which puts together the pieces of the puzzle on balanced life and leadership. The way the message is sent makes it worth reading – it is so illustrative as it is based on personal experiences.

Dr. Ulrich Lehner
Executive Vice President & CFO
And CEO Designate
Henkel KGaA
Düsseldorf
Germany

FOREWORD 2

I must admit that I was somewhat surprised at Vipen's initiative to write a book about power, because he is all but a man craving for power. On the other hand, I must congratulate him for the initiative and for the way in which he has analyzed the notions of power, including ethical power.

I am not a man attracted by power myself, at least not in the traditional sense of the word. As mentioned in the chapter on Charisma, how many charismatic leaders become their own worst enemies because they become obsessed by power not as a means, but as an objective. My personal remedy is simply not to take myself too seriously, but stay committed to worthwhile goals.

I also share Vipen's belief that people are our main assets, particularly in the retailing business. Therefore, I agree with his recommendation to dedicate more top management attention (not just rely on the Human Resource Department) to develop talent, and create the environment and provide the means, which allow employees to develop themselves to the upper limits of their capabilities! I also enjoyed the wit which he has sprinkled along with serious issues.

I hope that readers will have lots of fun as they discover the wisdon that Vipen wishes to share, based on an exciting career covering various jobs in several countries.

Luc E. VANDEVELDE
President/COO
Groupe Promodés
Paris

DEDICATION

- To my wonderful parents, grandparents and a special uncle and aunt, who tried to give me good values, and for their prayers.

- To the late K. Kuruvila Jacob, my revered headmaster, for showing that you can't have true leadership without character.

- To my darling wife, Kuko, my inspiring partner in life and sounding board since 1970. It was her encouragement that made me start this project in the first place.

- To my mother-in-law, whose patience and quiet courage are worth emulating.

- To various family members, friends and colleagues, young and old, who gave me additional insight in human relations and who believe in progress through clean methods and fair play.

- To our children, Ratika and Arjun, for their love and for making us proud, and our loving son-in-law, Viren for making us feel so special.

- To sincere politicians, an endangered species, who genuinely serve the people.

[I consider all of the above 'stakeholders' in such a book.]

- And finally, to Life, the ultimate teacher.

ACKNOWLEDGEMENTS

As mentioned in the Dedications and Introduction, I would never have written this book if it had not been for Kuko repeatedly telling me, "you must write". My reply would be "you are the teacher, the principal... you should be the one writing books". Kuko would counter my defense by saying, "but you have the flair!" Finally, when I took the plunge, Kuko played her part in carefully reading chapter after chapter, night after night, correcting typos, but more importantly, debating the issues. More than anything else, she would frequently say, "that was well written" or "that's a nice idea" or "keep it up, my love". All I can say is "thank you my love; thank you my 'Rani', for your spirited and spiritual backing throughout.

Our daughter, Ratika, has an excellent command of the English language. I used to send her the manuscripts in Hongkong. Her corrections and suggestions were invaluable. But, what I enjoyed even more was her challenging some of my thoughts. This was not only stimulating, but helped me in improving clarity and context. "Thank you my darling, for your loving support, here also."

I owe much gratitude to the Widjayas of Sinar Mas for their trust and support. I especially wish to thank my good friends and colleagues – Gus Nilo, Teddy Pawitra, and Sukrisno Njoto for their very useful comments on important issues. A big thanks is also due to Ken Gibson of McKinsey who took great pains to review the manuscript and make very meaningful suggestions.

I also wish to sincerely thank the following world-class companies for permitting me to present and discuss their corporate values and philosophies: Henkel, Promodés, Toyota, Singapore Technologies,

Matsushita and Acer. Their cooperation has enabled me to give real examples on these important issues.

I have to express my special gratigude to Mr. Shiv Nadar, Chairman & CEO of HCL and NIIT for sharing his views and personal experiences, which add value to this book.

I am also deeply indebted to Mr. Luc Vandevelde – President of Promodés, Dr. Ulrich Lehner – EVP & CFO of Henkel, Mr. Sat Pal Khattar and Mr. Victor Frank for diligently reading the book and making encouraging comments thereon.

Two young, bright and attractive ladies have really sweated it out for me. My cheerful secretaries, Linda Tanos and Yunni Gunawan, managed to squeeze sufficient time between their daily routines to type the manuscript. They coped very well with my subsequent fastidious corrections and frequent 'touch-ups'. They know that I cannot type to save my life. "Thank you, Linda and Yunni for your outstanding work and dedication. I sincerely hope that you see me less as a task-master and more as a mentor."

The list of acknowledgements is actually endless. However, I had better stop before this becomes a "Book of Acknowledgements"!

INTRODUCTION

"Experience is the mother of wisdom"

(Proverb)

With a short prayer, soft music and these very words, I have commenced a journey - - - a journey to express my thoughts, apprehensions, recommendations on the human side of business, based on reading books by acknowledged authorities on the subject, attending seminars and conferences, and especially through personal experiences.

Ever since I put together a collection of my poems and short stories into a book in 1996, my wife has encouraged me to write another book. Frankly, I did not have the courage to embark on such an ambitious project. I did not think I had it in me. During a weekend in August 1998, I was working on a seminar on 'People and Leadership'. As I was preparing my notes and 'bullet points' for the transparencies, I suddenly heard that inner voice: "if I write down my thoughts and ideas in detail and in chapter form, I could well end up writing a book!!" I actually froze for a few seconds at this thought. I asked, "what if I fail?" The inner voice said, "nothing ventured, nothing gained. Moreover, the skeleton (presentation format) for the seminar would cover about half the topics for a book anyway, and this would make the task lighter ". Thereafter, I began to write an average of three pages per day - - - and *voila!* Here's the book.

MAIN OBJECTIVE / MESSAGE

In the traditional sense, power has been viewed as military might, political power, totalitarianism, economic wealth. Occasionally, people talk of power in terms of span of control and technological capability.

On the other hand, there are quite a few people who have gained tremendous influence, which translates into unselfish power. Shining examples would be Lord Krishna, Moses, Jesus Christ, the Buddha, Prophet Mohammed; and in our century, Mahatma Gandhi, Mother Teresa, Master Cheng Yen in Taiwan, Nelson Mandela.

The book has been divided into four parts relating to power in different settings and to cover my impressions and feelings of various aspects of life, with special attention to corporate life. In my mind, this book is something like a general guide on corporate values, integrity and living a balanced life, with respect for nature and genuine concern for the less fortunate.

I have tried to convey my messages with anecdotes, historic examples, punctuated with verses and humour. This is, perhaps, a way of distinguishing my book from other books on similar issues.

Lessons I have learnt, consciously and unconsciously, through observations and experiences at the office and home will dominate this book. The reason is simple - I am not an academist or a psychologist or a consultant - I am a regular practicing manager and family man, aspiring to enhance my leadership qualities. I consider myself a permanent student of management and leadership. I have used anecdotes, some of which are autobiographical, to illustrate the thoughts and concepts that I am trying to convey. In some cases, I have been able to research and reactivate the 'dusty', 'mental archives' buried in nooks and corners inside my middle-aged cranium. Many of the ideas 'dawned' on me, when I was half-awake in bed, just before sunrise. Also, several interesting concepts 'seeped' into my 'gray-matter', after sunset and after work, while I (a typical 'Aquarian water baby') was swimming my habitual laps in the serene waters of the beautiful pool at the Grand Hyatt, Jakarta.

I believe that I enjoy people. Through bed-time stories (wherein good triumphs over evil) related by my parents and elders, history books and inspirational anecdotes by my high school principal, my little brain soaked up sufficient ideals. I began to admire great heroes and the achievements of the human spirit, especially if accompanied by humility and compassion. At the same time, I started developing a soft corner for the underdog and the under-privileged. These feelings were reinforced as I began to appreciate a little more of the deeper meanings of some holy scriptures, including the ancient but still relevant Bhagvad Gita, which conveys the essence of the even more ancient Vedas and Upanishads. Deepak Chopra has done a fine job in conveying these spiritual lessons for modern living.

Among the great pundits and writers who have opened my mind and inspired me include Swami Vivekananda, Peter Drucker, Stephen Covey, Spencer Johnson and Kenneth Blanchard.

The great practitioner Jack Welch is unquestionably a wonderful model to follow. Also, the subtle Tao Te Ching principles, so skillfully interpreted by James Autry and Stephen Mitchell, have greatly contributed towards giving me deeper insight, clarifying my thoughts and improving my approach to people and business.

I am grateful for having so many illustrious Gurus - who don't even know that I exist! (at least so far). If you find that some of the concepts are repeated in certain chapters, it is because of the unavoidable linkage between PEOPLE, PRINCIPLES, POWER, LEADERSHIP and STRATEGY. Some repetition also helps to drive home a point. On the other hand, if you feel that you are adequately familiar with a particular aspect, and that reading it again becomes boring, or a chapter seems too long, please don't yawn - - - just skip to the next paragraph or page.

My privileged association with the Widjaja family that controls Sinar Mas Group of Indonesia has been a tremendous eye-opener in understanding what makes pioneering entrepreneurs 'tick'. The

Widjaja's have some fine businesses and a great vision. My close interaction with all of them, especially with Teguh and Franky, in developing and implementing the **'Reaching the Sky'** management innovation programme has been a highly stimulating, educational and rewarding experience. This exposure was enriched, thanks to our inducting the services of McKinsey & Co., which brought in some truly top-match consultants, led by Carel Paauwe, and subsequently Ken Gibson, both first-class professionals with fine values. Our combined job has been to make Sinar Mas a modern, high performance company with an 'Olympic culture'. This entire process of change management, with all its ups and downs, has improved my understanding of management and people, as we tried to convert theory into practice.

In writing about people, power and principles, there must be at least a few references to historic leaders who deserve to be admired, emulated and remembered. However, I see no need for 'blindly' hero-worshipping our heroes, because this leads to personality cults, and the consequent 'I am infallible' syndrome, that eventually backfires and destroys the hitherto great hero.

We are all 'sinners' or potential sinners when allured by 'enticing' temptations. The main purpose of this book is to honour great people in various fields and to learn from them. While there are examples of a couple of 'villains', we should realize that no man is wholly bad. Let us learn from their mistakes, as we should do from our own.

This book is not addressed to any one specific type of person. In fact, I truly hope that it will attain a wide readership including managers, bankers, academics, entrepreneurs, union leaders, bureaucrats, military officers, politicians and young people who aspire towards leadership in any of these careers. Please feel free to read these chapters in any order, depending on your own priorities and 'moods' from time to time!

When a man has remained married to the same woman for twenty-eight years, and she has been a school teacher during all this time, at least a few of his thoughts or approaches would be influenced by her. I am proud to mention that her 'flavour' is present in parts of this book, although not necessarily in a conscious way.

I look forward to suggestions, criticisms or contrary thoughts that will improve my own learning, and help me write a better second edition or sequel. (That seems quite fashionable!).

It is not very easy to write on human relations and principles. On the other hand, it is far more difficult to put these 'ideals' into practice. I am bound to err from time to time, and I must remain open to sincere, constructive criticism to bring me back in line.

This is intended to be a book on serious subjects with serious intentions. However, I hope that my readers would agree that the content or the style of writing does not have to be serious all the time. Humour is welcome - - - as long as the joke's not on me! (just kidding!). I am a great fan of **Art Buckwald**, whose witty and insightful stories have added 'colour' to quality newspapers, including the International Herald Tribune. Additionally, I feel that I might be making another exception or aberration, by sprinkling, for 'better or *verse*', a few of my **poems** to, hopefully, add a little more meaning and fragrance to this anthology.

I hope that my readers feel good after reading this book. I genuinely believe that there are a lot of good people in this world and plenty of goodwill for us to tap. There does however, seem to be a global shortage of leadership - - - but there is hope.

"*Spell Bound*":
I apologize to readers educated in British style spelling for using some American spellings. Similar apologies are due to readers educated in the American system, for my British spellings. Perhaps, my expressions are also affected by both nations. I worked for many

years in both British and American Banks, and enjoyed both. Therefore, I am still under the **spell of divided loyalty** and drifting <u>literally</u> in the Atlantic Ocean on latitude 38° W, or mid-way between USA and its former colonizer and presently great ally. Please, therefore, accept the Anglo-American accent or flavour/flavor of this nomadic Indian. I know that you'll both be tolerant. Right Limies?! Right Yankees?!

Table of Contents

PART C ~ BUSINESS MINUS PEOPLE = ZERO

PART D ~ WHISPERS IN MY HEART

ഌ഼ **PART A** ഒഅ

CORPORATE
CULTURE & VALUES

CORPORATE CULTURE & VALUES

SYNOPSIS

1 Corporate Culture:

This chapter sheds light on the culture of colonial British banks in India and the dramatic change that has taken place in them since 1970. The appendage talks about the importance of culture compatibility, especially in the case of mergers & acquisitions.

2 Corporate Values and Philosophy:

Discussion on the Sinar Mas motto of 5 Qs&Ps - Quality People, Quality Principles, Quality Planning, Quality Products and Quality Profits, which I developed. I also talk about balancing corporate life and personal life. I have then summarized corporate values/principles of famous companies. These beautiful declarations should not be confined to glossy brochures or to decorate walls of corporate offices and hallways.

3 Importance of Stakeholders:

The importance of balancing stakeholder needs, even though they are often conflicting. The successful CEO is one who can 'walk the tight rope', keeping an eye on short-term issues, including cash flows, and building a great company with longevity.

4 Change ... and Coping with Change:

Emphasizes that change is unavoidable, and is in fact, necessary to progress. A few examples of successful change agents and the pitfalls of refusing to change. Includes a short tongue-in-cheek verse on the omnipresent lap-top computer.

5 Culture Change in a Family Controlled Asian Group:

Highlighting my personal experience as a Group Managing Director of Sinar Mas Group, a leading conglomerate in Indonesia with operations in various parts of Asia. How the first attempt at broad culture change failed, and how the second attempt has been more successful because of stronger commitment of the shareholders and better preparation. Appendage explains how Sinar Mas developed MBOS – Management by Olympic System and Olympic Club. The next appendage talks about SMG's "green gold mines", i.e. oil palm plantations and forestry operations.

6 "Psst, I heard on the grapevine that...":

This mentions the reality of the informal organization and importance of building the institution through good leadership and communication, whereby there is little difference between the formal organization and the grapevine.

1

CORPORATE CULTURE

"Men do more things through habit than through reason"
(Proverb)

Corporate culture is generally defined as a blend of values, beliefs, mind-set, policies and work styles which people in a particular corporation follow quite consistently in their day-to-day job performance. This culture identifies them and also acts as a binding factor. It also reflects how this group of people will capitalize on opportunities and face threats to their business. Using a more casual expression, corporate culture is how people in an organization *tick* and what makes them *tick*.

My first immersion in corporate culture began on December 1, 1966, when I started my first job as a Management Trainee in **Grindlays Bank** in Madras. I was still short of my 21st birthday, very much a 'greenhorn'. During the selection process, I was interviewed by about ten executives, mostly British, who still held almost all the top positions. They were all congenial and asked questions on economics, politics and commercial topics. However, the interviewers' main probing was on family background, schooling, character/personality issues, etc. At that time, I was surprised that my final examination grades were not of that much concern to them.

It was many years later, that I realized, that while the Bank wanted at least average college grades, the primary issue was whether the candidate would fit into and flourish in 'Grindlays culture'.

I remember that within a few days of my starting work, my Branch Manager, a polished and kind Englishman, named John Boase, invited me to his home for 'supper'. I had the pleasure of meeting his charming wife, Molly and delightful daughter, Carol who was visiting from London during the Christmas holidays. They all made me feel most welcome. By candlelight, I ate English style roast duck for the first time. It tasted good but since the bird was a little tough, the hostess announced, "you may lay down your forks and knives and use your fingers". At the end of the dinner, the gracious host said, "shall we adjourn to the drawing room for some coffee and sherry, it's too warm for cognac". All in all, this evening was a most pleasant and memorable one for the aspiring young banker. I was made to feel wanted and quite important.

By the way, Carol was then working for one of London's most prestigious hospitals. When I asked Carol if she had looked after any V.I.Ps, she half shyly and half *Boasetingly* replied, "Just a couple of months ago I gave Marlon Brando an enema! - - - what an handsome man." I wonder if Marlon remembers her tender loving care in 1996.

After the first phase of training in India the 'successful' trainees were sent to London for a year of Head Office training and exposure. Again, I realized much later that we were being immersed further in the bank's culture and we got 'soaked' in quite a nice way.

An interesting and controversial policy in the old Grindlays was that the young officer (all male officer cadre in those days) had to complete about three years with the bank before he could be given 'permission' to marry. Furthermore, the young hopeful was required to submit an application to Head Office, giving a résumé of his intended bride and her family for 'approval'. 'Respectability' was the issue. (Today this rule will be deemed a violation of human rights! It was put to rest around 1975). Most applications were approved; but a couple of my colleagues had to go through the indignity of waiting while Head Office asked the concerned Branch Managers to make additional inquiries on the in-laws-to-be, before giving its blessings. After 'due process', when the newly married couple returned after their honeymoon, the Manager's wife would host a nice 'coffee party' to introduce the latest Grindlays bride to the rest of the hens and make her feel welcome into the Grindlays family. About the period 1963-65, a young Scotsman, named Bill Crawford, working for the **Chartered Bank** (now Standard Chartered) fell in love with a young lady named Deepak Singh, who was half English and half Sikh (Punjabi). When he informed Chartered Bank of his intention to marry her, he was given an abrupt and legalistic warning, somewhat on the following lines – if you marry her, we divorce you! Bill broke his charter with Chartered Bank, and as a happily married man, carried the 'standard' of Bank of America, before too long.

Also, in those days all officers ate lunch together, which regularly exposed the trainees to senior officers. This was an informal setting for the 'Burra (big) Sahibs' to chat with the 'Chhota (small) Sahibs'. These interactions promoted some bonding and also gave the seniors the opportunity to assess the potential of the youngsters even away from the work place. Conversations covered banking topics, politics, golf, cricket, and of course the prevailing weather 'back home'. Today, we may call all this 'casual mentoring'.

Next to the officers' dining room, was a relaxing lounge which included a billiard table, which was popular with young and old. The Bank also had golfing, rowing and swimming teams in some cities. All these were opportunities to build a sense of belonging and _esprit de corps_.

Bachelors shared 'chummeries' (large apartments) which also served as good platforms for bonding. Suffice to say that those walls have great stories to tell of the extra-curricular or chummy activities!

The colorful Grindlays culture had its roots in India since the 1850s and it evolved and spread in neighbouring colonial territories and East Africa. This cohesive way of life remained more or less the same for over a century. Another sign of the old orientation was that the 'house magazine' of Grindlays was first called **'Monsoon'**, while that of Chartered Bank was **'Curry & Rice'**.

In mid 1967, I was transferred from Madras to Bombay, for the second leg of my training. Around December that year, our Regional Manager, Ronny Rees announced that our Chairman Lord Aldington (at that time also Chairman of the Tory Party, in Opposition at that time, and probably an early mentor of Margaret Thatcher) would be arriving in about two weeks to visit the Indian branches and top government and Reserve Bank officials. Also, there would be a formal 'black-tie' cocktail reception. So we had sufficient 'notice' to buy (or borrow) tuxedos. I spent almost a whole month's salary to get a tailor-made vicuña suit and my uncle taught me how to tie a bow-tie. I discovered that actually tying a bow-tie (not the clip-on version) is far from easy. Until then, we did not have to learn that art, in our *'neck* of the woods'!

I felt very honoured and inspired when Mr. Rees introduced me to his Lordship and said a few nice words about my performance and potential. "Jolly good and keep it up!", were the words that escape the 'stiff upper-lip' of this 'pucca' gentleman.

Then, around 1971, something quite unheard of and dramatic happened - Citibank bought 49% of Grindlays and took management control. A few Americans were seconded to Grindlays, and MBO - Management by Objectives was introduced. Suddenly, management functions were split basically into 'Credit & Marketing' and 'Operations'. All officers were given specific targets called Key Result Areas. There was tremendous chaos and uncertainty for a period. Some of the traditional style officers could no longer hide behind woolly performance measures or rely on relationships or family background alone. Due credit must to be given to old timers who did their best to learn new skills and adapt to the new work style paradigm. Many of them flourished in the new environment. Meanwhile, most of the youngsters foresaw better career prospects thereafter and were enthusiastic.

I should also acknowledge and commend the excellent leadership and communication that helped to bring about the culture change relatively smoothly and quickly. There was pain but the gain began to emerge within a comparatively short period of two or three years. Grindlays was the first of the colonial banks to make a successful culture change. It stole a clear lead over its peers. It became a more competitive and streamlined institution but also retained some good traditions on the human side. Additionally, I felt that Grindlays had also become a **learning organization**, of which I was a beneficiary.

One thing is clear, Grindlays, like some of the banks with colonial foundations, had a distinct culture. The strengths of the culture was its human orientation and customer relationships. The weaknesses, perhaps, were a bit of the old hierarchical boss attitudes; conformity - rather than creativity; mainly time scale career progression, and a lack of competitive spirit. These areas improved with the introduction of Management by Objectives, in the 1970s.

One sign of the changes in Grindlays' colonial culture was I never wore that beautiful tuxedo again in the tropics.

I left Grindlays in 1976, in response to an attractive offer from Bank of America. However, I still have a great affinity for my old Grindlays friends, with whom I worked as far back as twenty two years ago, thanks to that collegiate culture that continues to bind us.

Message:

The main point is that every entity has some sort of culture that cannot be ignored, regardless of its imperfections. A newcomer should be able to willingly adopt the organization's culture. If you don't like it, stay out or wait patiently if you see signals that a meaningful culture change has been initiated.

Conversely, an organization should be able to mold or even change its culture when the business scene changes - - - or get left behind. Real leaders are astute and open-minded, and they take the initiative. It is up to the leaders to promote (not force) a culture, whereby people have pride of association, look forward to coming to work, and can enjoy the spirit and rewards of superior performance.

Notes:
(i)   Grindlays is now part of ANZ Banking Group.
(ii) ANZ, through Grindlays, bought a great franchise in India. Another major asset gained by ANZ was a pool of well trained bankers, some of whom were elevated to senior positions at ANZ's Headquarters in Melbourne and overseas.
(iii) Chartered Bank subsequently merged with Standard Bank (strong in West and Southern Africa, with HQs in London) to form Standard Chartered Bank (SCB). The tremendous culture change in SCB is reflected in its appointing, in 1998, Rana Talwar – an Indian - as CEO. Talwar, an alumnus of Citibank, was recognized for leading Citibank's highly successful consumer banking business in Asia.

I now wish to add a sub-chapter on possible clash of corporate cultures and the importance of pre-empting such a painful problem.

Appendage

AVOIDING 'CULTURE CLASH'

It is important to recognize the cultural difference even between apparently similar or related businesses.

Note the difference between the mentality of a construction team vis-à-vis a property management team. The constructor's focus is on completing the project on time and within budget, handing it over to the client, and moving on to the next construction site. On the other side of the coin, is the property manager's frame of mind. His job is to maintain the property well and provide superior service to the occupants, on a sustained basis. He even looks different and speaks at variance, compared to his construction counterpart. There is no great synergy to be attained by merging their businesses. On the contrary, culture problems will come in the way, especially if a hasty merger is consummated, for short-term gains.

Now, let us look at a commercial bank and an investment bank. Both are in related financial services and both carry the word bank. However, we generally recognize that the commercial banker will be the more conservative type, with focus on risk reduction and long term relationship building with his customer. Bulk of his income is in the form of salary. The investment banker, on the other hand, is the consummate deal maker, underwriting share or bond issues, arranging mergers and acquisitions, promoting the 'D-word' - derivatives, etc. This person's main compensation comes from his share in the commission from the transaction which he helped consummate. He then moves to the next opportunity. Therefore, we can see that there are two different types of mind-sets, accompanied by dissimilar behavior. The commercial banker's working hours are relatively more predictable (it does not mean that he is less hard working). His investment counterpart travels a great deal - - - from deal to deal (boy, I'm dealing out puns!), including on weekends, to please his clients and meet tight deadlines. Therefore, great thought should be given to culture before considering a merger between the two types of institutions.

Finally, let's compare a well-established pharmaceutical company with a medical biotechnology firm. Both deal in 'medicine', one way or another, and are concerned with therapy, cures and health. However, the pharmaceutical corporation will focus mainly on production, marketing, brand building, distribution of its drugs, vitamins, etc., with secondary focus on new products in the pipeline. This type of company is already profitable, paying steady dividends and has multinational orientation. Meanwhile, the typical biotech firm is an upstart, with relatively low amount of high-risk capital, full of PhDs who spend hour upon hour, day upon day - - - year upon year, peeking through microscopes at their favorite microbes and cultures, and tinkering with test tubes, burners, shakers, etc. In fact, their culture is to play with cultures. (I seem to have got stuck in the pun culture). These scientists work painstakingly and patiently for what I may call the 'presto effect' or the magic of discovery, or isolation of a deadly 'bug', or creation of a new radical cure. Profit is not an immediate concern to them. Also, while these scientists may be from various countries, they are inwardly focused, and the firm does not (need to) have an international presence. It is therefore, plain to see that these two types of 'medical' firms have to have very different cultures. After discovery or invention, the bio-tech company will seek patents and laborious FDA approvals. It is clear that profits are a long way off in this business. The pharmaceutical firm could become a good customer of the biotech counterpart. They could even have a long term supply contract. The pharmaceutical company generally has deep pockets and could even provide some venture capital during the 'delicate' years. In other words, these companies could synergize through a kind of strategic alliance. However, a full merger could end up with negative synergy because of the big divergence of corporate culture.

A fairly recent example is the initially much touted merger plan between two very successful companies - American Home Products (AHP) and Monsanto. This merger was valued at over $ 30 billion.

AHP is a solid pharmaceutical and consumer products company. Meanwhile, Monsanto is re-inventing itself from a traditional chemical producer into a high-tech life sciences company, focusing on genomics and related sciences to develop high yield, high nutrition, pest resistant crops etc. Monsanto's own culture is undergoing a dramatic change. This new culture will make it even more different from that of AHP. Therefore, cultural integration could have become a big problem, or they might not achieve the desired 'chemical reaction'. It is just at well that this merger was called off in October, 1998. While it is not very pleasant to cancel a highly publicized merger proposal, we know that it is far better to abort an engagement (just return the ring) than to break up a marriage, in this case, involving many thousands of 'family members'.

2

CORPORATE VALUES AND PHILOSOPHY

"He that will enter into (corporate) Paradise
must have a gold key"
(Proverb)

One evening in 1994 my young but highly capable and enthusiastic boss, Franky Widjaja and I were talking about the need to improve the attitudes of our people. Franky expressed frustration that a significant proportion of our employees, including executives, were at an 'average' level of motivation. Important performance reports were quite frequently late or inaccurate. They also lacked proper variance analysis and/or proposed corrective action to improve performance. I suggested that we hold a few workshops explaining the vital importance of **MIS as a vital management tool** rather than a mere information gathering exercise. As a result of various deliberations between shareholders and executives, Sinar Mas Group is presently in an advanced stage of implementing SAP/R3 Enterprise Systems in two of its largest divisions.

I also offered to conduct seminars on **Teamwork** and **Leadership.** Franky thought that it was a good idea and suggested that I talk to his eldest brother, Teguh and obtain his support to cover all senior executives in the group. Teguh, who is always on the look out for such stimulation, readily approved the proposal and I held a few seminars in the hill resort of Puncak. The seminars were very successful, thanks to the excellent support of two HR professionals - Sharukh Marfatia and Gautam Chakrabarty.

The same night after Franky and I had that chat, I began to think a bit more seriously about **quality** as a way of life in Sinar Mas. I reminded myself to look at all our **stakeholders** to develop our values and then encapsulate them in a 'quality' based motto that is catchy and easy to remember. I then decided to 'sleep over it'. (I get some of my best ideas when I am slightly awake between 3a.m. and 5a.m.). Around that time I began to focus on people and quality and suddenly my mind went back to my childhood when we were taught our **'Ps 'n' Qs'**. Just as the sun was rising, the motto of **Qs&Ps** 'dawned' (ouch, pun again) on me. I scribbled the ideas on a scrap of paper, lest I did not remember them on awaking later. When I finally woke up that morning, I felt very inspired and quickly refined the thoughts which are reproduced below:

SINAR MAS MOTTO
6 Qs & Ps

QUALITY
PEOPLE

QUALITY

QUALITY
PROFITS

QUALITY
PRINCIPLES

PARTNERSHIP

QUALITY
PRODUCTS

QUALITY
PLANNING

I felt very honoured when all shareholders approved the motto. I subsequently designed the plaque which is now prominently displayed at our offices and factories. Shortly thereafter, I was requested by

Franky to develop a Handbook which would explain the motto and our corporate values and philosophy. The highlights are shown below:

1. **QUALITY PEOPLE**
   - We mean attracting and retaining **high calibre people** at all levels. We shall give our people adequate induction and ongoing re-inforcement/immersion to cultivate the new Sinar Mas Culture.
   - We have people from at least 15 nationalities representing diverse races, religions and cultures. We are **proud of this diversity** and treat it as a strength.
   - We shall provide them progressive **training** and **development,** backed by good **career planning** and **competitive incentive oriented remuneration**.
   - We place special emphasis on **team-work** because the ultimate success of an organization is based on channeling individual skills and contributions in a cooperative spirit towards the common **Corporate Goal**.
   - Senior Managers must display real leadership and serve as **top-class role models**.
   - We shall emphasise that **professionalism is not complete without integrity**.

2. **QUALITY PRINCIPLES**
   - We continually want to be an institution that flourishes on the foundations of **high values** and **fair play** - as an employer, as a partner, as a borrower, as a buyer, as a seller and as a responsible corporate citizen.
   - Since some of our businesses have direct environmental impact, we must ensure that we use **eco-friendly** practices, consistently.
   - We want to be viewed as one of the **ideal employers** that rewards hard-work, efficiency, creativity and professionalism. We shall strive to build **trust** and **credibility** both internally and externally.
   - We shall endeavour to create an environment whereby people look forward to their work day and **enjoy productive camaraderie**. We want our people to have **fun at work**.

- People as humans deserve **respect** and have a basic right of dignity, regardless of seniority. Moreover, we shall **celebrate the human spirit.**
- People should be able to disagree with respect and without fear of reprisal. Sinar Mas people should be able to **walk arm-in-arm even when they do not see eye-to-eye.**
- Our shareholders are willing to treat our top performing officers as **partners.**
- Such principles would naturally win the **loyalty** of our employees and the **respect** of the institutions we do business with.

3.   QUALITY PLANNING
- This covers the full spectrum of planning both for **short-term** and **long-term goals.**
- We would optimize the use of our **manpower, machines, materials** and **money.**
- We shall expand and create **strategic alliances** with other leading industrial and financial institutions in order to update our skills and technologies and to grow in important international markets.
- We shall maintain a proper **balance** between **profitability** and **risk.**
- Our **organization structure** must be effective and flexible to address the demands of changing times to facilitate free flow of communication, leading to better **staff morale** and **decision making.**

4.   QUALITY PRODUCTS
- The **customer** is the real reason for our existence and we must never lose sight of this fact in our deliberations and actions.
- We shall deploy highly trained and motivated teams using state-of-the-art techniques, processes and systems to produce top quality products, at lower cost, to **gain market share** and **improve margins.**

- We shall enhance our **market research** and **product development** to meet changing life-styles and demands in the market place.
- For us, **international competitiveness** is a key watchword and **customer satisfaction** a major aim.
- Since **speed** of decisions and **time-to-market** have become even more crucial, there should be a sense of urgency in all our activities.

5. QUALITY PROFITS

- Having done a quality job in the critical areas of PEOPLE, PLANNING, PRINCIPLES and PRODUCTS we would be rewarded with QUALITY PROFITS.
- Profits shall be allocated in the following manner:
  (i) Promptly re-paying loans & interest to financial institutions that support us
  (ii) Building reserves to strengthen our financial condition and for expansion
  (iii) Compensating our shareholders who entrust us with their money
  (iv) Rewarding deserving employees who achieve high corporate goals
  (These allocations were specially proposed by the Chairman - Pak Eka).

6. QUALITY PARTNERSHIP

It is our goal that the above Qs&Ps will result in the ultimate QP, which is the highly coveted **Quality Partnership** between owners and employees. (This idea came later from APP's Core V-Team)

The handbook was very well received (and a second edition will be printed shortly). I even held several workshops to explain the concepts and to implement them. At first, Franky and I thought that things were going well and were disappointed to discover a little later that while nobody disagreed with the values in the Handbook, implementation was slow and superficial. The bosses were still not practicing what we were trying to preach.

We then realized that two critical ingredients were missing:

- The shareholders and top executives, including myself, 'hoped' that since the Handbook had been 'blessed', distributed and explained, that it would begin to change our corporate culture and work style. In other words, the bosses were busy with expansion projects in several countries and did not find the necessity or time to constantly <u>push</u> to realize the new spirit and concepts.

- We wanted to change values and behaviour. However, we realized only later that our performance evaluation and reward system had not simultaneously changed to introduce any formal incentive which would encourage our people to adopt the new mind-set, approach and work style. It was after this realization that we went about the change process in a holistic way. This process and experience is described in the chapter titled 'Culture Change in an Asian Family Owned Group'.

Being a catalyst and very much involved in this culture change process, I am gratified that our 'second push' is making good progress. The enthusiasm and commitment of our people is improving. On the other hand, I feel that while corporate life or career or profession are vital aspects of our lives, we have to remind ourselves that these are not the only reasons why God put us on this planet. There has to be something more to life than just 'livelihood'.

CORPORATE LIFE VERSUS PERSONAL & FAMILY LIFE

Modern corporate life with its material rewards has increased stress all around. Ingenious inventions like laptops, mobile phones and E-mail have made people more productive. But, because of these very 'conveniences', people have less relaxation, less family time, less renewal time and more tension. Stress related diseases are rising and so are the cases of unhappy family lives and broken-homes, which again compound stress levels.

Long work days and work loaded week-ends have affected the mental and physical health of knowledge workers, and divorce rates have shot-up, at least in part due to over-ambitious or over-worked people not spending even 'quality time' with their spouses. They get carried away by prospects of bonuses and promotions. The husband says, "honey, I promise that after I finish this high visibility project in twelve months, I can spend more time with you." But after one year, another exciting project comes up with great financial incentives. The poor guy again gets 'trapped' by ambition and money. The rat-race continues with its impact on health, family and other relationships.

Moreover, this intense pressure leaves little time for spiritual up-lift or personal renewal, or 'sharpening the saw', in the words of Stephen Covey. If we keep on using the same saw without finding time to sharpen it, we would be left with a blunt, ineffective saw. It is also important to remember that tired people become irritable and their thinking becomes cloudy. All these factors, which focus only on short-term or narrow objectives, will eventually hurt corporate performance.

How to achieve balance? How to earn the promotion and bonus without 'killing' or at least undermining other important aspects of life? Does life only mean money and power?

Employers can at least do a few things to mitigate the problem. Some corporations encourage physical and mental fitness by providing or sponsoring health club memberships, even yoga/meditation classes. (This aspect is covered in the chapter titled 'Personal Health and Fitness'.)

Furthermore, top bosses should encourage more of 'work smarter rather than harder' ethic.

I have also written a chapter titled 'Success & Morality' to emphasize the need to listen to our conscience when we take decisions and actions.

At this stage, it is helpful to reflect on the corporate values of leading institutions who have made conscious changes to cope with the needs and challenges of today and tomorrow, including Henkel, Toyota, Singapore Technologies, Promodés, and Matsushita.

HENKEL'S VALUES *(formalized in 1995)*

Germany's Henkel is one of the world's largest and most successful chemical companies with a history of over a hundred years. Here, I am summarizing Henkel's major values and principles under two groups - (i) Teamwork & Leadership and (ii) Principles.

TEAMWORK AND LEADERSHIP:

1. **Cooperating in mutual trust**
   Trust is essential for successful and personally satisfying teamwork. Trust is based upon all Henkel people observing rules of conduct.
2. **Making decisions where competence lies**
   Decisions should be made by those empowered to do so, with necessary competence and awareness of consequences.
3. **Working and managing towards results**
   Managers and their staff formulate challenging goals as teams. Each individual must understand how best to achieve these goals. A regular dialogue between the players focuses on the contributions made by individuals and teams and their value for Henkel.
4. **Assessing performance conscientiously**
   The performance of all employees, including leadership where relevant, must be conscientiously assessed. Individuals learn about their strengths and where they need to improve. Superior performance will receive appreciation. Managers should in turn be prepared to be assessed by their staff.
5. **Communicating frankly**
   Open communication breaks down potential barriers between people. If things need to be addressed, no one should hesitate to do so immediately.

6. **Actively share and not withhold information**

   Sharing of information is critical to performance. Information must be shared appropriately and quickly. Sharing information also improves learning.

7. **Addressing emotions as well as arguments in conflicting situations**

   Conflicts may arise because of opposing interests, opinions, prejudices or emotions. It is important to address causes of such conflicts clearly to facilitate pragmatic solutions.

8. **Making use of diversity of opinions, arguments and different cultures**

   The diversity of ideas, emotions and perceptions amongst employees presents a valuable opportunity to avoid one-sided, over-simplified solutions. There should be an open mind-set for new approaches.

9. **Commitment to new ideas**

   New ideas, improved solutions to problems, including the speed of implementation, are pre-conditions to succeed against growing competition. Employees have to take this challenge with courage. Mistakes must be addressed openly to improve learning.

10. **Giving assignments/opportunities on merit**

    To succeed against competition, Henkel must assign tasks to employees with the highest capabilities. This also ensures equal opportunities for all employees.

11. **Practicing partnership**

    Successful interaction within the group is based on the spirit of partnership. In internal working relationships, everybody should be treated as a customer who expects the best service.

12. **Commitment to Leadership**

    Managers have a special responsibility to provide vision and values, as well as to direct the processes of target definition and active leadership. Employees, in turn, are entitled to seek guidance and assistance from their managers. Leadership means setting an example.

Principles:
1. Henkel is the Specialist in Applied Chemistry
2. Henkel is customer and market-oriented in all fields
3. Henkel utilizes its worldwide market potential
4. Henkel's market success is based on innovation
5. Henkel wants to attract the most competent people
6. Henkel is the ecological leader in the chemical industry
7. Henkel respects the social values and standards of the countries where we operate
8. Henkel's structure enables rapid response to change
9. Henkel makes all decisions with the goal of assuring the long-term continuity of the Company
10. Henkel preserves the tradition of an open family company

Comments:

People familiar with the traditional way in which German companies have been run will find the new Henkel style most refreshing, and it is bound to affect its compatriots. In 1996, Franky, Jo Liat Tjiang (Head of SMG's Strategic Ventures) and I had the privilege of meeting the top management of Henkel in Düsseldorf and learning about its technical and managerial innovations. We were most impressed and inspired by the way in which the above mentioned ideals were being implemented in this unique company.

TOYOTA
Toyota 2005 Vision – Harmonious Growth

Recognizing the scale of responsibility and degree of influence commensurate with being one of the world's top automakers, Toyota will seek harmony and balance in pursuit of our twin goals: 'Realization of Harmony with Society' and 'Enhancement of Management Foundations'.

Under the universal theme 'Harmonious Growth', which is to be shared by everyone, Toyota's personnel are expected to act on the local level, think globally and disregard bias when evaluating the views of their counterparts, wherever they happen to be.

Realization of Harmony

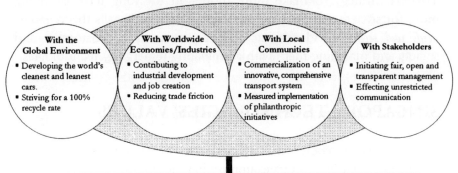

With the
Global Environment
- Developing the world's cleanest and leanest cars.
- Striving for a 100% recycle rate

With Worldwide
Economies/Industries
- Contributing to industrial development and job creation
- Reducing trade friction

With Local
Communities
- Commercialization of an innovative, comprehensive transport system
- Measured implementation of philanthropic initiatives

With Stakeholders
- Initiating fair, open and transparent management
- Effecting unrestricted communication

HARMONIOUS GROWTH

- Respond in timely fashion to the universal desire for safe, convenient transportation.
- Nurture new-generation business – alongside the manufacture of automobiles – aiming at providing society as a whole with a palette of diversified amenities.
- Maintain a degree of corporate growth that will ensure Toyota remains capable of consistently creating new standards of value and contributing to society.

Global Stabilization
of Sales Volume

Effective Use of
Management Resources

Assure of
Appropriate Profit

Enhancement of Management Foundations

Comments:
Team Toyota deserves to be saluted not only for world class cars at competitive prices, but also for its great business philosophy and business practices, which are well ahead of most other Japanese corporations. What is highly appealing in the case of Toyota is the special effort to create a happy balance (harmony) between conflicting goals and stakeholder needs. Toyota's culture seeks to give great importance to people and society from the widest possible prospective. Toyota is also willing to sacrifice some short-term profits

in developing cars that are not only safer for their occupants, but also cars that are safer for the environment. It is on the forefront of developing some of the world's 'cleanest' cars. All this is part of Toyota's strategy to make more money in the long term by doing more for society and the environment. Toyota aptly calls this *combining needs and seeds* i.e., identifying new requirements of customers and society and matching them with germinating (emerging) technologies.

SINGAPORE TECHNOLOGIES' VALUES

Singapore Technologies (ST) is one of the largest and most successful groups in Singapore. Let us examine what 'drives' this company.

VISION
To be a technology-based multinational conglomerate, headquartered in Singapore, contributing to the development of Singapore and the world through successful enterprise.

TO SEEK, TO STRIVE, TO EXCEL
This sums up our philosophy, our commitment and our expectations of ourselves and our businesses. We endeavor to play a positive role in bringing value to our business, our ventures, our customers and our fellow men through successful enterprise.

We Seek
To offer superior products and services
To delight our customers
To build our people
To stand by our reputation

We Strive
To deliver value to our customers
To build long term partnerships
To maintain outstanding operations
To achieve the highest standards of quality
To achieve superior performance

We Excel
Through fostering a strong ST spirit
Through maintaining a professional culture
Through caring for our people and our society
Through creating a successful future together

VALUES
Values are beliefs we consider important. These beliefs will influence our thoughts, decisions, judgments and actions. Values are the 'software' in us that will drive our thinking process and determine our approach and actions.
- Integrity
- Value Creation
- Courage
- Commitment
- Compassion

Comments:
Readers would note several compelling items in ST's philosophy and values. I highlight those that really appeal to me:
- ST people have high expectations of themselves.
- They give great importance to integrity.
- They recognize the value of courage – the courage to pursue their vision and stand by their beliefs.
- They have a strong human bias. This company values and practices compassion in its treatment of people. There is an inspiring story of how an employee with leukemia won tremendous support of ST and its people. They even found a matching bone marrow donor to save his life. Moreover, during this difficult two-year period, his job was retained for him. ST has a heart, and I salute it.
- Overall, I really like the way ST believes that its values are the 'software' which makes it 'tick'.

PROMODÉS' CORPORATE VALUES

QUALITY
The customer   =   The ultimate judge of our performance
                         Expects a professional approach

EFFICIENCY
Competence + action

ADAPTABILITY
Openness + innovation + flexibility

INITIATIVE
Capacity for action + responsibility

RESPECT
Appreciation of the individual + mutual understanding

Comments:
This global retailing giant, headquartered in Paris, is a great competitor
that is customer-focused. It deems consumers the ultimate judge of its
performance. It also gives strong weightage to respecting people,
while demanding flexibility and initiative.

Promodés has opened three very popular hypermarkets in Jakarta, in
a joint venture with Sinar Mas.

MATSUSHITA'S PHILOSOHPY

"Each one has his own path to follow. No one knows where it will
lead, or if it will easy or difficult. At times it may be wide; at others
narrow. Now it is smooth, now rocky. Even so we have no choice but
to continue. It is the only path open to us."

■ From *THE PATH*, by Konosuke Matsushita
(Founder)

BASIC MANAGEMENT OBJECTIVE

"Recognizing our responsibilities as industrialists, we will devote ourselves to the progress and development of society and the well-being of people through our business activities, thereby enhancing the quality of life throughout the world."

THE COMPANY CREED

"Progress and development can be realized only through the combined efforts and cooperation of each employee of our company. United in spirit, we pledge to perform our corporate duties with dedication, diligence, and integrity."

SEVEN PRINCIPLES

1. **Contribution to Society**

   We will conduct ourselves at all times in accordance with the Basic Management Objective, faithfully fulfilling our responsibilities as industrialists in our community in which we operate.

2. **Fairness and Honesty**

   We will be fair and honest in all our business dealings and in our personal conduct. No matter how talented or knowledgeable we may be, without personal integrity we can neither earn the respect of others nor enhance our own self-respect.

3. **Cooperation and Team Spirit**

   We will pool our abilities to accomplish the goals that we share. No matter how much skilled we are, without cooperation and team spirit we will be a company in name only.

4. **Untiring Effort for Improvement**

   We will constantly strive to improve our ability to contribute to society through our business activities. Only through such untiring effort can we fulfill our Basic Management Objective and help to realize lasting peace and prosperity.

5. **Courtesy and Humility**

   We will be cordial and modest, always respecting the rights and needs of others in order to strengthen healthy social relationships and improve the quality of life in our community.

6. **Adaptability**

   We will continually adapt our thinking and behaviour to meet the
   ever-changing conditions around us, taking care to always act in
   harmony with nature in order to ensure progress and success in
   our endeavours.

7. **Gratitude**

   We will act out of a sense of gratitude for all the benefits we have
   received, confident that this attitude will be a source of boundless
   joy and vitality, enabling us to overcome any obstacles that we
   encounter.

Comments:

Up to the early 1950s, Matsushita was dwarfed by the likes of Hitachi
and Toshiba in consumer electronics. During the advent of the
Television era, while Hitachi and Toshiba concentrated their selling
efforts on selling TVs in the glitzy department stores in affluent parts
of Tokyo, Matsushita's sales force performed house-to-house sales
calls in the villages and captured huge market share. After this success
Matsushita has never looked back. Since the 1970s, its brands like
'Panasonic' and 'National' are popular throughout the world, and
ahead of Toshiba and Hitachi in several products.

Matsushita is not resting on its laurels. It realizes that it has to succeed
in a highly competitive globalized industry, with a high rate of
obsolescence and changing tastes. Its management realizes that
respect cannot be earned without good corporate citizenship, fair play
and humility, both internally and externally. Its culture emphasizes
that skills without team spirit are not meaningful. It nurtures an
environment for continuous innovation – technical and managerial –
and the need for harmony and adaptability, particularly in the fast
changing times. A rarely stated principle is having a feeling of
gratitude, job satisfaction and joy that raises people's confidence and
strength to accept and overcome greater challenges.

ACER CULTURE

A FRESH PERSPECTIVE
Acer, as a world-renowned high-tech conglomerate, has always emphasized the importance of applying a 'fresh perspective' to every situation it encounters. We believe that 'fresh' is better than 'new'. 'New' technology, for example, connotes unproven, untested and expensive, whereas 'fresh' technology and products will offer the best value.

ACER CULTURE, A SUSTAINABLE CULTURE
Acer corporate culture rests on four major pillars:
- Human nature is basically good
- Customer is No. 1
- Put knowledge to work for the company
- Be pragmatic and accountable

HUMAN NATURE IS BASICALLY GOOD
When Acer started-up 23 years ago, four young founders cultivated a unique set of corporate culture guidelines that have distinguished it among its global competitors. They aimed to create an efficient work environment through mutual respect and trust. Besides not having to clock in, Acer employees are encouraged to freely express their opinions, take risks, and most importantly, learn from their mistakes. The company viewed any costs incurred from an employee's inexperience as 'paying tuition'.

To date, Acer employees are still proud to continue the tradition of 'integrity, open-mindedness, partnership and ownership' that has been passed down from the company founders. With firm faith in the goodness of human nature, Acer has created and delivered many human-centric benefits to its staff.

CUSTOMER IS NO. 1
All Acer operations follow the successful 'Acer 1-2-3' business philosophy: customers are first priority, employees second and

shareholders third. The logic is that if customers are satisfied, it follows that employee and shareholder satisfaction will be met as well.

Acer is committed to providing the 'freshest technology' to be enjoyed by everyone, everywhere. The company believes that the benefits of high tech does not lie in laboratory breakthroughs, rather, in how much it can improve the quality of our lives. If technology fails to achieve that, it is meaningless.

PUT KNOWLEDGE TO WORK FOR THE COMPANY

Through proper empowerment in the workplace, employees are strongly encouraged to and rewarded for developing skills and 'know-how' that help sustain Acer's long-term business growth. As the company motto goes, Acer employees will always 'tackle difficulties, break through bottlenecks and create new opportunities that bring real value'. Acer's intangible assets such as intellectual property will be turned into tangible rewards and managed to foster the corporate strength.

Acer has the tradition of 'si-fu' (means 'teacher' in Chinese), a respectful title given to senior employees who are obliged to pass on the know-how and experiences they have accumulated along their career path to the next generation.

Acer employees, at the same time are encouraged to maintain an entrepreneurial spirit so that they can be entrusted with responsibilities and make business decisions in a sensible way, with minimal supervision.

BE PRAGMATIC AND ACCOUNTABLE

'Down-to-earth' is an important quality in the personality of Acer employees. As the IT industry is highly competitive, Acer emphasizes the importance of conducting business like a relay-marathon race. In any business process, each employee plays an important role in doing the right things right the first time, and passing on the baton to the next employee who will be picking up the responsibility and adding his/her contribution (value) in the business/production process, and so on.

Everyone is encouraged to calculate risks and avoid taking the risks that the company cannot afford. Flexibility is extremely important when running a business. Acer believes it is more important to keep the business alive than save face.

COMMON INTEREST AND COMMON GOALS

Acer has been linking employees' interest with the company's future. Since the company's introduction of the employee stock ownership program and employee intrepreneurship (means employees start up a new business operation internally within the organization and be the head of that operation), it has successfully encouraged its staff to work aggressively towards the common goal and vision of providing fresh technology to be enjoyed by everyone, everywhere.

Stan Shih, chairman and CEO of The Acer Group states, "In a perpetually changing IT industry, what principles can Acer count on? First, we take care of all stakeholders; second, we continuously improve and create value".

Comments:

It is not surprising that Stan Shih is one of the most respected 'new-wave' business leaders in Asia. He and his co-founders have built Acer Group on solid principles like shared vision; human beings are basically good and trust begets trust; empowerment with incentives helps develop entrepreneurship. Practising such values helps lift an organisation to a state of effective 'self-governance', mentioned in chapter 12 on How to 'Control' People. Acer's 'fresh' and value based approach is also re-freshing. All these are ingredients of a success formula.

CONCLUSION:

In all these cases – Henkel, Toyota, Singapore Technologies, Promodés, Matsushita, Acer and Sinar Mas – there are lots of well meaning expressions. However, they will remain just words in corporate literature or on corporate walls if they do not enter and remain in our **heads** (mind-set and goals) and **hearts** (feeling and passion), and affect our **hands** (work and behaviour). This begs the need for real leadership to embrace and implement these important and positive concepts. Like the others, Sinar Mas is also working very hard to make it all happen.

Shiv Nadar, the founder-supremo of HCL and NIIT, two of India's leading information technology companies, says that many large companies had their days in the sun so long as they stuck to their values and implemented them honestly. Whenever these values were diluted the companies hit rough patches.

3

IMPORTANCE OF STAKEHOLDERS

"Goodness in not tied to greatness,
but greatness to goodness"
(Proverb)

An enterprise, during all times of its existence, has to endeavour to meet certain needs, demands and expectations of various segments of society, often referred to as stakeholders. Some of their needs are explicit while others are implied.

Hereunder, I have tried to make a general list of stakeholders and their respective needs.

STAKEHOLDERS	NEEDS/EXPECTATIONS
Customers/consumers	Quality products, quality service convenience, competitive price
Employees, career-seekers	Association, development, progress, reward, appreciation, respect
Suppliers of raw materials, components, services, consultants, etc.	Reliable long-term customers, fair profit
Technical collaborators, joint venture partners	Reliable partnerships, new markets, new technologies, new brands
Government, society	Taxes, law and order, healthy environment, building human capital
Investors/shareholders	Superior returns with low risk

Business history tells us that strategies which do not respect the key stakeholders and their expectations will meet with:
- limited success, or
- short-term success, or
- failure

It is important to remember all the time that these stakeholders are **all people** one way or other – people who are consumers and workers, and people who represent organizations/institutions, which in turn are owned by people. Why I am emphasizing this point is because we often see corporations and legal entities as 'faceless' or 'non-human' structures and systems. But they are all owned and run by people to serve people.

It is not too difficult to prepare such a list of stakeholders and their demands, and present it in fancy corporate brochures. The great challenge for us is to recognize that the stakeholders have different, and often conflicting needs. After this recognition, we have to organize our priorities, principles, structures, systems and energies to actually **serve these stakeholders in a balanced way**.

I believe that strategy should start with the customer, because the customer is the very reason of our existence. Every effort must be made to please the client, and even exceed expectations, in certain cases. This has to be balanced with the stockholders' desire for superior returns on equity. A few years ago, Daimler-Benz had difficulty in selling its Mercedes cars because they were 'over-engineered' and many customers felt that they were over-priced. Daimler-Benz had to re-work their production processes to meet the quality expectation of the market and at the same time control costs.

A frequent temptation for executives in the mining, chemical and similar industries is to 'save' money on pollution control, and thereby give a nice return to shareholders, and to 'earn' fat personal bonuses. The Union Carbide tragedy in Bhopal, India is a startling example. Yes, for a couple of years higher profits were reported because initial subtle warning signs at the insecticide plant were 'ignored' and the corrective action and related expenses were postponed. When the highly poisonous gas leaked to set off the world's worst chemical disaster, the company put up alibis and strong defenses against claims on behalf of thousands of people, who were killed or permanently injured. This lack of attention to the stakeholders in the form of (i) the government, which prescribes safety rules and standards and (ii) the community, which needs safe and peaceful living, were violated. Result: Union Carbide's plant was shut down (probably) permanently – no more income; its reputation as a reliable and environmentally conscious company was severely damaged; its top managers' energies were spent in fighting lawsuits; it had to pay huge compensations and its share price tanked and stayed low for quite a long time.

I have written about employees' needs as stakeholders in various chapters and, therefore, this aspect need not be repeated here.

Many companies in developing countries create, with a lot of fanfare, joint ventures with leading international companies to get access to technology, solid brands or even to find new markets. Some of these companies really treat their foreign partners with respect and fairness and the relationship flourishes for mutual benefit. However, it was disappointing to observe that a few local companies (e.g. including, but not limited to Saudi Arabia and Indonesia, where I observed this) have a strategy to indiscriminately blame the foreign partner for anything and everything that goes wrong for the joint venture. Even worse can happen when the joint venture is doing well and generating good profits, and where the locals have learnt the techniques, and the outlook remains bright. Here, the locals use 'tactics' to make the foreign partner and its seconded staff 'uncomfortable', in the hope of buying out the foreign share at a discount. In some instances, the local company 'high-jacks' key seconded personnel, as it gets rid of the partner. Such people are obviously not giving balanced treatment between the stakeholder in the form of the local stakeholder (owner) vis-à-vis the stakeholder in person of the foreign partner, who has a right to fair treatment and long-terms gains, based on contributions.

On the other hand, there are cases where the foreign partner does not fulfill its part of the bargain. We have cases when obsolete technology or machines are supplied by the foreign partner. In other instances, the foreign party supplies raw-materials or components at inflated prices to the joint venture. There are also situations wherein the foreign party buys the joint venture's products at unfairly low prices to boost its own profits. Again, we have conflict because of unfair and unbalanced treatment meted out to different stakeholders.

Also, some corporations treat their suppliers in a very shabby way, as if suppliers belong to a 'lower caste' of corporate society. Sometimes, the big company acts as if it is the sole reason for the survival of the supplier. The attitude of the Purchasing Manager is to 'squeeze' the supplier as far and as much as possible by reducing prices and/or delaying payment unreasonably. Here again, one stakeholder's interest has been undermined. This strategy may succeed for a while. Eventually, this supplier will build other reliable outlets and will have no loyalty to this difficult buyer. Moreover, these suppliers start 'padding' their prices in order to negotiate artificial discounts with the difficult customer. Sometimes, product quality can also suffer to the detriment of the buyer when the buyer wants unreasonable discounts. Furthermore, the supplier may increase prices for habitual slow paymasters to compensate for the interest cost on such receivables/dues. Last but not least, in times of shortages this supplier will direct more products to the customers who treats him consistently well.

On the other hand, it is gratifying to see that several enlightened companies treat their suppliers like 'partners' or stakeholders. They work out long-term contracts with reliable suppliers, to mutual advantage. This customer gets the right quality products or raw materials, in the right quantities, at the right times and at a fair price (not necessarily the lowest price). The supplier gets the satisfaction of having a solid, 'captive' customer, who helps him with constructive feedback on quality etc., gives him a fair margin, and pays him on time. Examples of such best practice companies are WalMart,

Unilever, Colgate-Palmolive, Shell. They and their suppliers have benefited from such long-term associations based on fair play and trust. Such stakeholder trust has progressed into joint R&D work, between the customer and supplier in several cases.

It should be noted that there is a common thread running through many of these stakeholder situations. There is a universal need for being balanced, fair and ethical, not acting against one's conscience. In other words, long term success, *inter-alia*, flies on the wings of fair play and business ethics, as is discussed in the chapter titled "Success and Morality".

No person or institution can be perfect, but we can, at our own levels or fields, endeavour to be 'least imperfect', reaching as closely as possible, that state of personal or corporate **'ANANDA'** or higher joy.

❦❦❦❦❦

On a personal note, three of our most important stakeholders have reached the twilight of their lives – my ultra-special parents and very wonderful mother-in-law. As mentioned elsewhere in this book, while my wife and I were 'born under a wandering star', we hope that our next and 'final tent' will be pitched in the environs of Delhi where most of our 'personal stakeholders' reside. We have proposed - - - and may God dispose, accordingly.

4

CHANGE . . . AND COPING WITH CHANGE

"The only constant is change"
Heraclitus, Greek Philosopher, 6ᵗʰ Century B.C.

Every time I read or make the above statement I am struck by its profundity. I simply marvel at Heraclitus, one of the great founders of western thought, who could have such tremendous perspective and foresight even in the days when people thought that the earth was flat or square, or that it was the sun that revolved around the earth!

On the other hand, recall the lyrics of the popular Billy Joel song, "Just the Way You Are", which says, "Don't go changing, to try to please me....".

I don't really see a big contradiction in both these messages. We simply need to recognize the areas where we need to change. We must retain our basic values like fair play, integrity, respect for human dignity and the like. But where we need to adapt or change, we should do it on a timely basis, winning the understanding and commitment of the vast majority of our people at all levels of the organization.

At this stage, I wish to talk about a few changes of historic proportions that have taken place before our very eyes. We have to realize that we are in the **age of discontinuity**. Things considered almost impossible or most unlikely only 50 years ago have happened.

Chairman Mao despised all things American and called Americans and their allies capitalist and imperialist running dogs. Then Henry Kissinger found the 'window' through **'ping pong diplomacy'** and the course of history changed remarkably.

The **Cold War** was 'heating up' for a long time. Then, within a very short time (in historic terms) the Cold War was over – in our life time. Now the world seems to have just one 'policeman'. While the risk of a 'global' war has receded, there are new risks as a result of the weakening of Russia. It is no secret that the Russian military is demoralized and that there are huge arrears in salary payments. There is real fear of nuclear technology and materials being illegally sold to rogue countries. Governments have to cope with the changed situation of new opportunities coupled with new risks. There will be more investment opportunities and joint ventures from the 'peace dividend' in certain countries previously considered off-limits. At the same time, governments will have to cooperate to prevent smuggling and proliferation of dangerous goods (not just drugs). Meanwhile, defense contractors have to change their strategies.

Many defense industries are consolidating (e.g. Lockheed-Martin) and building alliances. Again, some will adapt 'military technology' for civilian uses. Examples: GE and Rolls Royce jet engines for power systems; composite materials to make lighter and stronger cars; microwave applications for wireless telecommunications and in the domestic kitchen.

Germany was the feared and despised enemy of the World Wars and had destroyed so much of Europe. Today, this nation is at the forefront of a united Europe. Germany is holding hands with France, its enemy until 1945, to lead the change for a single currency – **EURO**. These erstwhile bitter European rivals are uniting and cooperating in an unprecedented way with their neighbours to reduce in-equalities. The implications for Europe and the world are simply enormous. Things are, after teething troubles, going to be simplified by not having to deal in 15 odd currencies. Banks and moneychangers will lose 'FX' income that came from changing moneys of countries now coming within the EURO AREA or EUROLAND. The all-important US Dollar will also lose some of its importance in that region. Yet, the new system may simplify things and encourage more investment from America.

Taking an example from Asia, Soeharto ruled over Indonesians like an undisputed depot for 32 years. Then in May 1998, within a tiny span of a few months, he had to quit in disgrace.

These are just a few of examples of dramatic and 'quick' changes and their impact on governments, societies and corporations. Those who can foresee the change, or at least adapt quickly to the trend, will be better armed to cope with the discontinuity of the status quo.

Sometimes, a person or a group becomes the agent of change in a pro-active sense. Here, we have to commend various NGO's – Amnesty International, Greenpeace etc. on how they have worked relentlessly and against heavy odds to bring about awareness and change. Governments and institutions that learnt from such volunteer groups and changed their ways, have benefited. The slow or short-sighted or arrogant corporations have lost prestige and shareholder value until they corrected the situation. Examples – Exxon Valdez; Shells' old oil platform in the North Sea; France's (old) barbaric attack on the protest ship 'Rainbow Warrior' near the nuclear test site in the South Pacific.

I now wish to focus again on the corporate world where I have had personal experience. (Another detailed chapter is devoted to culture change in a specific corporation.) Some ambitious CEOs are in such a rush to push for change. An otherwise excellent vision attains limited success because sufficient time and effort was not spent to explain the dream and make it a shared vision. A critical success factor is re-training people to match the new work style, technology, etc.

I have a playful little verse for you on how lap-tops may change the scene in some executive suites. First, I apologize in advance to the ladies who may feel somewhat offended. Ladies, please give me some charity in the form of your indulgence and smiles.

LAP-TOP

> The lap-top is a great invention;
> It's handy during work or vacation.
> But some will admit with hesitation:
> They miss good old lap-dictation!

Whichever way we look at it, change affects people – people with feelings, apprehensions and aspirations. It is the critical challenge of the top managers of the organization to pool their creative and communication skills, involve people from all levels in evolving and creating the vision. By all means, the top brass or generals should articulate the big dream, but let the capable majors and lieutenants and sergeants give their inputs to come up with a vision that belongs to vast majority. A real shared vision can achieve corporate miracles. History has taught us that a solid rallying point, with good leadership, has helped smaller and lesser-equipped armies (Davids) defeat otherwise superior forces (Goliaths). We are seeing several such cases in the corporate world in recent years.

5

CULTURE CHANGE IN A FAMILY CONTROLLED ASIAN GROUP

"He that looks not before, finds himself behind."

(Proverb)

Since 1993, I have been working as Group Managing Director at the Corporate Office of Sinar Mas Group (SMG) which is headquartered in Jakarta.

The founder and Chairman of SMG is Mr. Eka Tjipta Widjaja whose family migrated to Indonesia from China about 70 years ago when he was just a boy. Even before he was 12 years old, young Eka acted as a house-to-house salesman for his father's little provision store. Pak Eka, as he is affectionately known, started his first formal business in copra and coconut oil trading over fifty years ago.

During this initial phase he was hit by World War II related problems and recession, which was further compounded by Indonesia's violent struggle for Independence. The young entrepreneur went virtually bankrupt twice and sold many personal and family assets to fully honor his debts/dues. It was this display of integrity that won him the trust of the business community and banks. They were subsequently happy to trust him and do business with him when conditions improved.

To cut a long story short, SMG is today one of the strongest and most respected groups in Indonesia with dominant positions in Pulp

& Paper, Oil Palm Plantations & Refining, Financial Services and Real Estate. Pak Eka has been well received and honoured by presidents and prime ministers of several countries. But the crowning glory came when he was awarded 'Emerging Markets CEO of the Year - 1996' at the IMF-World Bank Conference in Washington, D.C. It is also noteworthy that Pak Eka has never forgotten his humble beginnings and has supported several worthwhile charities, and his children are keeping up this tradition.

How did this happen? I have already mentioned how he won trust and respect in the business community. I need not go through the full history but wish to highlight some of SMG's success factors. In addition to his own business acumen, he was able to train his highly intelligent and hardworking children. Pak Eka's dynamism and high intellect genes are very evident in six children who hold top posts in SMG. He was also ably supported for several years by his son-in-law, Rudy, who passed away in 1988. The main growth opportunities came after the 1968 Investment Law when Indonesia started to become pro-business. SMG's vision focused on the 'essential' industries especially where there would be a distinct competitive advantage. The docile and inexpensive labour at the forestry and plantation level was an added 'plus'. Hence the huge investments in resource based pulp & paper and oil palm. While the banking and real estate divisions have been struck badly by the political-cum-economic crisis which started in the summer of 1997, the resource and export-oriented businesses are flourishing and give stability to the whole Group. The bank – BII's re-capitalization was completed in June, 1999.

In 1995, during one of our Thursday morning Board Meetings, we decided to do more serious SWOT analysis even though all four core divisions were making good money and the future looked very bright. The Widjajas are open-minded and generally listen to their senior executives. I summarized our strengths, mainly those mentioned above, but also stated that in some of our businesses there were hidden inefficiencies, which were being veiled by 'easy' profits. These super profits were being made because of cheap raw materials and natural resource advantages vis-à-vis our competitors in North America, Europe, Japan and Australia.

Since my observations were being received quite positively, I went on to suggest the need for BPR and culture change. Teguh, the first son, and heir apparent, who chairs these meetings asked "what do you recommend?" It was proposed that we select one of the leading international management consultant companies to help us with this process because this would be a three to five year programme. Very quickly the Board approved the search for a consultant.

We narrowed the choice down to three firms based on reputation and cost. Of these finalists, the best one carried the highest price tag - several million dollars over two years. I was directed to urge this firm to accept only around 25% of the total amount as regular monthly fees and to accept the balance as a 'success fee based on tangible savings and gains'. The firm was reluctant to accept this contingency feature as a 'never done before'. However, we then offered them a juicy premium on top of the success fee. The conditional compensation package looked very attractive and here was the opportunity for the consultancy firm to win their biggest account in Indonesia. The firm's head office gave exception approval and we were ready to go.

Unfortunately, this project collapsed in about four months. Since I was one of the prime movers, I felt terrible. Also, in spite of my best efforts, I was unable to bring the project back on track.

All we could do was to analyze the causes of failure so that we would be better prepared if there were a 'next chance'. We summarized the causes into two groups - where SMG was responsible and where the consultant came up short.

SINAR MAS

1. Even though the shareholders gave their support, they and key executives were focused on growth opportunities in Indonesia and abroad. Others were pre-occupied with short-term issues.

2. Many old timers were comfortable with the status quo.

3. Several others could 'justify' resistance to change because we were making better profits than many sophisticated competitors.

4. The originally strong message for change from the top was not given consistently and repeatedly.

5. Attitude of some people was that if the Consultants know so much, let them implement the projects (shift in ownership and responsibility).

6. Mind-set: the financial risk was 'low' because the bulk of the cost was contingent on big savings/gains. So let the consultants do 'all' the work.

7. While SMG formed a steering committee of capable people to support the effort, most were part-timers, including myself.

8. SMG appointed the IT Department Head to be the day-to-day contact person. He was very bright and committed but did not have the seniority to influence the senior 'generals' who head the big operations.

9. Since participating in or supporting the change programme was not in the performance criteria for raises and promotions there was no special 'incentive' to do so.

10. Many traditionalists felt insecure and were afraid of losing their power. Cynicism and skepticism spread and even the spirit of several enthusiasts was dampened.

CONSULTANT *(old)*

1. Due to SMG's perceived production bias, they appointed a senior technical industry specific person, who had virtually no experience in Asia, to head their team. With hindsight, they should have chosen a senior generalist with Asian experience and the technical expert as deputy.

2. In some of their diagnostic reports, they (mostly) accurately but bluntly highlighted SMGs weakness. The presentation did not take local sensitivities into account. 'Loss of face' for some SMG executives made the attitude towards the consultants even more negative.

3. They did not have a senior generalist like a Country Head based in Jakarta. This decreased the opportunities to have top level discussions 'as equals' on progress and de-bottlenecking.

4. Since progress even on worthwhile projects was slow, the firm began to suspect that it may not be able to earn the big success fee element, and that the discounted monthly retainer would be insufficient to warrant their commitment to the programme. They proposed re-negotiation of the contract - to drop the back-end success fee/bonus and significantly boost the monthly retainer. But, SMG felt it had a good low-risk contract and refused any change in the payments.

5. The consultants did not give enough weightage to suggestions given by our senior officers in the diagnostic and initial implementation phase.

The BPR project was sadly abandoned. The only benefit was the lessons that could be learnt from failure.

Henry Ford said, "Failure is a chance to analyze one's mistakes and start all-over." Taking my cue from this advice, I got over the heartburn surprisingly quickly.

For about 4-5 months after the termination of the above-mentioned contract we lay low on this subject and continued with our normal activities. Then, in another Thursday Board Meeting in early 1996, Teguh who is an 'empire builder' at heart, but also a believer in innovation, said that we cannot afford to be complacent, and to give 'culture change' another try. This was just what I was craving to hear. This time I suggested McKinsey & Co. as my first choice with two alternatives. I also suggested it would now be 'impossible' and indeed inadvisable to force a first class consultancy firm to agree to the contingency fee. No decision was taken and it was agreed that we would 'sleep over it' until the next meeting.

As chance would have it, the Mr. Koo - Chairman of the respected LG Group of Korea (good partner of SMG) visited Jakarta within a few days. Pak Eka hosted a fine dinner in his honour, which was attended by SMG's Board Members, including myself. Mr. Koo briefly described LG's successful change management programme. They also invited us to visit their V-Team and operations to learn from their innovation processes. When we asked him if they used any consultants, he replied "McKinsey". That was it. I was quickly given the mandate to bring in the great firm of management consultants.

Within a couple of weeks, we negotiated a mutually acceptable contract with McKinsey on behalf of SMG's biggest division - Pulp & Paper. With the real and solid support of Teguh, I made a series of presentations on how to make our Management Innovation Program work. Fortunately, people were more open-minded this time when we discussed the failure factors of our previous BPR initiative. Gus Nilo (Group Managing Director, an excellent 'big picture' man with about 13 years experience in SMG) also jumped on board as one of the active sponsors. This generated additional momentum.

Shortly thereafter, we launched our **Management Innovation Program** with an 'Ideas Competition' over two consecutive weekends, wherein heads of the major profit centres and their selected team members made enthusiastic and creative presentations. The judges included all the Widjajas – Teguh, Vice Chairman and

President of the Pulp & Paper Division; Sukmawati, Vice Chairman and CEO at the Group level; Indra, President of Financial Services; Muktar, President of Real Estate Division; Franky - President of Agribusiness, Foods & Consumer Products Division, and Group Managing Directors like Gus Nilo, Hendrik Tee (one of the brightest CFOs, particularly at that age) and myself.

Since, Teguh and his youngest brother, Franky (the 'dynamic-duo' of Sinar Mas) wanted to initiate the Olympic spirit, I proposed and they approved real gold medals for the winners. Accordingly, I purchased Krugerands of one troy oz. and half troy oz. for the first and second prizes, respectively. Everybody, especially the winners, felt great about the whole affair and proudly wore the Krugerand medals like Olympic Champions.

On this occasion, I also introduced the McKinsey team, most ably led by Carel Paauwe. With the level of enthusiasm that had built up, I was confident that McKinsey stood a much better chance than the previous firm. Also, in order to avoid the pitfalls of the previous exercise, we had a few candid discussions with McKinsey's senior officers of what and how things went wrong earlier. In fact, at Gus' suggestion, we even stopped mentioning the now 'dirty' word 're-engineering', and used the expression 'Management Innovation'. The name of the programme, **"Reaching the Sky"**, was chosen, based on Teguh's sky high goals. One of Teguh's favorite sayings was 'I want not just chemical reaction - I want nuclear reaction.' By this expression, he meant that we already have the benefit of low cost pulpwood. Now, if we can enhance our technical capabilities, strengthen leadership skills & teamwork, and develop policies and systems that encourage creativity and sense of entrepreneurship - all under an Olympic culture, we would have improvement in performance of nuclear proportions. Wow! He has emphasized this concept on many occasions and the message is getting home. It also makes the consultant's job a bit easier. He also frequently says that normal synergy may be 1+1=3, but in nuclear reaction 1+1=11! Talk about high aspirations! During some of his inspiring speeches, Teguh reminds us to exceed customer expectations, so that the customer will say 'WAH!'. Thereafter, we referred to this concept as the 'WAH! EFFECT'.

At the invitation of LG Group, our Board Members and senior executives made several visits to their offices and plants in Korea to study certain aspects of their programme that could be applicable to SMG (I made three trips). First, we learnt how they instituted a team at the corporate level to act as the main change agent. They called it the Core V-Team ('V' for vision) headed by a fine professional - Mr. Nam. They had also set up several secondary V-Teams at the major operations to accelerate, deepen and broaden the roll-out of ideas and concepts. The objective was also to encourage innovation and facilitate de-centralization and empowerment.

During one of my presentations on how to adapt the LG experience to SMG, I mentioned 'V-Team'. One of the shareholders asked, "What does V-Team mean?" I responded, "In LG, 'V' stands for 'vision', but we may also use it for 'victory'". During the next round of presentations by the profit centres, Suresh Kilam (Marketing Supremo for Pulp & Paper) - probably prompted by Teguh - displayed a slide which showed 'V V - Team' meaning Vision & Victory Team. He then added with a beaming smile, "If you put 'V' and 'V' together, you get 'W' which stands for 'Widjaja', which means victory." Everybody cheered. Next Hsu Cha Ming, the big 'general' for production of pulp and paper, fired off a very stimulating presentation on improving productivity and reducing pulp cost further. Also highlighted was the fast growing hybrid acacia trees which could be harvested in 7 years versus 15 to 20 years for 'normal' trees.

It was obvious that the innovation fever and fervour had reached a new high and the happy contagion was spreading. We felt most gratified but knew that this was just the start of our virtually endless uphill (relay) race.

Next, was a fine presentation by Tan Siauw Liang, the 'big chief' of the oil palm plantations. He laid out ambitious plans and strategies to make Sinar Mas the world's largest and most profitable plantation company which is respected for its best practices! He told us how his team would expand planted areas and boost yield per hectare.

The third presentation was made by the Financial Services team. Bank Internasional Indonesia (BII) explained how they would continue to build on our bank - BII's reputation as Indonesia's best managed and most profitable private sector bank. They would especially expand consumer banking. Willy Nusantara also made an interesting pitch on how the Insurance Division aimed at becoming the top life and non-life insurance group in the country.

Finally, Julius Keke made a presentation on behalf of the Real Estate Division. He detailed how they would maintain their lead and grow market share, especially in the lower-middle income housing sector - which still had good prospects.

At the end of the presentation, all shareholders got together to compare their scoring. Eventually, it was my honour as M.C. to announce the first prize to Pulp & Paper (they were much more than paper tigers!), and second prize to Plantation Division (their efforts bore fresh fruit in big bunches!).

Great progress has since been made throughout the group in the Reaching the Sky programme. Each of the four core divisions has a V-Team of its own. The V-Team for the Agribusiness, Foods & Consumer Division has Matti Karinen as its head. Matti was one of the top McKinsey consultants working with this division. Franky was able to convince him to join us and McKinsey to release him. His intellectual power, matched by high energy, have enhanced the capabilities of this V-Team, and some encouraging results are showing. We are continuing to 'beef-up' our Core V-Teams. K.C. Chan is a welcome addition as Matti's deputy. The objective is to develop many secondary V-Teams in order to accelerate the 'roll-out' of improvement ideas, processes and practices, as well as generate new ideas at the shop-floor and field levels.

For many months we had been feeling the dire need for top Human Resource specialists so that the human side of the organization did not fall behind, while we were progressing on the 'operations' side. Franky was also able to attract Sukrisno (Kris) Njoto to join us as Director of Corporate HR in the Agribusiness, Food & Consumer Division. Kris brings tremendous experience in human resource development. He has both academic and practical managerial experience. Kris had previously worked as a lecturer in the National University of Singapore, researcher for NASA and subsequently as a senior HR practitioner in a major Indonesian company, before joining Sinar Mas.

I have encouraged Kris to synergize for the overall benefit of HR activities in the group. Based on my past experience I have suggested that we have to balance persistence and patience. As the first Roman Emperor, Augustus Caesar (63B.C. – 14A.D.) admonished – "Make haste slowly". One of the challenges of management is to be able to 'walk the tight rope' between conflicting approaches and cope with ambiguity, because we cannot always avoid it. I have great confidence that such professionals will oil the wheels of Sinar Mas' culture transformation process. I also feel very honoured that Kris considers me a mentor, and I hope that I will not let him down. On the other hand, I must say, without hesitation, that Kris has already made a tremendous impact in the one year that he has been with Sinar Mas. In addition to introducing sound ideas, Kris has the sincerity and personality that builds bridges and team spirit.

Appendage I

MBOS

Over the last two years, a new performance and reward system has been instituted after the usual process of fine tuning. Since the idea was to use Olympic principles and ideals, Teguh coined the acronym – MBOS, which does not stand for Management by Objectives in plural. In our context, it means Management by Olympic System, which is explained as follows:

We drew inspiration from the Olympic spirit as our guiding light to fulfill our dream of becoming a world-class organization. Here is a summary of how Olympic Principles are converted into Sinar Mas' MBOS, reflecting our new management style and corporate culture.

Olympic Principles	M B O S
Clear 'Rules of the Game'	▪ Identify 'Key Performance Indicators' (KPIs) ▪ Regular and large scale communication
Aspiring for world's best, challenging the 'impossible'	▪ Set high aspiration 'Olympic Targets'
Constantly comparing yourself against high targets and records	▪ Identify benchmarks/world class performance ▪ Track and review quantitative business performance
Trained by professionals, very often former medalists themselves	▪ Invest in establishing structured coaching/training (Olympic Support System)
Fair-play, open evaluation	▪ Secure reliable data and establish a fair/open 360° evaluation process
Sportsmanship, competition	▪ Establish a healthy internal competition mechanism, create an exciting atmosphere
Winners are respected/rewarded, become role models. Losers seek next chance and work harder	▪ Provide handsome rewards/incentives to high performers, while sending clear signals to 'C' performers to improve

FEATURES OF MBOS

I do not wish to go into details of this high achievement - high reward programme, due to confidentiality reasons. However, I can say that it consists of four key elements, which together, would form the pillars of an Olympic culture in Sinar Mas Group.

OVERALL OBJECTIVE:

Achieving High Aspiration 'Olympic Targets' under the banner of Key Performance Indicators (KPIs).
- Meeting monthly and annual targets.
- Developing and implementing breakthrough ideas.

Vehicles:

1) **Personal Performance Objectives (PPOs) – Annual basis**

   Individual officers' evaluation on 360° basis. Rewards are based on annual achievement of individual targets as well as People Leadership, Teamwork, Strategic Thinking, Management Innovation.

   Examples :

   i) Produce XXX tons of high-grade oil or paper, etc. at cost below $xxx per ton, or, increase market share of cooking oil to 32%.

   ii) People leadership: Improve career development and succession planning system. Be a good mentor.

   iii) Promote teamwork through more cross-functional meetings to improve understanding and problem-solving e.g. reduce free fatty acids in palm oil.

   iv) Nurture management and/or technical innovation.

2) **Performance Incentive Targets (PIT), monthly or quarterly for on-going operational performance**

   Example : Incentives on improving yields per hectare, or increasing output of paper machines over agreed benchmarks.

3) **League Competitions** on specific indices which can be compared based on apple-to-apple

   Example :   Competition between similar oil palm estates and mills on yields and cost per ton.

   In this competition, front-runners are shown on monthly or quarterly intervals to encourage competitive spirit. Awards are given annually to the winners.

4) **Skill Development Activity** (SDA - Cross-functional team work) Competitions based on significant incremental impact through business process re-design, breakthrough ideas and innovations.

   Examples:
   - Management processes to boost quality and yields through quantitative management tools.
   - New methods in 'production areas' to achieve zero defect, quality enhancement.
   - Dramatic cost reduction.
   - New marketing strategy and system to boost market share.
   - Product innovation.

Special rewards and awards are given on individual and team basis. There is growing emphasis on team-based rewards which are given with pomp and ceremony.

Significant additional benefits of the SDA concept are the development of **skills** like leadership, team-spirit, problem solving, flexible attitude, with respect for others. In addition to 'business oriented' themes, we also have a couple of SDAs on community welfare. We have to thank the LG Group of Korea for introducing SMG to this concept.

The Widjajas are totally committed to MBOS. In order to ensure the broad and deep understanding, acceptance and implementation of MBOS, Teguh and Franky have mandated compulsory MBOS training for all managers. Similarly, their brothers, Indra and Muktar are promoting MBOS in the Financial Services Division and Real Estate Division respectively. Simultaneously, Frankle   –   the immaculately dressed Widjaja – is spreading the MBOS message in Singapore, where he resides. Therefore, I am hopeful that MBOS culture will flourish in transforming Sinar Mas and help it become better and emerge stronger from the Asian Crisis. In his opening speech for one of our MBOS Training Seminars, Teguh quoted an inspirational Chinese saying:

> *"Knowing there are tigers in the mountain,*
> *I am determined to walk towards the mountain;*
> *There are no insurmountable tasks in the world,*
> *With dedicated people, God will always be by our side."*

Then, he added with emphasis "Do not become proud or complacent when you win, and never be discouraged if you fail."

Key members of this culture change process, myself included, feel very gratified by the progress made by this family-led group in a developing country. I also get the feeling that to really emerge successfully, not only do we have to learn new methods and attitudes quickly, but equally quickly we have to 'un-learn', forget and abandon the archaic practices and behavior. As a matter of fact, we must have the courage and commitment to promptly 'slaughter sacred cows' which can hamper our progress on the exciting but fairly long MBOS voyage.

OLYMPIC CLUB

In order to accelerate the culture change process and to further incentivise excellence and commitment on a durable basis, we felt the need to create a special identity and 'grouping' for our top performing executives, the *crème de la crème* of Sinar Mas. I remembered that my friends who worked for IBM, used to put in great effort to become 'HPC' members. HPC stood for 'Hundred Percent Club' and it was a great honour for IBM officers to be admitted into this exclusive group and to retain this most coveted membership.

Through my discussions with Teguh, we developed the concept of Sinar Mas' Olympic Club. The choice of name became quite simple because we were introducing MBOS based on Olympic ideals and high aspiration targets. The objective was to create a profit sharing pool or trust for the benefit of the outstanding performers. The trust would be funded through the 'extra' bonuses earned by these officers. The trust would invest in listed companies of Sinar Mas Group as and when it receives funds. By this process, the 'nest-eggs' for our executives would be linked with the price performance of the group's listed stocks. Also, an officer could encash his/her shares only after serving a minimum vesting period. The Olympic Club is still under development but should be implemented fairly soon, given the sincerity of our owners who wish to treat the best executives as 'partners'.

While the Olympic Club Member becomes part of an elite corps, his behavior must be far from 'elitist'. The selection criteria will include excellent track record on operational targets and 'soft' issues, on a consistent basis. The member will also have to be a great role model who can take · on the assignment of a **corporate missionary**. Additional benefits of Olympic Club membership are: exposure to shareholders and top executives (mentors), attending special courses, fast-track opportunities, etc. Incidentally, the concept of corporate missionary has been flourishing in ABB, Shell and Nestle's for many years. Citibank's IS cadre (International Staff cadre) serves the same objectives in spreading Citibank's culture, and ensuring uniform systems throughout its huge international network of branches and offices.

It would be quite obvious to readers that I am personally very enthusiastic about Sinar Mas' MBOS and Olympic Club. In fact, I feel a great sense of ownership towards these concepts, with which I have been so intimately involved. However, my colleagues and I must not forget that MBOS, Olympic Club and similar management concepts are **not destinations** in themselves. They are, no doubt, extremely effective performance enhancement tools. Nevertheless, these concepts or aids are just important steps or landmarks in the never-ending journey of corporate development and progress. We have to keep improving them and looking for even better ideas in the years to come, if we wish to maintain our leadership.

Shiv Nadar rightly cautions us that success is an 'endless marathon' and emphasizes that the patrons and participants of such clubs and programs should be people who enjoy the 'chase' more than the 'kill'.

Appendage II

"GREEN GOLD MINES"

As the whole world is aware, Indonesia is going through one of the worst periods in its modern history. People below the poverty line have surged dramatically from the already high thirty million to ninety million or 45% of the population. Due to the current devaluation of the Indonesian Rupiah to 20-25 % of its value of June, 1997 and local interest rates over 60% per annum, more than 90% of companies in this country are technically bankrupt. It is now clear that some of the IMF 'cures' have been worse than the 'disease', at least in the short-run. (The exchange rate and interest rate have improved since April 1999.)

Sinar Mas in not immune to the 'Krismon' and 'Kristal' I refer to in the chapter titled 'Adaptability'. In fact, the Real Estate and Banking Divisions have been badly bashed by the tidal wave of this crisis. Tremendous concerted efforts are being made to re-vitalise these businesses and I am confident that these efforts will succeed eventually. Meanwhile, Sinar Mas continues to gain great strength from its sensible diversification because its other two core divisions - Pulp & Paper under Teguh, and Oil Palm Plantation and Refining under Franky have emerged as the solid engines of Sinar Mas.

In fact, the Widjaja family considers the oil palm plantations and industrial forests (for pulp wood) as our **green gold mines.** Generally speaking, gold (or diamonds) in the ground is only potential value. Moreover, while the usual mines are depleted over time, these forestry and plantation 'mines' are renewable. The magic is to have the **minds to mine** this potential wealth and convert it into real wealth (like converting potential energy into kinetic energy), in a profitable and sustained way. Recently, Franky came up with a powerful slogan: "Let's Dig the Green Gold Mine" to demonstrate his passion for extracting the highest yields of oil per hectare of our oil palm plantations.

Sinar Mas men, money and machines are being concentrated in these areas which are still generating employment, while most companies have started down-sizing. The concepts of MBOS and the forthcoming Olympic Club are/will be used to enhance value in these extremely difficult days. These businesses have and will earn even greater export earnings for the country in the years to come. (This is not a sales pitch to buy our stocks!)

It is important to note that several other Indonesian companies had similar opportunities to develop oil palm plantations and industrial forest. Only some succeeded during the 'comfortable' days under Soeharto. Still fewer companies will survive in the current crisis situation. Ultimately, given equal opportunities, success will boil down to the first two **Q&Ps** i.e. **quality people** and **quality principles**, which I mentioned in the chapter titled 'Corporate Values and Philosophy'.

The message to our executives is simple but poignant:
Be grateful that Sinar Mas is still strong and will emerge stronger when the 'smoke' clears. Work hard, reduce waste, optimize capacity utilization and improve collections. In one of our recent board meetings, Franky emphasized "be confident, but also be humble".
As mentioned earlier, there is no end to improvement and innovation in human endeavours. (We had thought that the **'Kama Sutra'** had covered all options and positions! The human mind continues to innovate even in the most basic functions!) In 1969 I saw, on black and white television, NASA's 'Eagle' landing craft make its 'soft landing' on the moon. Anxious moments later, the hatch opened and as Neil Armstrong stepped on the lunar surface, he made a profound historic statement that still resonates in many minds: "A small step for man - - - a giant step for mankind." Taking the cue from these unforgettable words, I say that the Sinar Mas version of the Eagle, namely Icarus will continue 'Reaching for the Sky'. Just like the Moon or Mars are not the final destinations for space scientists and cosmonauts, Sinar Mas' shareholders and executives will achieve great landmarks along the way in their never ending journey for the much

coveted, but illusive Olympic excellence, as standards and challenges keep rising.

I apologize if some readers feel that I have written too much about Sinar Mas. It has been a great privilege for me to be one of the main change agents in this large and diverse conglomerate, with many cultures. Also, it was a personally satisfying and great learning experience for me - - - and I survived to 'tell the tale'.

OLYMPIC CONFERENCE

The **Agribusiness Olympic Conference** to adjudge and honour the best SDAs, was held on March 31, 1999.

As readers will observe, I like to write poems. One day, while I was visualising our Olympic Conference, suddenly the thought came to me - why not do a song which captures the **MBOS spirit** and our conference Theme **"Digging the Green Gold Mine."**

Then, that same Sunday afternoon, while I was having home made 'Soto Ayam' (Indonesian chicken and cabbage soup) with my wife, I suddenly yelled – "I've got it!" My wife got a start and enquired, "What's the matter?" I again exclaimed, "I've got it. I am going to change the words of Louis Armstrong's beautiful song 'What a Wonderful World', as the theme song for our Olympic Conference!"

Fortunately, I received tremendous support from twelve young men and women within the company to form our chorus. And believe it of not, they asked me to be the conductor! (for the first and probably last time in my life). I was also asked to co-ordinate and direct a model role play which would show the SDA process of building a team, identifying a high impact theme, research, depicting problem solving exercises, disagreements and search for consensus, experimentation, pilot project, achieving break-through and celebrating success. Directing this play was another first time experience for me, very educating and great fun.

On that exciting day, several high quality SDAs were presented and prizes were awarded to winning teams. Towards the end, our team presented the model 'SDA Drama' titled "Man and Buffalo Partnership for Greater Productivity", in which we proved that the value of human harvesters would be boosted almost 100% if they were supported by buffalo-drawn carts to move the harvested palm fruit bunches to collection points. Even in this modern age of satellites, automation and robotics, the buffalo is still the best 'transporter' in certain types of plantations or topography.

After presenting our SDA, I had to announce our song. I heard myself yell with Olympic gusto:
"Ladies and Gentlemen:
It now gives us great pleasure to present 'What a Beautiful Goal',
by the Golden Chorus of Sinar Mas."

Our Golden Chorus sang with expression and in harmony. After the singing was over, the crowd of three hundred executives cheered loudly. I felt a pleasant lump in my throat. Two of my colleagues told me that they saw tears in Franky's eyes, as he heard this 'anthem'. What more could I ask for! I profusely thanked our wonderful actors and singers for their excellent performances.
The song is presented as follows:

The song is presented as follows:

What a Wonderful Goal

We grow palms of green
With fruit that's bright,
We love our palms
By day, by night - - -
And we sing to ourselves...
Our <u>Green Gold Mine</u>[1]

The MBOS spirit
Shines in our eyes
As we go higher
<u>Reaching for the sky</u>[2] - - -
And we sing to ourselves...
What a wonderful goal.

The color of our Filma[3]
So golden to our eyes,
Is used in kitchens
Far and nearby.
We are friends holding hands
Saying we'll help you,
In all <u>Strategic Ventures</u>
We're there for you.

We are friends holding hands
Saying we'll help you
In all <u>KPI's</u>[4]
We're there for you - - -
And we sing to yourselves...
What a wonderful goal.

And - - we - - sing - - to- - your- - selves...
What - - a - - won-der-ful - - g-o-a-l

O.... YEAH.....

Inspired by the song 'What a Wonderful World'
by Louis Armstrong (SACHMO)

---

[1] Oil Palm plantations referred to in Appendage
[2] Name of Sinar Mas' Management Innovation and Culture Change Program
[3] Brand name of Sinar Mas' leading cooking oil
[4] Key Performance Indicators under MBOS – Management by Olympic System

6

"PSST, I HEARD ON THE GRAPEVINE THAT..."

"He who speaks much of others burns his tongue"
(Proverb)

People, by and large, don't like to feel isolated. People want to be kept informed, particularly on topics that are important or meaningful to them. People do not like to feel left out or feel insignificant. A good portion of us humans also like an element of gossip or an exchange of sensational news, especially touching the 'Room at the Top'. In other words, every corporation has an informal organization - groups of special friends - with the 'grapevine' as the medium of communication. A Chinese proverb cautions us: "Whispered words are heard afar".

The challenge of the institution is to have a well-structured organization - but with fewer 'walls' and more **'bridges'** supported by effective internal communications. This means that the 'formal organization' should be able to 'satisfy' the reasonable information needs of the vast majority of employees and make them feel like. **'insiders'**. Consequently, people will not need to rely on the informal grapevine, resulting in a reduction in the gap between the formal and informal organization.

Corporate communication must be **clear** so that there is no room for misunderstanding or different interpretations. The communication must also be **timely**. If the board has made an important decision on, say, employee benefits or approved a significant promotion, etc., the news should be disseminated quickly and efficiently before the rumour mill starts to grind.

Various media should be used. A senior officer or department head can call a quick meeting and personally make the announcement. Sometimes, the public address system is a good 'broadcast' tool. Many companies video-tape messages or interviews with the CEO and circulate these tapes to give important signals to employees on matters affecting the corporation and its people. Newsletters presented creatively are an excellent medium to keep staff 'in the know'. But do not only use such printed material, because of time delays at the printers to convey urgent news. The verbal or PA system should be used for the main announcement and details may be released in the 'Staff News and Views'.

In the newsletter, it is also a good idea to invite people from the mainstream to contribute stories of common interest. Don't rely solely on the communications department who are not directly involved in the main operations, where the money is really made. This is a good medium for recognition and motivation. Success stories and congratulatory themes enrich the newsletter and people look forward to it.

Having stated the above-mentioned media of communication, there is no substitute for direct one-on-one, face-to-face discussion between the supervisor and subordinate, or among peers. Such contact is **personal** and is key effective **two-way** communication.

Whatever we do, however we communicate - we should keep the people in mind … and heart.

හහ **PART B** ශශ

TEAMWORK
&
LEADERSHIP

ಖಖ **Part – B** ಇಲ

TEAMWORK & LEADERSHIP

SYNOPSIS

7   Power of Passion:
There is tremendous enthusiasm if the leaders have passion. Passion can be used to win 'just' wars or it can be abused if it is misdirected.

8   Strength through Humility:
Leaders can enhance their strength through humility. Contrarywise, lack of humility can hurt a leader. I have tried to distinguish humility from timidity by focusing on 'positive humility'.

9   Teamwork: Camaraderie-In-Action:
Underlines key aspects of high performance teams. Emphasis on the need for respecting each other and pooling resources to achieve shared goals.

10   Welcome aboard 'Mentorship':
The manager's job is incomplete if he does not mentor his people. Also, the onus is on juniors to develop themselves.

11   'Head Man Walking':
Management by walking around is a good idea, but the ground should be prepared for making employees welcome the boss' visits.

12   How to 'Control' People:
It is important for bosses to have control. The key question is how a boss acquires or uses his power or authority. Bosses, through their behaviour, should create an environment of 'self-governance'.

13 People Leadership:

Debates whether leaders are 'born' or 'made'. Leadership can show in early childhood through the power of genes or early influences. Also, the impact of environment and mentors on nurturing potential leaders.

14 Charisma:

The mystique and value of charisma and how it can be used beautifully for progress, or how can it be abused. The artificial image of a person is described as 'Max Factor Charisma'. But, if we merely focus on the frail frames or wrinkled faces like Mahatma Gandhi, who would say that they had charisma.

15 The Buck Stops Here:

Highlights the need for the boss to take responsibility for his decisions, instead of shifting the blame to his juniors. Mentions my personal experience (mis-judgement) in Bank of America, where I let my conscience guide me.

16 Motivation:

A key attribute of a leader is the art of inspiring his people. There are pointers on the traits of a motivator. Also, how a junior looks up to his senior.

17 The Art of Reprimand:

Some old fashioned bosses feel their power increases when they scold or shout at their people. The idea of reprimand is to carefully criticize the action and not the person, and give proper guidance. The subordinate should feel that he was treated fairly.

7

POWER OF PASSION

"You can do anything if you have enthusiasm.
Enthusiasm is the spark in your eye, the swing in the gait,
the grip of your hand, the irresistible surge of your will
and your energy to execute your ideas.
Enthusiasm is at the bottom of all progress!
With it, there is accomplishment.
Without it, there are only alibis."

Henry Ford

For our present purposes, I would define passion as strong enthusiasm accompanied by emotional energy.

Many of us would have read about Henry Ford and/or seen actor Cliff Robertson play the role of Ford, the illustrious founder of Ford, the world's second largest automobile manufacturer. Recall the scenes where Ford is working passionately day and night to make his internal combustion engine work. His passion was such that he refused to be defeated by failure. In fact, he used failure as a teacher to re-think his design and concept, and start all over again. Ford jumps and dances and yells in delight when his engine suddenly starts chugging. This dramatic breakthrough has changed the world of transportation.

Similarly, many of us would have read or seen Shakespeare's Henry IV. King Henry is eager to recruit the right kind of people to help him achieve his objectives. He describes to one of his trusted aides the kind of men he needs to win the war:

"Will you tell me, Master Shallow, how to choose a man? Care I for limb, the thews, the stature, bulk and big assemblance of a man? Give me the spirit, Master Shallow."

Falstaff, Henry IV

This clearly shows that physical strength alone is not enough to win. A physically strong man may not have the courage and spirit at the time of combat or in a crisis. One may have all the physical attributes but if one lacks the spirit or passion, not much can be achieved.

In fact, I cannot think of a single worthwhile or world-class goal that can be successfully pursued without enthusiasm or passion. I don't know of any successful leader who lacked zest or could not bring out the zeal of this people. Bill Gates says that his greatest strength is his ability to transfer his enthusiasm to his people.

Let's take a look at David Copperfield — not the victim of circumstances created by Charles Dickens, but one of the greatest magicians the world has known. Copperfield says, "Passion is everything", then he adds "...Dreams aren't a matter of chance, but a matter of choice. When I dream, I believe I am rehearsing my future" Wow! I say, what a profound statement and this is no illusion by the unequaled illusionist in the world.

I simply cannot see how excellence or success in any field of human endeavour can be attained without passion.

The physically frail Mahatma Gandhi 'fought' his bloodless war of freedom with passion. He was able to unite and galvanize his people with passion. His passionate non-violent demonstrations eventually made the colonizers feel guilty about controlling India. He became one of the greatest team builders of all time — without offering any financial incentive!

Also, if two young men with otherwise 'similar credentials' eye one and the same young lady for a (special) relationship, it is the one with a healthy display of passion that stands a better chance. We have also heard or experienced that marriages and similar companionships become routine or boring when passion evaporates.

Having said all these passionate things about passion, it is equally important that our zeal or zest be coupled with wisdom and a dose of humility. Uncontrolled passion without balance can be highly destructive and harmful. E.g. Nazi or Ku Klux Klan movements; Saddam Hussein's invasion of Kuwait.

8

STRENGTH THROUGH HUMILITY

'God, grant me the serenity to accept the things I cannot change,
The courage to change the things I can,
And the wisdom to know the difference.'
Serenity Prayer attributed to Saint Francis of Assisi.

In the chapter titled 'Power of Passion', I mentioned that this quality was exemplified in Henry Ford and Mahatma Gandhi. However, they were 'poles apart' in another key attribute - humility.

Ford's success also bloated his ego to the point that he did not listen to some of his key lieutenants. Ford became too sure of himself based on his past achievements and closed his mind to new trends in the automobile business. It is said that this driven man felt that he was virtually infallible and he lacked the humility to recognize that his subordinates had good ideas. His humility was 'stunted' so much that he even ignored customer choices. His arrogance became famous by his insisting that the customers could have any colour car they want 'as long as it is black'. Apparently, he also did not feel the need to upgrade or replace his Model-T car in time; and therefore lost market share to competitors like General Motors.

Another interesting example of success blinding the entrepreneur is that of John D. Rockefeller, arguably the father of the American petroleum industry. In his hey-day he was the richest man in the world and the head of Standard Oil Company (the forerunner of ESSO/EXXON). Rockefeller made his initial mega-bucks through kerosene and did not believe in the importance of petrol (gasoline), because the automobile industry was in its infancy, and its future was not clear. At that time, the steam-based external combustion engine still ruled the railroads, high roads and high seas. Rockefeller's inability to foresee the future money making products of his industry, coupled with his arrogance, made him 'fire' (thank God, without igniting kerosene!), the manager of his unit - Standard Oil of Indiana, because this manager wanted to focus on gasoline production. We all know of the huge profit gasoline generated for the petroleum refining industry, and how it changed the world.

Most people agree, at least with the benefit of hindsight, that it is difficult to be humble especially if you are at thé peak of success or epitome of your industry.

Now, let's take a look at Mahatma. Gandhi was a non-violent fighter for human rights and the leader of India's freedom struggle. He was respected and admired even by his opponents, and often feared by his enemies. Millions of his followers literally worshipped him. Yet, this man who aroused unprecedented passions did not let Mr. Ego taint his character. Gandhi's humility was part of his greatness. He believed in the 'round-table' style of debating issues. His humility kept him close to India's poor masses. It is also this humility that gave him the flexibility to negotiate in a peaceful way with the British Government. Being humble does not mean being weak. On the contrary, he was a tower of spiritual strength.

I remember a Hindi proverb which my mother told me when I was in my early thirties: 'The more fruit the mango tree bears, the lower it bows down'. This implies that the wealthier or more powerful a person becomes, the more humble he should also become.

People with humility are approachable, and therefore, get the benefit of diverse opinions and the best ideas. Also, a boss with a humble approach becomes a good motivator and role model. By the same token, companies with arrogant CEOs have more 'yes-men' and lower employee morale.

Here is a short but significant story[*] of Thomas Watson, Jr., former supremo of IBM. As Watson tried to enter the IBM building, the security guard noticed that he did not have his ID and promptly (but courteously) requested the boss to come back with his ID to gain entry. Now, instead of being offended and firing the guard, Watson praised him for doing his duty well. That is leadership with a generous sprinkle of humility.

On the other end of the scale, is a similar start to a story, but with a radically different end. Charles Revson of Revlon was stopped by a receptionist for removing the sign-in (attendance) sheet. The boss' ego was hurt and he fired the woman. Very often the top executive's ego can result in (mis-) management by fear. These examples often show the organization's culture. They tell whether the corporation is being governed by fair principles or by egoistic principals.

Another important area that can be impacted by humility or lack thereof is learning. Some young people can get a 'chip on the shoulder' after attaining a Kellogg or Harvard MBA. They feel that they have already reached the pinnacle or ultimate in learning. Their egos or dearth of humility 'blinds' them to the fact that learning should be continuing and that true learning comes from trying to apply academic knowledge in real corporate life or other practical situations.

There is a beautiful Indian prayer in which the devotee asks God, 'Oh Creator and Protector of the universe, give strength to the weak, and grant wisdom and humility to the strong'. I am sure that there are similar themes in most preachings.

---

[*] Adapted from Thomas A. Stewart's insightful 'The Leading Edge' which featured in Fortune magazine in 1998.

One could summarize the key advantages or gains of people who are 'armed' with genuine humility:

- They are more popular and enjoy better relationships.
- They can make better decisions by considering differing opinions.
- They can step into others' shoes to understand them better.
- They are generally found to be more trustworthy.
- They are usually less tense.
- Their subordinates feel they have more 'space' to progress.
- Their subordinates can learn the benefits of humility from their bosses' behaviour.

I wish to clarify that I am not talking about false modesty or humility, or similar behaviour which is affected by weakness, poverty or juniority. It is very easy for a poor person to be humble. I have yet to see a beggar who is egoistic. Similarly, I have noticed some executives who are very humble in front of their bosses but who 'enjoy' talking down to their subordinates.

It is also important not to confuse humility with timidity. Can any right-minded person say that Gandhi was timid - - - humble, yes, but timid, no.

At the same time, I must admit I have had my share of knocks in this sensitive area. I have generally tried to be considerate and understanding of others. But I have not consciously tried to be 'humble'. On a few occasions, my enthusiasm was interpreted as arrogance. Now, being aware of this pitfall, I have tried to display a softer, more accommodating demeanor. Recently, one of my bosses did not give me a certain assignment because, as he told me to my face, 'You're too timid for this'. That was a real shocker and I actually felt deflated for a few minutes. I later smiled and said to myself, 'Courage or timidity can sometimes lie in the eyes of the beholder!' Lesson: I have to do my best to maintain high values and not lose my balance - - - and just hope that the others see me as I am. My style should be flexible to suit varying conditions but time honored values and principles must not be side-tracked for 'image purposes' or short-term gains.

I believe that there are important lessons to be learnt from the tragedy of the 'unsinkable' luxury passenger liner, **Titanic**. The main ones are, that size is no guarantee for survival, and being too sure of oneself or being complacent will lead to disaster, sooner or later. In fact, the mighty Roman Empire was at its weakest when it reached its biggest size. The Romans became arrogant and lazy, corrupt and selfish. In the Titanic's case, the owner was so sure of the invincibility of the largest ship on the world, that he apparently questioned the need for life boats because they would ruin the aesthetics of the 'wonder ship'. His pride made him disregard his chief shipwright's recommendation for many more lifeboats and other safety measures. The rest is history.

I am reminded of a thought provoking proverb: 'The first degree of folly is to hold one's self wise, the second to profess it, the third to despise counsel'.

From what I have read and heard, Andy Grove, the maestro of Intel, and Rajat Gupta, the highly respected President of McKinsey & Co., have the positive humility that I have written about in this chapter.

9

TEAMWORK:
CAMARADERIE-IN-ACTION

"Many cobwebs can tie-up a lion"
(African Proverb)

More and more corporations are recognizing and harnessing the power of teamwork which I like to describe as camaraderie-in-action, focused action. In this context, I mean friendship in the work place. We do not have to be best friends outside the office in order to be good teammates. In fact too much personal friendship may sometimes hurt objectivity in the work situation.

I think that most of us in management appreciate the difference between a group and a team. The challenge now is to elevate the team to a distinctly higher level or to build a **High Performance Team (HPT)**. Listed below are some of the major characteristics of this powerhouse concept:

Characteristics of High Performance Teams:
Regardless of differences in nationality, race and religion and regardless of seniority:
- Members cherishing a common goal/vision
- Members befriending each other
- Members trusting each other
- Members respecting each other
- Members enjoying each others' company
- Members listening to each others' views, with open minds

- Members <u>learning</u> from each other
- Members <u>sharing</u> a 'WE CAN DO' attitude
- Members <u>celebrating</u> success together
- Members <u>passionate</u> about winning, achieving breakthroughs

The HPT would also have something similar to the Three Musketeers' motto - "One for all and all for one!" There will be a special bond, a special kinship between the team-mates. An additional feature of the HPT is its composition. A team may have all the above mentioned attributes but would still not qualify as a HPT if its members, no matter how good, are mostly of similar background or skill or function. In such a team there will be too much inbreeding of ideas - mental incest! They will not be able to look at the problem or opportunity from every angle. Take the game of soccer - all players appear to be doing the same thing - chasing the ball, kicking and heading it. Also, all players in a team have a common goal (pun intended). But they cannot all be strikers or defenders. They are a team of specialists.

Again, in the case of soccer, we witness how the whole team 'celebrates' each time a player shoots a goal. Such dramatic celebration is a tremendous energizer. In a corporate set-up, we need not jump all over each other and hug and kiss, but we can clearly felicitate the successful person or team and spread the euphoria.

The HPT will have a diverse membership. Pooling of expertise and experience is critical for top quality results. The leader of the team is not necessarily the senior most person. The member with the most important expertise needed for success <u>and</u> has leadership skills would be elected as leader.

There are so many forces that impact products, services and processes that it is vital for the team leader to recruit the relevant people. In this way, the team can look at the whole picture and come up with the best idea or proposal. Also, what is very important is that because members have joined from various relevant departments, we have 'built-in ownership' of the decision in all important areas - so implementation becomes much easier. This aspect of wide ownership cannot be over-emphasized.

Let me attempt a couple of imaginary examples to illustrate the process:

I get a thrill out of shooting wild animals with a - - - camera (not rifle). I enjoy taking photographs during holidays and special occasions. However, I don't, or really can't, use a high quality 'manual' or professional camera because I get confused between the implications of shutter speed, aperture, depth of field, light, distance and so on. I simply rely on the easy to operate **auto focus** cameras made by Canon or Minolta. Most pictures in natural daylight come out fine. The trouble is with night time pictures with the built-in flash. The people or objects come out too bright (over-exposed) when I click from near or too dark (under-exposed) when the distance is greater. I guess that the flash has only one 'fixed' power/wattage.

Supposing a Canon marketing expert called 'Wiz-san' gets a hunch that to make their auto-focus camera more user friendly and effective/versatile, his company should develop a self-adjusting flash. The flash would automatically judge and release the right amount of light depending on the subject, light conditions and distance, and *voila!* better night shots. The more he thinks about this feature, the more he feels that many amateur enthusiasts, like me, would love 'his new camera'. So, Wiz-san discusses the idea with his boss who's nickname is 'Pro-san' because he is a pro-active professional. Pro-san has an open-minded approach and actively encourages ideas from his subordinates. Pro-san feels that the idea deserves a 'shot'. Pro-san believes that this could be a great opportunity to surprise the competition, expand market share and boost profit margin to boot. Pro-san contacts his peers in Design & Engineering, Manufacturing, Cost Accounting, Market Research to solicit their reaction and support. Assume that all these department heads feel that this idea might 'click' and carve additional market share, with a slightly higher margin, because of the new auto-flash feature. Subsequently, permission is obtained from the COO for a pilot project.

At the next stage, the Heads nominate at least one of their best experts with analytical skills as well as team skills to join the cross-functional team. Since it was Wiz-san's idea he may be made the team leader. Or, the team may determine that since the main challenge is design, 'Dessy-san' from that department may be chosen as the leader.

The leader and entire team will be aware or made aware of the special attributes of the HPT. Their commitments will be full-time or part-time depending on the needs from time-to-time. A special, fairly spacious room, sometimes called a team 'laboratory' (LG calls it 'Tear-Down Room') will be provided to the team. Pro-san may also obtain the COO's approval for a special incentive to the team based on the level of success.

Now, the HPT for Project, named 'Flash to Slash the Competition' is ready to go, and let their creative juices gush! They will remain focused on the key issues but will maintain a holistic view. They will have daily get-togethers to exchange thoughts. They will also work in sub-groups, or even alone for specific issues or tasks. But they will always keep the whole team informed. They will probably take a key supplier into confidence and involve it in certain discussions. The leader, as well the department heads, will ensure that morale is high and offer encouragement, especially, when the team hits a stonewall. Even small successes will be recognized and celebrated enthusiastically. While I don't guarantee that the project will achieve commercial success, you may be sure that the HPT 'formula' will maximize chances of success.

Let us take a more personal example: Gillette, the greatest brand in shaving products has been a consistent innovator, especially in the last 20-25 years. Gillette developed the cartridge-sandwich blade - 'TRAC II' to displace the traditional safety razor blade, then upgraded to 'CONTOUR'; again graduated to 'SENSOR' and further improved to 'SENSOR EXCEL'. At each stage Gillette improvised or innovated for shaving convenience, to get the edge (oh, puns) over their competitors.

We can safely assume that Gillette expects competitors to play catch-up and yet is determined to expand its lead. It will certainly use all its marketing skills and promotion capabilities. Additionally, especially for its long-term vitality, it will want to keep on innovating. At this stage, Marketing and Product Development Departments look at what needs to be done (this is often a continuing process with new phases or thrusts). Let us say that they feel that the consumer would like two additional features:

1. The lubra-strip should also release a good antiseptic/disinfectant;
2. The effective life of the twin blades should be extended by at least 25%.

(Actually, I get only two shaves these days, compared with four to five shaves, five years ago. Maybe, at the age of fifty-three, my beard has suddenly become harder. As you would note, I have a vested interest in this subject!)

This would be viewed as a project to please the consumer, expand market share, and increase margins. In any event, an HPT would likely be formed at Gillette on similar lines as mentioned in the CANON case. Additionally, the HPT may include a member from Purchasing to talk with the steel suppliers and the people who supply/develop the machines that sharpens the blades and gives them the further 'edge' (advertising slogan) over the competition. He may also contact the people who make the protective coating that protects the blade's edge.

A friend of mine in America recently informed me of the shaving pleasure he derived from Gillette's latest 'MACH-3'. I am looking forward to its introduction at my supermarket in Jakarta. Hopefully, my wife will feel the difference!

(Oh, I just thought of another advertising line for Gillette's shaving foam/cream "I'd lather shave with Gillette!")

Both CANON and Gillette probably do much more than what I have described. In any case, these are hypothetical cases. But the point is to emphasize the benefit and importance of real cross-functional cooperation if we are aiming for world-class status.

General Electric under maestro Jack Welch, EDS under the ebullient Ross Perot have made teamwork a fine art. Some years ago, LG Group of Korea under the leadership of Chairman Khoo introduced such organized teamwork under the banner of SDA - 'Skill Development Activity' to great advantage. LG has annual Skill Olympics where the best 15-20 SDA teams present their projects and results. Attractive prizes are awarded to the winners and runners-up. LG has achieved some really valuable break-throughs by this process. Moreover, there is great improvement in its corporate culture with greater motivation and empowerment down the ranks.

The idea of replicating a good idea developed in a unit, in other (similar) units within an organization is not new. However, some narrowed-minded managers do not like to share their good ideas. Such people get short-term gains by depriving their 'internal competitors' and looking better than them. In the process, they do not grow out of their 'local mentality' and they 'surrender' the opportunity to emerge as team building leaders on a corporate-wide basis. Therefore, their careers become stunted after a few years.

John Reed, now Co-Chairman of the gigantic Citigroup, credited Rana Talwar with popularizing the concept of **'success transfer'** at Citibank, while Talwar was Head of Citibank's Consumer Banking Division for Asia. Talwar's former subordinates also consistently commend him for supporting and standing up for his people and promoting teamwork. I'm sure that Rana's leadership skills stand out among the factors that contributed to his being appointed (the first non-British) CEO of Standard Chartered Bank.

Sinar Mas Group has embarked on a major management innovation programme - **Reaching the Sky.** This name was inspired by Vice Chairman, Teguh Ganda Wijaya. Here, Sinar Mas is very grateful to LG for its help in introducing the SDA concept. Lots of exciting and profitable ideas have emerged from these SDA competitions, in which many teams participate. I'm sure that several of these teams will attain HPT status. The Widjaja family and their top executives are providing the push and support to ensure success. Details are found in the chapter titled "Culture Change in a Family Controlled Asian Group".

TEAMWORK SEMINARS

In 1994 and 1995, I had to conduct seminars on 'Teamwork' for our Top Managers. On the morning of the seminar, I pondered over how I would create an atmosphere of equality and humility, that are important, especially for team building skills. I wanted to do something different than just making the usual statement that we are all equal in the classroom. Suddenly, an idea struck me. After the group settled into the room, I briefly explained the objectives of the session. Then I said to the attendees, "please write your titles in neat big letters on a clean sheet of paper. Then neatly fold the paper twice - - - Now tear-up the paper!" Many were surprised at my 'command', but all of them dutifully tore their papers. I followed that by saying, "for the rest of the seminar, let us learn with a sense of equality and enthusiasm of children. Let's have fun, while we learn about each other and human relationships."

To highlight the importance of friendship which cements teamwork, I offer you the following poem:

FRIENDSHIP

Friendship is a profound and enormous word;
Its explanation could fill a whole white-board.

Friendship is love, friendship is sharing,
Friendship is warmth, friendship is caring.

Friendship is support through thick 'n' thin;
It's a feeling that comes from the heart within.

Friendship is giving honest, sound advice;
You cannot just buy it for any old price.

Friendship is a non-profit institution,
Requiring sincere, selfless constitution.

Love begets love and trust begets trust;
To be a complete human, a friend is a must.

Friendships never appear on a silver plate;
Search and make some before it's too late!

Where can we find true friends to harbour?
Start with the family and thy neighbour.

A true friend is worth more than gold;
Hope I can be one, before I'm too old!

10

WELCOME ABOARD "MENTORSHIP"*

*"The best horse needs breaking,
and the most able child needs teaching"*
(Proverb)

We all need someone to look up to; someone who cares for our welfare; someone who can be trusted; someone who one can turn to for help. In short, everybody needs some sort of mentoring at some time or other.

One of my most important non-family mentors was **T.S. Gopal**, our teacher in the final year of high school, and a mathematical 'wiz'. He had a great sense of humour and in his own words, "my appearance is not my fault." He would grin and say, "I smoke forty cigarettes a day, which has helped me become a great ninety pound (41 kg) skeleton." Indirectly, he was cautioning us against smoking. Mind you, a tight slap from his bony hand could bestow bigger marks on our teenage cheeks than on some of our examination marks. Also, he very rarely reprimanded without sufficient reason. In fact, he was definitely my favourite teacher after the great headmaster, Mr. Kuruvila Jacob.

On one typical dull, wet, monsoon day, he must have got up on the wrong side of the bed. This time he walked into our classroom with an unusual frown on his face. He asked to see our homework

---

* Please permit me to coin/launch this new word. 'Stewardship' and Leadership have been sailing beautifully for many years.

assignments. He did not say 'good' to the boys who had done a good job. The boy just before me had not done his homework and Mr. TS mercilessly tore this boy's book and said, "your book is returned in TWO VOLUMES!" When he examined my book, he must have impatiently opened the wrong page. Thinking that I too had skipped my assignment, he yelled at me and launched my duly completed homework with the correct answers, out of the window! Obviously, the book had a very wet flight and an even muddier landing, two floors below. All the boys were amazed at what had happened. I was truly devastated, because my favourite teacher did not believe that I had correctly and duly done my homework. I tried to hold back the tears that had swelled up in my eyes and could only say, "but Sir, I….". Before I could say more, he now tenderly said "Vipen, go and retrieve your book quickly and see me in the staff room, after class." Later, when I showed him my book (fortunately the ink had not 'run' on the two important pages), he first said, "correct-answers", then he put his hand on my shoulder and said, "Vipen, I'm sorry that I acted thoughtlessly and suddenly. I respect you for not reacting sharply. Something tells me that regardless of your grades, you'll do well in life. Now go back to your class with a smile." My faith in Mr. TS had been fully restored. He truly was a class act among my class masters.

On reflection, he also taught me that only a noble-minded boss, a real leader, has the courage to apologize to his subordinate. There is no loss face or decline in dignity, in a sincere apology. In fact, such a 'humble' boss rises in stature in this process.

In the chapter titled "Corporate Culture", I wrote about the Grindlays Bank Manager in `whose branch I had my first training. However, my first professional mentor was an unassuming Indian gentleman, named K.V. Sitaram (Sita), whose job title was 'Accountant', the forerunner of today's 'Operations Manager'. This gentleman, about eleven years my senior, took me under his wing. He did not have a great physical or outward personality but I was quickly impressed by his quiet confidence. In those days (1960s), bank unions, which were dominated by the Communist Party, were very powerful; perhaps too powerful for their own good. Also, there was an adverse relationship between the Bank's management and the union. But, Sita, my mentor, had a more cordial relationship with the union leaders than most other officers.

I could clearly tell from day-one that Sita showed a personal interest in me and my progress as a Management Trainee. On my very first day of work - December 1st, 1966 - the union went on an All-India 'go-slow' (a sort of sit-in strike when workers do the bare minimum). In those days, the bank had no computers and so customer ledgers and accounts were all done manually. Therefore, the officers would end up doing a lot of clerical work, even as late as midnight, sometimes. On certain occasions, even wives of officers would put their shoulders to the wheel. The idea was to show the union that they could not paralyse the bank, and at the same time to show our commitment to our customers.

The go-slow and following full strike action was an opportunity for me to work even closer with my mentor than my normal training programme called for. Everyday, we had lunch together in the Officers 'Tiffin' Room. Another person who naturally became my mentor was an intelligent and chubby Scotsman called George Cuningham. (George eventually became the Regional Director of the Bank for South Asia.) These gentlemen told me many interesting anecdotes about the Bank, its staff and customers. Many of them were funny, but virtually all carried subtle messages on do's and don'ts in a banking career. Also, I began to see the benefit of humour in corporate life. Additionally, I got a better idea of what was important to the Bank - what we, nowadays, call values. I could clearly see that Grindlays' goal was to remain the number one foreign bank in India and become top in customer service. All this made me very excited, since I felt that I was becoming a part of this great effort.

I felt proud that senior officers were sharing business strategy with a kid-trainee like me. I was inspired in being considered a member of the team. The Bank Manager, John Boase and Sita would also give me periodic tests to monitor the progress of my department-by-department training programme. Even after thirty plus years, I have warm feelings for my first banking mentor, Sita.

Management Trainees who successfully completed the 18-month training programme in India were sent to London for about one year, for Head Office exposure, because we 'needed some final polishing up', before becoming 'covenanted officers'. All trainees were housed at the Bank's club called Minerva Lodge in Blackheath, south-east of London.

At the Head Office's Staff Department was a 'jolly good' English lady called Pat Jolly, whose job was to help us settle in. After being introduced to her, she asked me to complete a Personal History Form. The third or fourth question was 'State your tribe'. I chuckled and asked the lady, "What is your tribe?" - - - She blushed and said, "Oh, that question is only for African trainees. You may ignore that one." At least I did not have to go that far back into my ancestry to reveal my tribal affiliation!

The Trainees were under the wings of two Scotsmen - the first was, Mr. Gordon Fleming, the Staff Manager and the second was a well-matured man, George Miller, who was Manager of the Foreign Trade Department (Letters of Credit, Negotiations, Bill Discounting, Collections, etc.). Both took good interest in us and reviewed reports on us from the various department heads. Mr. Fleming, would also conduct seminars on general management and 'practice of banking'.

Mr. Miller would tell us useful stories or case histories on how the Bank supported trade between Britain and its former colonies. We were told that the major imports into Britain were tea, jute (burlap), sugar, logs/timber, hides and skins, mica, manganese, spices, cotton, wool. Key exports from Britain were machinery, cars, cotton and woollen textiles, branded consumer products. We were taught the principles behind foreign trade transactions and precautions to secure the Bank and its customers. Several of those stories helped us subsequently when we returned to India to positions of responsibility.

These three individuals acted as our mentors, although the expression was never used in those days. As and when our H.O. training was completed, we were appointed as covenanted officers on the way to eventually becoming 'Burra (big) Sahibs' in India. On the eve of our return, a senior General Manager would give each new covenanted officer a pep talk on how the Bank had faith in him and wished him a successful career in the Bank. We all got a good send-off as we returned to our home countries, as bank executives.

Another person who I would consider a mentor during my younger banking years at Grindlays, was Tej Sarwal, my branch manager in New Delhi. I addressed him as 'Sir' in the office and 'Tej' after-hours. He had a very sharp mind and was respected as a good banker. Although he was quite busy, he did take interest in my progress. On one occasion, I showed him a few advertising ideas which I had developed, more as a hobby. He quickly felt that I had a flair for copy-writing and recommended these ideas to the Country Head. Before long, the big boss wrote me a letter of appreciation and some of my ideas were used in the bank's advertising campaign. Tej was also my boss subsequently in Bombay. When he resigned from the bank in 1975, I certainly missed the mentor in him.

Formal mentoring has gained more universal acceptance and is consciously applied in best practice companies like Shell, Unilever, GE, etc. It is expected that understudies who have benefited from good mentors, will in turn become fine mentors themselves. In other words, **mentorship** (sounds a little more meaningful to me than just 'mentoring', as a noun) becomes part of the corporate culture.

Overall, **Jack Welch** is arguably the best example of the corporate mentor. He takes great interest and delight in lecturing at the GE Management Development Institute in Crotonville, several times a year to new recruits and up-coming managers – the future 'generals' of General Electric. Additionally, he personally reviews the targets and achievements of his top one hundred or so executives, to monitor their progress and to ensure that they are given suitable career development opportunities and rewards. Welch says that he spends as much as 60% of his time on such management issues. Another noteworthy feature of Welch is his hand-written notes to his managers to inspire them and to show support and empathy regarding their personal problems. Through this great style, Jack has been able to identify and develop several potential successors and most of them have also became excellent mentors themselves. This means that Jack's ideas and style are very much in evidence in GE's culture. It is noteworthy that GE has nurtured and 'provided' more CEOs to other organisations than any other company. This in itself is a testimonial to GE's ability to develop leaders, especially under Welch's stewardship and emphasis on mentoring.

Welch himself was fortunate to have a great, insightful and objective mentor in Reginald Jones. Jones who had already been CEO of GE for eight successful years, wanted to find a successor who would completely transform GE, to meet the increasing technological and competitive challenges in its core businesses. Jones had instructed one of his senior confidants to prepare a short list of candidates for the elite **Executive Management Staff** or EMS, from whom Jones would nominate his successor to lead the 'self-revival' of GE. Jones immediately noted the conspicuous absence of Jack's name. Apparently, Jack was not included because of his somewhat abrasive style. However, Jones clearly felt that Welch's overall brilliant track record heavily weighed in his favour. Moreover, in tough situations there is no harm in sounding a bit abrasive, if one is sincere and not insulting. To cut a long story short, Welch no doubt deserved to be 'crowned', but due credit must also be given to Jones, the mentor. The rest is history.

An example of good but indirect 'mentorship' becoming incorporated in the company's human resource development policy is the employer - employee partnership at **Motorola**. Motorola has developed the **Individual Dignity Entitlement Programme**, a broad-based approach to identify, resolve and even elevate employee issues to get proper attention.

Parents can also be great mentors. **Bill Gates** has had great mentors in his parents. **Martina Hinggis** the Czech-Swiss tennis sensation, is blessed with a highly inspiring mother-cum-coach. **William Pitt**, the Elder, a great orator and statesman was the mentor and father of William Pitt, **The Younger**, the youngest and highly successful Prime Minister in British history. **AP Gianini**, the founder of Bank of America was an entrepreneur and philantrophist. At one time, he was also one of the largest shareholders of First National Bank (Citibank). 'AP' is regarded as a fine mentor to his son and able successor, Mario. Mario is credited with the internationalization of Bank of America. Mario too was a born leader, nurtured by a great father-mentor, who had already proved himself to be a born leader.

I have mentioned in certain parts of this book about how my mother was trying to 'mould' my values through bed-time stories which contained important morals. Her deep and unfailing faith in God is evident to everyone who knows her. My father is not what you would call a 'religious person'. However, he has frequently told us, "I do not pray for my children to be wealthy. My prayer is that you may be healthy, happy, have good friends and earn real respect."

One morning, in 1979, I went to the Makati Medical Center in Manila for some tests. While I sat to wait for my turn, I heard what was then to me only an amusing inter-action between an elegantly dressed and ambitious mother and her bright, precious son, who could not have been a day over nine. The boy had to take a 'barium meal' test to check if he had any ulcers, but was very reluctant to swallow a whole glass full of this less than appetising, unappealing liquid chemical. Everytime his mother brought the glass to his dip, he would giggle and playfully push her hand aside. Subsequently, the mother looked him in the eye and said in a firm but still cordial tone, "Jun, if you don't get well and strong soon, how will you be able to take-over the business from your father." The boy, promptly gulped down the barium meal. Today, when I recall that incident I can tell that the mother was not just getting the little boy to imbibe an unpalatable potion; she was also being a mentor in regard to the longer term goal of making her son a good CEO of the large family business.

Readers would note that I have talked about mentors in other chapters as well. I would like to end this chapter by talking about Mahatma Gandhi as the great mentor and 'guru' of India's first Prime Minister, **Jawaharlal Nehru**. Nehru was the only son and favourite child of Moltilal Nehru, a prosperous and aristrocratic lawyer. Young Nehru had schooling in England and his doting father treated him like a prince. In other words, Jawahar (meaning 'gem') was used to the good life. It was Gandhi's ideals and his humble style of leading by example, coupled with the great national cause of freedom, that 'converted' Nehru. The convert became a great secular and unifying leader under Gandhi's patient guidance. To this day, Gandhi's understudy, Nehru is remembered as a great international statesman.

Shiv Nadar is also a great believer in mentoring. At the same time, he reminds us that we have to be "very careful in letting go of birds that have grown wings. My best successes and failures have occurred when I have made judgements on when the wings were strong enough". Nader has the integrity, courage and humility to admit that NIIT and HCL Infosystems flourished because he knew when to withdraw from their day-to-day management. On the other hand, this fine entrepreneurial leader confesses that he made wrong timing decisions in the cases of Network and HCL Office Automation, which failed. These kinds of experiences tell us that bosses must learn **when** to let go and in **whose** favour to let go.

For **James Bond** fans, an example of a good mentor is **'M'**. Although M, who is Bond's boss, is mostly in the background and kind of invisible, he has a subtle, but effective way of inspiring *007*. M emphasizes how much Her Majesty's Secret Service depends on Bond's capabilities and gives him a little pep talk before each challenging assignment. Similarly, on Bond's successful accomplishment of a mission, M does not fail to appreciate or congratulate Bond for a job well done. There is no backslapping or significant celebration between them or special financial reward for the glamorous hero, but the mentoring is very much in evidence in the charming, old British style of understatement. On the other hand, one has to admit that the colourful super-agent is largely self-motivated. He finds his own 'job satisfaction' and 'intangible rewards', thanks to the beautiful damsels he encounters during his, otherwise, life-threatening missions.

Here is a little sampling of some conversations from two of Fleming's famous books/films which show the warm informality, intimacy and cordiality between boss and subordinate:

Book: Dr No[*]
Scene: Bond doesn't want to leave his Beretta behind and M tells him this:

> M   :   If you carry a 00-number, it means you have license to kill, not get killed!!

Book: Thunderball[†]
Scene: M has just told Bond that he is to be sent to a health farm for two weeks:

Bond couldn't believe his ears. He said, "But Sir, I mean, I'm perfectly all right. Are you sure? I mean, is this really necessary?"

"No," M smiled frostily. "Not necessary. Essential. If you want to stay in the double-O section, that is, I can't afford to have an officer in that section who isn't one hundred percent fit." M lowered his eyes to the basket in front of him and took out a signal file, "That's all, 007." He didn't look up. The tone of voice was final.

Bond got to his feet. He said nothing. He walked across the room and let himself out, closing the door behind him with exaggerated softness.

It is noteworthy that mentors do not have to be only bosses, teachers or parents. Any experienced or wise person can fulfil this role. It is interesting to note that Mr. Konusuke Matsushita, the founder of the Japanese consumer electronics giant – Matsushita Electric viewed his chauffeur as a mentor and frequently referred to him for advice during their drives to and from work.

11

'HEAD MAN WALKING'

"When the Master governs,
the people are hardly aware he exists - - -"
(From Chapter 17 of Tao Te Ching)

Generally, 'management-by-walking-around' is a good idea. It is useful for top executives to come down from their executive suites to directly feel the 'pulse' of the people by walking around the shop floor and other similar operating areas, including the customer service departments. Top executives at successful companies like Coca-Cola, Unilever, Proctor & Gamble visit major supermarkets with their Sales Managers to make personal observations and talk with the staff, and clients as well, to get a direct 'feel' of the consumers.

However, the timing and psychology of such visits is vital. In times of industrial relations problems or recessions one has to be extra judicious. Also, in some companies, due to historical or cultural factors, the workers get petrified when the boss 'inspects' the work place. Sometimes workers freeze at the sight of the big boss and operations are disrupted. Some workers, with indoctrination by union leaders, believe that these maybe fault-finding visits, or precursors to downsizing programmes.

Therefore, it is the responsibility of the seniors and HR Department to make employees believe that they are in an organization which values its people - that the organization cares for the welfare of its employees - that top management encourages employee participation and empowerment. Such a sincere approach will magnify the benefits of management-by-walking-around.

There is another interesting approach inspired by the *TAO TE CHING** - the **'Invisible Leader'**. Here, the real leader knows that his power is ultimately based on the skills and motivation of his/her people. Therefore, such a leader does not have the 'face' of a boss. The Invisible Leader's behaviour towards subordinates and employees puts him/her in the light of a coach, a facilitator, a supporter and even a cheerleader. Such a leader can walk around, inspire the 'troops', and unleash their tremendous creative energy.

---

* I took guidance from the excellent book 'Real Power'- Business lessons from the Tao Te Ching, written by James A. Autry and Stephen Mitchell.

12

HOW TO 'CONTROL' PEOPLE

"When you are right, you have no need to be angry.
When you are wrong, you have no right to be angry."
                                            Mahatma Gandhi

Generally speaking, people like to be in control. Many bosses want to show that they are 'hands-on' managers by exercising control. Generally, pioneers and second generation entrepreneurs like the feeling of control even more than others. It is difficult to find fault with such people because they have put in a lot of personal sweat and majority of risk capital.

In marriage also, when the husband is the sole or major bread-winner, he is accepted as the 'head' of the family. Naturally, the husband has the main say, and often, the only say on important issues. Since the 1970s, we have more and more cases of wives making virtually equal financial contributions to the family unit, especially in rich OECD countries. This development and other social factors have significantly balanced the 'spouse vs. spouse landscape'. There is no longer a big shortage of wives who are equal partners. In fact, at least in developed countries, there are a good number of wives who 'wear the pants' at home, due to their education, incomes and/or personalities.

Coming back to the corporate set-up, every executive needs a degree of control if he/she has to function effectively, especially through subordinates. Broadly, an executive can achieve control and discipline in one of two ways:

1. By an **iron-hand**, also known as **management-by-fear**, or
2. Management by **inspiration**.

Let's examine these approaches:

Management-by-fear may be fairly effective in the short run. Decisions are highly centralized and can be made quickly. All employees come to work on time and they take very few and short breaks for coffee and lunch, for fear of being reprimanded, or even fired. The 'hard' boss may actually feel happy and proud because he has control, and employees are at his beck and call. Such a boss also uses anger to exercise discipline and control, and for his own 'ego massage'.

However, most of us are aware of the weaknesses of this management style:

- Decisions are made without consultation. Sometimes even relatively senior and experienced managers are treated like clerks.
- There is no sense of wide 'ownership' in the business plan.
- People feel that they are treated like slaves or robots, and morale is low.
- Employees keep good ideas to themselves.
- People are so afraid of making mistakes that they do the bare minimum routine work.
- Employees become 'clock-watchers'.
- There is no sense of loyalty, and good workers will seek alternate employment. Those who remain are order takers with low self-esteem.

Over a period of time, these factors will hurt the corporation's productivity, profitability, and even viability. Fortunately, this kind of iron-fisted or hot-tempered boss is on the 'endangered list', at least in developed economies.

Along with the profound advice quoted at the start of this chapter, from the great soul, it would be worthwhile for our hands-on friends to listen to an important message from the Bhagvad Gita and the Tao Te Ching, which tell us to practise 'detachment'. In our modern situation of careers, family life and daily routine, detachment does not mean staying aloof or not getting involved. It certainly does not mean that top management should remain isolated in ivory towers. To me, this kind of detachment means non-interference, to give people time and space to think, and do their jobs sensibly, without feeling undue pressure. Yet, the 'detached' boss is very approachable - he acts as an advisor and supporter.

Management-by-inspiration is a totally different style, as the name suggests. In this scenario, top management discusses its fundamental beliefs and values with a wide cross-section of people, including representatives of junior cadres. It also shares and articulates the grand vision and explains broad goals. Doubts are clarified and good suggestions are welcomed and incorporated in the final document or declaration. Consequently, the organization has a strong foundation cemented by and at all segments and levels of membership. This kind of corporation has a greater chance for sustained success because of the shared values and common vision. Some indicators of this style are:

- Employees are viewed in a positive manner and they in turn view senior management in a positive light.
- Employees are shown benefits of the vision or culture change programme or business plan.
- Since employees' ideas are also represented in the plan they feel a sense of ownership and become more responsible for its success.
- Senior executives conduct 'management-by-self-control'. They control their own egos or need for power and give people more discretion on how to achieve results.
- Employees become motivated to improve quality and productivity with less supervision. They feel that they have more 'space' without the boss constantly looking over their shoulders.
- Morale is distinctly superior because the employees focus on reward rather than punishment.

- Management tolerates genuine mistakes; seniors counsel and train staff like happy coaches.
- Employees feel that there is a fair reward system.
- Employees learn to appreciate that the organization should not accept wrong attitudes or conflicting values or goals. There is a fair procedure on disciplinary action.

CREATIVE EMPLOYEES

Creative employees need 'special handling'. In recent years, I have come to appreciate, even more, that the best way of 'killing' creativity is to 'control' employees who are doing creative work e.g. advertising, story/script writing, research, product development, etc. In my own case, I have found that I get my best ideas when I am not **'in the office state of mind'**. As mentioned in the Introduction, the ideas come me when I am relaxed – half asleep or while swimming. In other words, the creative juices flow much better when one is not pre-occupied with office routine or tension. I subsequently organize those thoughts and implement them when I am back in the office.

I especially feel that creative employees must not be bound by strict office hours because their minds are frequently 'working' even better when they are not in the formal office. I have referred to the SDA teams (cross-functional task forces) in their Tear Down Rooms ('labs') at LG Group in Chapter 10. The teams working on breakthrough projects have no fixed hours. Their gymnasium and bedrooms are right next to the Tear Down Rooms. It is up to the members to work through the night when they are all pumped-up, and relax the next day to recuperate. Generally speaking, rooms of creative people have very different décor when compared to normal offices. It has been proved that office layout, color schemes, music, and general environment play a great role in inspiring creativity. As mentioned elsewhere in this book, creativity cannot be mandated or suddenly increased by financial incentives alone.

RESULT - PROMOTING SELF-GOVERNANCE

If the top management is able to create the right environment, as mentioned above, the result is genuine loyalty and much more. Employees enjoy coming to work and they demonstrate a strong feeling of 'membership' or pride of association. The organization has created the climate for top performance. Things start 'ticking' by themselves because of natural or spontaneous controls based on personal commitment, which may also be called self-governance.

Ultimately, it is up to the boss to decide what kind of boss he/she wishes to be. The boss can choose to be a **mentor** or a **tormentor**.

13

PEOPLE LEADERSHIP

"The history of the world is but the biography of great men"
(and women)
Thomas Carlyle

Since this book is essentially about people, I am writing about leading people here. Moreover, where there is good **'people leadership'**, the potential for excellence and developing future leaders increases. Another outcome of good people leadership is that the organization develops capabilities to become a market leader, as well.

Some experts say, "Leaders are born, not made." On the other hand, certain authorities on the subject say, "Leaders can be developed." I have to admit that I have 'one foot in each camp' and hope that I can justify my 'forked-tongue'!

Let's examine these theories:

Scene: First few days at kindergarten, the 5-6 year old kids have not known each other before. If we observe this group playing or interacting at random, we would notice that it will not be long before the majority of the kids look up to <u>one</u> as their leader. This could be because he is the biggest or fastest or strongest. It could also be the result of one kid being the friendliest, the peace maker, the one who plays fair and can hold the group together. Of course, the kid who has some of the physical attributes of the first type with some of the human values of the second type - such an exceptional kid would meet the definition of a **born leader**.

The leadership which may have been 'inborn' in this child, is a combination of inherited leadership genes and the 'messages' the child receives and the 'examples' it observes, consciously or sub-consciously from parents, elder siblings, (pre-school) teachers, classmates, etc. We may describe these two groups of factors as the **power of genes** and the **power of early influences**.

Now, if our **born leader** gets the continuing benefit of good parenting, good education, team sports, activities like boy-scouts and generally positive re-enforcement, the leadership qualities get refined and stronger. Also, the confidence gained builds positive ambition. Subsequently, if he/she gets into an organization - civil, commercial or military, which recognizes and nurtures this leadership talent, the 'full' leadership potential could well be realized. In my mind, Jack Welch, the CEO of GE and General Colin Powell are fine examples of this type of born leader.

The above three paragraphs support the 'born leader' view, but even this type of leader needs nurturing and mentoring.

Now, let us look at a person who did not demonstrate early/natural leadership qualities. Our candidate did not have the leadership head-start through genes or early influences. But, he/she is basically bright and motivated. In any event, it is difficult and, perhaps not advisable, for an organization to find and retain all born leaders. The organization will also look for many good 'solid technicians'. Among those technicians, persons who show supervisory or managerial potential are given planned training and development exposure, on and off the job, and increasing responsibility that would help them be aware of and imbibe leadership skills.

The born leaders and latent leaders in a progressive organization will be given general management and leadership training although the first category would probably get accelerated training & development assuming that they are fast-trackers, as discussed in the relevant chapter. They will initially be 'taught' efficient management. Not much later, these candidates will be exposed to effective management and how to focus on real issues and how to multiply or leverage their skills through subordinates. Considerable emphasis will be given to the importance of teamwork and on how to be a good team player.

During these on-going development programs, these candidates and young officers will get a further grounding in the company's vision and values. They are 'encouraged' to align their own career ambitions with the corporate vision and values. Again, the better corporation's values will be demonstrated by its real belief and investment in its people. They will be taught the values and virtues of fair play, and building genuine loyalty, etc. These officers will be helped to find the **motivator** inside themselves. In other words, the candidates of both categories, in addition to improving at least one technical skill, are consciously given opportunities to learn or improve managerial skills to at least become a 'competent manager', combining efficiency and effectiveness. Hopefully, some will also have or gain charisma as they develop and move up the organization.

At each stage, there are regular reviews to monitor the candidate's/officer's progress, with counseling in appropriate ways. They have to be able to take on increasing responsibility, including responsibility for the performance of their subordinates. They have to learn to take 'ownership' of projects or problems and to **carry the ball all the way**. They must understand and practice the concept of **'the buck stops here'**, and learn to give attention to solving and preventing problems rather than assigning blame. (Exception: frauds and the like)

It is my belief that given the above-mentioned 'treatment', at least some of the officers who did not have/display very early leadership attributes or potential, will discover the hidden leader inside. This, then is the case for 'leaders are made'. This is the second part of my rationale for being split between the theories - 'leaders are born' and 'leaders are made', and I recommend that neither school of thought be ignored. Otherwise, the world will have a much smaller reservoir of real leaders.

Bill Gates' brilliance showed from a very young age and he enjoyed strong parental support. (I have not heard or read that he was into team sports in any significant way.) The world's richest man ever, and the world's most successful college drop-out ever, in addition to natural or self-taught technical excellence, displayed unique leadership from his early twenties. I think that for all practical purposes, he had earned his 'doctorate' by the time he finished high school. I am not referring to academic brilliance alone. At twenty-three, he started Microsoft with the tremendous and clear vision of **'a computer on every desk and every home'**. He was among the first people who recognized that in this Information Age, software will become more powerful than hardware. (Or, if I may say so, hardware is now 'softer' than software). Bill's crystal ball told him of the speed of the coming software explosion. Bill foresaw very early how software could magnify mankind's brain power. He could not 'afford' to finish college or get work experience before starting Microsoft because someone else would grab the initiative. In fact, it's no exaggeration to say that he was and is one of the world's prime accelerators of software development and application. Bill's leadership also shows that he is not nervous about hiring the best brains in the business. He enjoys associating with very smart people; he does not feel threatened or intimidated by them. In fact, unfortunately, many founders or pioneers, because of ego, do not like their lieutenants to be very brilliant. While they desire competence, they give more importance to personal loyalty.

Another sign of Gates' leadership is his statement, "My greatest strength is my ability to transfer my enthusiasm to my people." - the sign of a great team builder. Furthermore, Bill or Microsoft has made many more employees millionaires than probably any other company in history. Bill, in my mind was and is of the 'born leader' type in a very original way.

I do hope that he and the authorities can resolve the antitrust issues for the benefit of Microsoft, the software industry, and the consumer. This calls for a sort of mercantile statesmanship on his part and less paranoia on the part of his competitors. As Peter Drucker says, no firm can remain a dominant monopoly for long in the free world.

Michael Dell, the dynamic and visionary creator of Dell Computer Company is to me a great symbol of a born leader. He has truly revolutionized how personal computers can be customized, and yet sold by mail order, in surprisingly short time frames.

Al Grove of Intel, and Time Magazine's 'Man of the Year - 1997', is another icon who shows great vision and leadership. The company, under his technical and people leadership, has achieved such a strong market position and reputation, that most computer manufacturers are proud to advertise 'INTEL INSIDE'.

People like Bill Gates and Al Grove have enriched their colleagues and shareholders <u>and</u> enriched the concept of leadership - - - tough but great examples to emulate!

Muhammad Yunus is an outstanding example of humanness, vision, dedication, commitment, organization and leadership skills, all rolled into one person. An economist by qualification, he was deeply touched by the plight of the poorest of the poor in a village called Jobra in his country, Bangladesh. While still a youth, he was deeply saddened that even those who tried to do some work like small farming, or handicrafts like making bamboo stools, baskets etc., were exploited by loan sharks or blood suckers who charged interest as high as 10% per week! Yunus still an economics student, managed to lend the equivalent of $35 to forty two artisans including many women, on a repayable when able basis. Just imagine, that by lending an average of 83 cents he was able to help so many, otherwise helpless peasants!

This little effort was the seed that germinated and branched into a highly successful and model rural financial institution called **GRAMEEN BANK** or village bank. Today, this bank has over 1,100 (small) branches. Through this unique institution, Yunus has given direct employment to over 12,000 staffers at the bank itself and helped raise the living standard and dignity of several hundred thousand villagers in Bangladesh. What's also most remarkable is that GRAMEEN BANK claims to have less than a 2% default rate, in spite of the fact that the vast majority of the loans are unsecured, not collateralised!! Citibank, Deutsche Bank, BNP, Tokyo Mitsubishi, ABN-Amro, HSBC, please take note ... probably you already have. This story also proves that poor people want make an honest living, if we give them a chance. They don't want pity from us - just timely start-up help.

I salute you, Mr. Yunus for blending business and welfare so beautifully. You have earned international admiration and our plaudits. You have real charisma. The Nobel Academy should have a special combined award for Economics, Peace and Nobility for such a fine all-rounder.

Anybody wishes to guess to which category of leadership **Richard Branson** of Virgin fame belongs? You got it! This maverick, daredevil, un-conventional dynamo of a businessman, is a 'dyed-in-the-wool' born leader. Ask the venerable British Airways and American Airlines about this competitor! When I was at Heathrow, London Airport in 1997, I was tickled to read this huge slogan painted across Virgin's jumbo jet: "NO WAY BA–AA". Richard certainly lives up to his lion-hearted name!

I have written about various attributes and examples of leadership throughout this book. Now, I need to make a special mention of the attribute of **bonding power**. Whether it is a family unit, military unit, business unit or a sports team, the leader must have the ability to hold the team together. He/she must be the cement to hold the 'human bricks' together and keep the 'relationship structure' cordial, strong and motivated.

To be a leader, one has to have followers and supporters. To be a great leader, the leader has to be able to hold his people together under a worthwhile common cause.

In the corporate world, there have been several **mega-mergers**, including:

- Swiss Bank Corporation merges with Union Bank of Switzerland to form United Bank of Switzerland
- Ciba-Geigy merges with Sandoz to form Novartis
- Bank of America merges with Nations Bank
- Citicorp merges with Travellers to form Citigroup
- Daimler-Benz merges with Chrysler to form Daimler Chrysler
- Exxon merges with Mobil (in process)
- British Petroleum merges with Amoco to form BP Amoco and BP Amoco and is trying to absorb Atlantic Richfield
- Renault bought the controlling 35% stake in Nissan Motors
- Hyundai Electronics merges with LG Semi-Conductor
- America Online (AOL) has acquired Netscape
- Yahoo! Is in the process of merging with Broadcast.comm.
- Banque National de Paris makes the most 'radical' bid for both Banque Paribas and Societé Generale, who are in advanced merger talks with each other. If this merger takes place, it would create the world's first trillion-dollar bank! I also hate to think of the number of redundancies it would create.

The leaders of these merged companies, in addition to their grand visions, must have the ability to mesh or bond the merging entities and cultures for the common good of the 'whole'. They should act fairly and sincerely in giving key positions to the concerned executives, without showing favoritism. Otherwise, many good people will leave or will lose their motivation, which would hurt the overall objective. The bonding power of key executives can help to minimize 'post-merger blues'.

Readers who follow 'M & As' would recall the spate of acquisitions of merchant banks and stock brokers by leading banks in the run-up to the 'Big Bang' in Britain in the late 1980s and early 1990s. Some of those acquisitions, where insufficient attention had been given to the human side, suffered from 'hangover' or 'indigestion', depending on what they drank and ate during the 'courtship' and early 'honeymoon' celebrations. (Gee, I can't stay serious for long.) In those cases of poor bonding, 'acquired employees' jumped ship *en masse*, and all parties involved suffered, except the sellers who cashed out with handsome premia (premiums).

Here, I wish to list some **historic** examples of great leaders (generals and politicians) with the unique bonding ability to build and maintain **energized unity** among their people, even in adverse situations or against heavy odds:

Leonidas leading his small Spartan force against the huge numerical superiority of the invading Persians in the Battle of Thermopylae;

Admiral Nelson in the Battle of Trafalgar against the mighty Spanish Armada;

Joan of Arc in leading the relief of Orleans, in support of Charles VII;

George Washington leading the American War of Independence;

Abraham Lincoln leading the 'Union' during the American Civil War;

Mahatma Gandhi who was able to unite and energize India's diverse ethnic and religious groups, rich and poor, in the peaceful and successful struggle for independence;

At this stage, I would like to make specific comments on a few more recognized heroes, who will also be remembered by future generations.

Nelson Mandela during the transition from *Apartheid* to relatively peaceful democracy in South Africa. About twenty-seven years of his 'best' years were spent in prison. Yet, he has not shown bitterness against the rich, white minority. He has been statesman like, with focus on nation building. He has presided over a much more stable and ethnically tolerant South Africa, a South Africa that is respected in the community of nations and enjoys great influence in the African continent. It is no surprise that Mandela won the Nobel Peace Prize. Now, he richly deserves a "Nobel peace prize for unselfishness" by not hanging on the presidency. Congratulations! President Mandela.

Colin Powell

I believe that General Colin Powel is a fine example of a born leader, whose potential was fortunately recognized by his superiors in good time. We should also give credit to his mentors, who helped groom him into an outstanding leader. It is worth quoting Powell's simple rules:

1. It ain't as bad as you think. It will look better in the morning.
2. Get mad, then get over it.
3. Avoid having your ego so close to your position that when your position falls, your ego goes with it.
4. It can be done!
5. Be careful what you choose. You may get it.
6. Don't let adverse facts stand in the way of a good decision.
7. You can't make someone else's choices. You shouldn't let some one else make yours.
8. Check small things.
9. Share credit.
10. Remain calm. Be kind.
11. Have a vision. Be demanding.
12. Don't take counsel of your fears or naysayers.
13. Perpetual optimism is a force multiplier.

Winston Churchill (1874-1965) Let me attempt a little thumb nail sketch of one of the finest examples of a born leader of our times. Although Winston Leonard Spencer Churchill kept 'flunking' Latin in school, he was truly a brilliant man of destiny whose impact was felt around the world for several decades.

From his young days Churchill displayed leadership. He belonged to a line of famous Dukes. After his initial grooming at the famous Harrow Public School, he attended the Royal Military College at Sandhurst. Quite soon he showed his fearless qualities in the battle-fields of colonial India and the Sudan. Later, in 1898, as a war reporter in the Boer Wars, he was captured by the Boers. But, this spirited man escaped and returned to London to a hero's welcome. It is an achievement for anyone to become a legend in his own lifetime, but Churchill achieved this status in his still youthful years.

To cut a long story short, Churchill became Prime Minister of Britain twice in its most critical periods. His cigar chomping personality was always present to raise the morale of his people whether they were soldiers, nurses or civilians. One could compile a solid anthology on Churchill's great speeches, but I would like to quote one of his oft quoted historic speeches that revealed the great leader in him:

> *"We shall defend our island, whatever the cost may be - - - We shall fight on the beaches, we shall fight on the landing grounds, we shall fight on the fields and the streets, we shall fight on the hills, we shall never surrender."*

Churchill was made a Knight of the Garter by Queen Elizabeth II in 1953, and was later awarded the Nobel Prize for Literature in recognition of his fine books and great speeches.

Churchill had great intellect, a deep understanding of history, a personal feel for the life on the battle fronts, a tremendous patriotic spirit, a great sense of humour, capped with his inspiring personality. I have already mentioned his oratory excellence. All these cherished qualities 'stuffed' in just one person are what gave Churchill the well deserved reputation of a charismatic leader and statesman. He was able to put this charisma to good use, especially during the World War

II, while the Nazis were bombing Britain, before America joined the war. While Churchill is one of the finest examples of a born leader, I hasten to add that 'environmental factors' and historic challenges of monumental proportions worked to heighten his legendary leadership skills. (This comes back to the earlier debate of whether leaders are born or made - - - it must be a combination of both factors, while the weightage may defer from person to person.)

Without trying to sound presumptuous, I have two qualms versus this great man: (i) He belittled Mahatma Gandhi as a half naked 'fakir' when the Indian was pleading the case for India's independence in London. Churchill feared that if Britain gave up the 'jewel in the crown', that it would mark the beginning of the decline of his dear British Empire. (ii) In 1944, the Viceroy of India, Wavell, telegraphed Churchill for help to supply emergency food for the starving millions during the famous Bengal Famine. Wavell's astonishment was recorded in his journal: "Winston sent me a peevish telegram to ask why Gandhi hadn't died yet! He has never answered my telegram about food." I suppose that even such a great leader had his blind spot. He just didn't care what happened as long as the British Empire was intact. The quality of humanness sometimes 'deserted' him, if the affected people were not his own compatriots.

Oliver Cromwell (1599-1658) could be described as largely a courageous, non conformist leader, with principles. As a member of the English Parliament, he was strongly opposed to the tyrant King Charles I's move to abolish major rights of the Parliament. Cromwell's belief in the principles of power through Parliament made him join the Civil War against his own King. As a result of this backlash, the tyrant King was forced to flee from London. Cromwell's character was such that his belief was firm in religion, firm in government and powerful in battle.

Although he had no previous war experience, he was able to garner support of the Puritan farmers. With these farmers, he raised a cavalry called Ironsides. Cromwell's latent military genius also helped him defeat the great Swedish general Gustavos Adolphos and subsequently Prince Rupert, the nephew of Charles I, in 1644.

Due to Cromwell's military exploits, discipline and fair governing principles, he was subsequently named Lord Protector of the Commonwealth covering England, Scotland and Ireland. He was respected throughout the western hemisphere, and loved and admired at home. Even though the Puritans helped him establish and consolidate his rule, Cromwell believed in the principle of religious freedom and tried to weed out the fanatical Puritans from his Parliament. However, this job remained unfinished because of his preoccupation in foreign wars and larger Commonwealth affairs. His firm belief in justice was fully tested when the army demanded King Charles' head. Cromwell first hesitated. Finally, he weighed the potential menace of Charles' remaining alive, vis-à-vis the larger interests of his people and country. He showed his personal <u>wisdom</u> and <u>courage</u> in co-signing Charles' death warrant. Cromwell is in my mind, one of the great and historic examples of power, people and principles. He had the rare courage of conviction and leadership to unite common people to preserve those principles and exposed himself to personal peril for his great causes. He was also 'flexible' at critical times, which may also be sometimes deemed as compromising his ideals.

The enigmatic Cromwell is delicately but aptly described by John Bucham as follows:

> *"A Devotee of law, he was forced to be often lawless; a civillian to the core, he had to maintain himself by the sword; with a passion to construct, his task was chiefly to destroy..."*

This kind of description earned him the appellation 'man for all seasons'.

Benjamin Franklin (1706-1790) was a born genius and principled leader. In trying to adhere to the theme of this book and chapter, I shall refrain from writing about his famous achievements as a newsman or scientist (e.g. proving that lightning is electricity).

Franklin became a colonial leader to protect the British colonies in North America against the French, who were supported by some (Red) Indian tribes. Subsequently, he was sent as a representative of Pennsylvania to the Mother Country, England, to argue for fair tax payments from (rich) people who lived in England but inherited huge land holdings in Pennsylvania. These taxes were needed urgently for the defense of Britain's colonies in America. The British respected him for his scientific work, humour and principles, and his mission was successful.

Some years later, following 'the Boston Tea Party', thirteen of the colonies wanted to break away from Britain, for which they could only turn to the French for help. Again, Franklin was the one entrusted with the job to elicit support in France. It was his great character, personality and principles that ultimately helped him win French support, in what became the American War of Independence.

The final testimony to this man, one of the greatest sons of America, is that he is the only person to have been involved intimately in drafting and signing the four most important documents in American history: (i) the Declaration of Independence in 1776, (ii) the Treaty of Alliance with France in 1778, (iii) the Treaty of Paris in 1783, and (iv) the American Constitution in 1787.

In essence, I would say that this man was so richly endowed with intellectual power; a burning desire for freedom, with responsibility; a profound belief in God, balanced with a sense of secularism; adherence to fair play and equal opportunity, and sincere preference for peaceful negotiations, instead of war. It is difficult to imagine that one human being could have all these coveted qualities and enjoy such genuine charisma, popularity and public trust. History acknowledges that Franklin's principle based leadership is a very, very unique and a tough act to follow. Small wonder that his face appears on American $100 bills (notes).

If we were to rate Churchill, Cromwell and Franklin, we would, indeed, give them all very, very high marks. However, in my humble opinion, Franklin scores somewhat higher points due to his humane spirit.

Kapil Dev

For cricket fans, I would mention Kapil Dev, one of the finest all-rounders the game has known, and the Indian team captain for several years. Kapil, in my mind, was the best cricket captain that India has ever had. He displayed that lion-hearted spirit and led by example. His never-say-die attitude was balanced with great dignity and a sense of fair play.

14

CHARISMA

You are what your deep, driving desire is.
As your desire is, so is your will.
As your will is, so is your deed.
As your deed is, so is your destiny.
Brihadaranyaka Upanishad IV.4.5.

This is an oft-quoted verse from the great Upanishads of India's ageless Sanskrit culture.

In the chapter titled "People Leadership", I talked about certain leaders and their special attributes. I now wish to delve deeper into **charisma**, the intriguing and poetic word of Persian origin. A unique attribute that gives a leader additional appeal is charisma. To me, the leader develops or 'earns' charisma by having charm; an appealing style; a powerful, yet endearing personality; an oratory gift, including wit; a certain presence and demeanor that radiates and inspires confidence. Sometimes, charisma may be inherited.

I view charisma as 'icing on the cake'. Attractive icing helps to 'complete' or 'dress' the cake and make it more appealing. But we have to remember that icing, like beauty, is only 'skin-deep'. There has to be a really **well baked person**, with the **right ingredients**, under the skin. The right ingredients are - the basic and solid qualities and skills, many of which I have referred to in various parts in this book. Additionally, gaining experience and confidence over time, and the wise use of these attributes, supported with time honoured principles and values, represent the well-baked or seasoned aspects required of a leader.

Charisma is a wonderfully useful 'aura', if reflected by a genuine leader. However, nobody is going to enjoy overly sweet icing only. Too much icing alone will soon taste bitter and even make us sick. Similarly, if charisma is only skin-deep like 'make-up', or 'hollow packaging', it can cause havoc through the weak, unwise or fraudulent leader to, at least temporarily, lead the followers astray. Caveat: if a person wins popular following, only or mainly by using artificial and superficial attractions, charisma can be a dangerous thing, unless we are only talking about **show business**.

In summary, what I wish to emphasize is, that in business, as in politics, charisma is a wonderful and powerful lever to have and use, as a **supplement** to the **real qualities** - - - not a substitute for them. Otherwise, misplaced charisma can be down-right wasteful or destructive in an unprincipled or unwise person. Cautionary examples are Adolf Hitler, Saddam Hussein.

Recent history, and even 'current history' tells us that when a charismatic leader's popularity **booms** to 'cult status', the time for him/her to **'bomb out'** is also not far behind. Sometimes, a few leaders, with the help of 'spin doctors' or other tools, become too popular for their own good. This ultra popular leader often becomes a law unto himself, and soon enough sows the seeds of his own decline and ultimate failure. We must remember that the rewards or punishments for our 'karmas' are due, sooner or later.

Two women who <u>inherited</u> charisma and 'blew it' were the late Prime Minister **Indira Gandhi** and former Prime Minister **Benazir Bhutto**. Indira won a significant mandate twice from the Indian people but committed at least four major follies: (i) She declared a harsh National Emergency in the 1970s for her 'self preservation'. Also, her arrogant second son Sanjay and cronies abused power to hurt and imprison many innocent people. (ii) She 'sponsored' corruption under the pretext of collecting election campaign funds for her Congress Party. (iii) She became too enamoured with and too close to the then Soviet Union, which was not helping India in the real sense. (iv) She committed the unforgivable sin of ordering a military assault on the most sacred 'Golden Temple' of the Sikhs, which is also deeply revered by many Hindus. By this order, she alienated many moderate and patriotic Sikhs. This was a great tragedy for all of India. Indira's sad story was ended by a couple of her own Sikh bodyguards who shot her in cold blood. This too was tragic and most regrettable.

Indira once made a beautiful and profound statement, "You can't shake hands with a closed fist." If only she had practised what she had preached, history may have been kinder to her and to India.

Her daughter-in-law, the attractive Italian born, **Sonia** (widow of the late Prime Minister Rajiv Gandhi) is presently enjoying a charismatic surge in India because of the family name and sympathy due to Rajiv's assassination, which are bolstered with the dignity and balance she has displayed so far. Sonia is also gaining centre-stage and is just a hair's breath away from the Pmship as BJPs leaky boat has almost capsized. Her daughter **Priyanka** is also basking in this charismatic sunshine. India's third General Election in three years, due around September of '99, will tell us how much this 'charismatic weapon' will work.

I hope for India's sake, that if this attractive mother-daughter duo wrests the Indian political crown, they would remember the good deeds and misdeeds of their senior family members, who were major political players:

Jawaharial Nehru
He was patriotic and honest; but leftist, arrogant and somewhat naïve.

Indira Gandhi
Intelligent; but less patriotic, less honest, more power crazy and reckless.

Sanjay Gandhi
Bright; but selfish, impatient, lacking integrity, very power crazy, brash, ruthless bully (e.g. forcing sterilisation even of young men

under the banner of Family Planning, granting liquor licenses to dubious people on a dubious basis). He did all this without even being a minister, leave alone prime minister.

Rajeev Gandhi

Started modestly and with good intentions; but favoured his Doon School Goons or cronies, lost his sense of balance, abused power, and got entangled in one of India's biggest corruption scandals – the Bofors Case – involving large kick-backs in a deal covering import of major weapons from Sweden to India. Despite Rejeev's attempts to make this arms deal look like an arms length transaction, the long arm of the law nearly got him. The 'nearly' is because he was able to twist many arms to get him out of harm's way.

Now, let's review a few more charismatic leaders:

Benazir also received a generous share of charisma, thanks to her father, Zulfikar Ali Bhutto, who became a martyr through a politically motivated death sentence 'sponsored' by the martial law President, Zia-Ul-Haq. The 'inheritance' was augmented because she was Harvard educated and good looking. (She did cover her head, but did not need to veil her face.) Anyway, it is creditable that Benazir became Prime Minister in a very chauvinistic and somewhat feudalistic country like Pakistan. Unfortunately, she did not meet many of her election promises. Furthermore, her marriage to an overly ambitious (and reportedly aggressive) businessman, Asif Zardari, did not help her reputation or her country's situation. For a long period, Pakistan's parliament had to spend inordinate time and energy debating the 'excesses' committed by the 'Benazir-Asif combo'. Before long, Benazir lost her job as PM and had to grace the Opposition benches in Islamabad. More recently, she has been living in Exile, presumably to avoid the jail sentence. Meanwhile, Asif seems to have received 'Black and Blue' treatment in prison.

It can only be hoped that Prime Minister **Chandrika Kumaratunga** of Sri Lanka (daughter of the first two Prime Ministers – Mr. & Mrs.

Bandaranaike - this is a record in itself) can end up using her family charisma and other attributes for the betterment of her poor, war-torn country, compared to her old counterparts of the Sub-continent. Her countrymen must be praying that the old KKN virus á la Indonesia will not infect her or her cabinet.

Dictatorial leaders frequently forget or ignore lessons even from recent history. There was a good lesson to be learnt from Ferdinand Marcos of the Philippines on how not to wield power. On the other end of the scale, there is an excellent lesson to be learnt from **Lee Kuan Yew** of Singapore. Senior Minister Lee realized his great vision on how to develop a small country without its own natural resources. He also had the good sense to systematically transfer power, and without personally enriching himself or his kith and kin.

Indonesia apparently did progress a great deal during the pro-business Soeharto regime. Infrastructure improved tremendously. Jakarta never had to face the infamous 'brownouts' of Manila (in the 1980s). Indonesia's per capita GDP zoomed from around $100 in the 1960s to nearly $1,000 by June 1997. The main problems were that this progress contained a serious element of 'KKN', described in the chapter titled 'Adaptability', and excess borrowings in foreign (dollar) currency, even for non-dollar earning projects. It is ironical, but not surprising, that the daughter of his predecessor (whom he himself deposed), Megawati Soekarnoputri finds that her star is shining now, with grassroots support. One can only hope that Mega, the front-runner or whoever wins the forthcoming, third presidential elections, will follow only the good policies and practices of Indonesia's first two President's and carefully avoid the pitfalls that trapped them. The next President must not let power and popularity cloud her/his judgment, priorities and sense of balance. I certainly hope to see a peaceful and prosperous period under the next President, who has a great challenge, but, also a great opportunity to re-build a great nation. Personally, I feel that a partnership of Mega, as President, and General Wiranto, as VP, is the best way to go forward.

Let us also not forget Eva (Evita) Peron and Imelda (Iron-Butterfly) Marcos who got intoxicated by their charisma-enhanced popularity and ended up abusing it, and eventually losing their charisma and lustre.

Talking about the late Argentinean icon-cum-bombshell, I cannot help mentioning that the South Indian state of Tamil Nadu can boast or complain (depending on your values) about its home-grown version of Evita. **Jayalalitha**, a Brahmin girl, was one year my junior at the Church Park Convent in Madras (Chennai). She was a bright student with good looks. After school, she soon found fame, glory and limelight through the silver screen of the booming film industry of Madras. At that time, several top story writers, directors and film heroes were deeply involved in regional politics through a party called DMK. Jaya's talents and looks charmed the audiences, and she managed to 'enter the hearts' of two princes of the Madras cine-political elite, namely Karunanidhi and MG Ramachandran (known as MGR to his fans, or rather followers). The 'filmy' eternal triangle became a real-life internal tangle, and consequently there had to be a parting in the party, a split in DMK. This 'Helen of Ploy' had the face that launched a 'thousand sheets' to announce the new splinter party headed by MGR, called AIDMK. Jaya had picked the AIDMK or MGR 'horse' (or stud) as her (by at that time) sole lover. Their new party won the next state election battle following the split, and MGR soon became the Chief Minister (C.M.) of that state. A few years later, this cinematic hero-cum-Chief Minister died, but Jaya had sympathy and charisma on her side which helped her beat MGR's legal wife in becoming the C.M. Soon she abused her power and her coffers were quickly swelling with multitudes of 'troy ounces' (I couldn't resist the temptation to say it, while she couldn't resist the temptation to make it.)

Anyway, to cut a long story short, Jaya got booted out at the following state elections because of her wide-ranging excesses, culminating in the overly regal and ostentatious wedding of her adopted son. As a result, her former lover (now enemy) Karunanidhi is back in the

C.M.'s chair. Many political pundits had written off Jaya as a politician and it was largely expected that she would retire and devote herself to 'quiet time' to protect herself against major lawsuits for corruption and abuse of power. But Jaya was no spring chicken. She waited for the right time to spring back. She recharged her battered batteries and kept herself motivated by one solid principle - the **principle of power over people**.

I could probably write a song for Jayvita, I mean Jaya. Let me just give you a little **'appeteaser'**:

> *"Don't cry for me dear Karuna.*
> *The truth is I 'barely' loved you.*
> *All through my wild days,*
> *My mad existence,*
> *I kept no promise,*
> *- - - Please keep your distance."*

As the filmy saga continues, Karunanidhi (Karuna) and his DMK bungled again, and Jaya's AIDMK won a small but significant block of seats in the 1998 (federal) General Elections for the Indian Parliament. The Bharatya Janta Party (BJP), under Prime Minister **Vajpayee** (frequently referred to as the right man in the wrong party) was short of a clear majority and needed, inter alia, Jaya's support to stay in power and remain as head of the Central Government. Therefore, we had a typical case of 'tail wagging the dog' which was even more painful for India because the 'dog' and 'tail' belonged to highly incompatible 'breeds'! They had radically different ideologies, but they had one thing in common - craving for power. In Hindi, this is typically called 'KISSA KURSI KA'. This literally means the case of the 'seat', implying what all politicians do to grab or stay in power.

Earlier, one of the most original ideas of Jaya's spin-doctors was to portray her as, guess what - - - Virgin Mary! Admittedly, our 'Santa Jaya Maria' is shy of taking formal marriage vows. She is entitled to her own (immaculate or otherwise) **conception** of wedlock. However, she has had at least three of her own well-known and virile 'Josephs', including the latest, Sohn Baba. Her spin doctors' virtual reality (or virgin unreality) gambit got trumped or check-mated when the public went up in arms.

Although, this **'queen bee'** of Tamil Nadu has a big sting, her narrow vision and questionable track-record will prevent her from wearing the national political crown. Having said that, the buzz-word is that this not so humble bee still has a 'bee in her bonnet' and she can *humble* New Delhi's **big bumble bee**, and his hive, I mean cabinet, of *bungle* and *fumble* bees. I hear a *mumble* that if 'P.M.ji' cannot help Jaya in concealing the skeletons (and troy ounces) in her Madras closet, she will pull that Persian rug to *tumble* him. (Here I'm rhyming with **know** rhyme and reason.) In fact, I saw on CNN, Mr. Vajpayee deliver his 51st Independence Day Speech at Delhi's Red Fort. Just as he finished with the traditional patriotic words "JAI HIND" (Victory to India) the aging leader could barely stand. We saw him *stumble* - - - there were concerns about Jaya's impact on his health - - - the *rumble* reverberated throughout his vast country and the stock market index took a dive at that time.

Personal letter to Jayalalitha

Dear Jaya,

Based on our old school 'bond', this is 'For Your Eyes Only'.

Hope that you're not too tired buzzing between Chennai and New Delhi. Please do not take this letter as a declaration of verbal war. In any event, you are very seasoned at dodging real and metaphorical bullets and brick-bats. You've also had your share of floral and verbal bouquets from your 'devotees'. Just accept these paragraphs as my little 'penmanship' and 'punmanship' - - - On my part, there is no guilt, I'm just adding some GILT to the charisma concept.

Seriously, Jaya, I also hope that if you gain the big 'kursi' (chair) again, some of these chapters will, hopefully, make you think a bit more, before you act.

And Jaya, your previous fall from grace should have taught you that superficial charisma alone will not take you far. Go for the real and sincere values of charisma and rely less on the filmy version. Remember the lessons you learnt at Church Park in moral science classes, and on human values. If you do a good job next time, your former Church Park mates will be proud of you again. You may also wish to re-learn the lessons of one of your first films 'The Epistle' (in which our common friend Deepak Singh Crawford was your supporting actress). Don't just rely on greedy spin doctors and fortune-tellers. You are still young (anybody born a whole year after me is young) and have not lost your sting, unlike the late high flying Eva, or the former and aging diva of the Philippines, who can hardly fly or float (let alone gloat).

And, finally Jaya, please read and re-read that definition of success in the chapter titled 'Success and Morality'.

Good luck, Jaya
Yours, etc.

☙❧☙❧☙❧

When I wrote the earlier letter and paragraph preceding it, I viewed the Jayalalitha-Vajpayee relationship as "the (naughty) tail wagging the (good) dog". Finally, in mid April 1999, this naughty tail wagged so hard that it tripped Vajpayee, and the thirteen month ruling coalition ended in collision. Now, I wonder how the Sonia – Jayalalitha relationship, if any, will develop. They 'conveniently' got together to conspire torpedoing Vajpayee's boat. However there is a big question mark on whether these very different prima doñas can work together.

The fresh general election results of October 1999 have returned the BJP led coalition with a convincing majority. Looks like poetic justice has been served with Vajpayee's position stronger than ever and

Jayalalitha's party among the defeated.

One faction in the Congress Party, by leading the revolt against Sonia's candidature as prime minister, has weakened Congress' changes at the national level. The Indian constitution requeries, inter alia, that the prime minister must be an Indian citizen. It does not disqualify people of foreign origin. This is a case of a great and secular constitution interpreted by un-principled politicians. In any event, I believe that Vajpayee's is the best person to lead India.

When I try to analyze these (and other) colourful, charismatic personalities, I find that they generally fall into one of two broad categories, although a few may 'qualify' for both with varying weightage. I would realistically describe these as MAX FACTOR CHARISMA, on the one hand, which refers to the cosmetic, put-on, artificial, hollow image; and the FACTS FACTOR CHARISMA, on the other hand, which is based on solid values and skills. As I write these lines I remember the proverb: "The face is no index to the heart."

I'm sure that my readers will be able to 'tell the sheep from the goats', quite easily. I hope that you'll enjoy this exercise, as I have. I would hasten to add that President Ronald Reagan was a balanced version of both factors of charisma. He must be credited for constructively using his tinsel-town experience to become California's Governor then, impose his political charisma as President and finally strengthening the military and morale of Americans, while weakening those of the Soviets.

Fidel Ramos *(knew when and how to take charge, and to retire with dignity)*
Among the leaders of developing countries in 1990s, Fidel Ramos proved to be a class act. But, first let me start with a little background. General Ramos was the Chief of Marcos' military machine in the Philippines and very much a confidant of the late President. Marcos' popularity had clearly begun to decline even while I was serving at the South East Asia Headquarters of Bank of America in Manila, during

1978-81. Civil unrest was becoming visible and we could feel the political heat.

One afternoon, my wife had just stepped out of the famous 'RUSTAN's' Store (associated with Imelda) when a bomb exploded at the check-out line, killing three or four innocent shoppers and staffers and injuring many more. I was at the office about half a kilometre away and can clearly remember Kuko's trembling voice on the telephone: "Honey, please thank God that your wife is still alive!" I panicked but she quickly added, "but I am fine, no injury, don't worry." Naturally, I was relieved that she was unharmed and no friends were hurt. I heard the horrific details later that evening, at home. This bomb was a sign of major problems to come.

We were transferred back to India in February, 1981. By 1984, Marcos' popularity and Imelda's charisma had almost totally worn-off, like old gold plating peeling off the - - - pig iron. Sensing this as an opportune time, Marcos' long time opponent Senator Benigno 'Ninoy' Aquino, the very popular Filipino who lived in self-exile in the U.S. for many years, felt that the timing was right for him to make a much heralded return home and apply pressure on Marcos to quit. However, as the door of his airplane opened, 'hit men' shot and killed this courageous son of the Philippines, before he could even set foot on the tarmac of Manila International Airport. This tragic and cowardly assassination made the nation hate Marcos even more. Before long, Ninoy's widow, Corazon (Cory) grabbed the initiative and started the famous **Peoples Power** which gathered tremendous momentum.

Meanwhile, General Ramos saw the handwriting on the wall and 'jumped ship' to join the Peoples Power movement. Some people accused Ramos of betraying his mentor and joining an inexperienced widow. Ramos' sense of history, judgement of the situation and sense of timing couldn't be better. Cory needed the military on her side, especially when Defence Minister - Juan Ponce Enrile, an ambitious Marcos crony and instrument, still showed loyalty to the frail Marcos and the still strong and ambitious 'Madame Iron Butterfly'. Ramos saw the clear direction of the wind and tide. He must have got a prescription from Dr. Jekyl and overnight switched his hyde, I mean hide.

Marcos and his cronies tried hard to convince the public that Cory was not qualified because she had no experience. In fact, I recall Cory saying something like "As Marcos has said, I do not have any experience. Yes, I am proud to admit that I do not have experience in corruption, nepotism and other crimes." This repartée worked like real 'zinger' and made old Marcos weaker still, politically and health-wise. Cory with her Peoples Power and vital timely support from Ramos succeeded eventually in the elections and moved into the Malacañang Presidential Palace. On the other side, the best that Marcos' former political ally, America could do, was to fly him and his family to Hawaii where he faded further, and passed away.

Cory rewarded Ramos by making him her Defence Minister. For a few years, the fortunes of the Philippines suffered because the economic woes and foreign loan defaults were compounded by one of the worst volcanic eruptions of Mt. Pinatubo, and typhoons with tidal waves in 1987. By 1992, Cory's term was over and it was in Ramos' destiny to become President for a six-year term.

Fortunately for Ramos, he was not Marcos' son-in-law like Soeharto's ambitious son-in-law and three-star general. If Fidel Ramos had been closely related to Marcos he would have ended up as Fidel Castrated. I am taking this liberty because Filipinos have a great sense of humour. I'm presuming that his first namesake in Havana will also smile rather than frown, because I believe that he too can take a joke.

As President, Ramos used his military discipline, not brute power, to consolidate the gains of the latter part of the Cory Presidency. He worked very hard and sincerely to mend the economy and provided incentives to foreign investors to return to the Philippines. Their country has had good human resources and managerial talent. The issue was to have peace, harmony and a pro-business environment to make things work. Ramos and his team were able to do just that. Not only has the economy been revived, it has become more broad-based to include hi-tech industrial parks. Tourists have also returned in droves. But, most importantly, democracy and political stability have been established. It is for these reasons that Philippines has been relatively immune to the 'Asian Flu' that has crippled and nearly devastated countries like Indonesia and Thailand.

Last, but very important: Ramos did not get tempted to amend the constitution and stay in power for another term. Another good lesson from a wise leader to 'otherwise' leaders.

Fidel Castro _(older but 'otherwiser')_

Having talked about the successful Filipino Fidel, I could be branded an infidel if I don't talk about his unique Cuban namesake. I had a 'dream talk' with the evergreen leader in his olive-green fatigues (by the way, he hardly shows any fatigue, even now - - - only 'fading glory'):

> _"Señor Presidente: First of all, please accept my congratulations on being the longest serving Presidente of any country in the whole wide world. There are barely a handful of Monarchs who have more years than the grey hairs in your presidential beard ⊸ Queen Elizabeth II, King Bhumibhol of Thailand, and the King of Tonga. But, while they have generally performed their regal duties with high grades, they were lucky to get their respective crowns and thrones because of their bloodlines. That's no special credit to them. Senior Presidente, may I call you Fidel, now that we have become friends, you deserve the real credit. Royalty got their thrones by **bloodline**. But you Fidel, grabbed the crown by **bloodletting** and dethroning the previous running dog of American capitalism! You 'used' (others) blood, sweat and tears to gain what the royals inherited! Congratulations again, Amigo._
>
> _But Fidel, I was as upset as you to hear that some biased reporters 'credit' you with only $100 million in your personal fortune, while Queen Elizabeth, Sultan Bokiah of Brunei, King Fahd of Saudi_

Arabia, etc. have billions in their royal vaults and accounts. Maybe, if you opened your (black) books to 'Author Anderson', or 'De Light of Touché' or 'Cooperative Lybrands' or 'Priceless Watershed', they could list and value or even re-value your translucent assets and help you qualify at least as a billionaire. You must catch up with late Marcos, as a minimum target, before it is too late. I know that you can do it. You did it against the American backed rebels at the BAY OF PIGS - - - now show them what you did in the PAY OF BIGS!

Another, humble pie, I mean humble advice from one non-cigar aficionado to a true addict: If you ever visit Singapore, please don't smoke your delectable hand-rolled Havana cigars, in non-smoking areas. Otherwise, they'll use your own sugar cane baton and administer a not-so-sweet caning to your sweet a.., you know what I mean.

Adios, Mucho Macho Amigo!"

❧❧❧❧❧

I have to tell my American pals – including CIA – not to get too excited about my great CUBAN DREAM!

I believe that there is a tremendous lesson for future leaders in these stories and 'personal letters'.

Notes:
As my writings would indicate, I have no political party affiliations. Firstly, I am a-political by nature. Secondly, I find it extremely difficult to choose from only one - - - billion people! Meanwhile, as a secular minded Hindu who puts India before religion, I am guardedly hopeful that BJP is trying to water-down its fundamentalist Hindu manifesto to gain a broader appeal. Time will tell. The nation is desperately crying out for an honest, efficient and secular party that can nurture peace, harmony and prosperity on an all-India scale.

15

THE BUCK STOPS HERE

"He who excuses himself, accuses himself"

(Proverb)

I think I read this little story in the Reader's Digest:

An attractive woman tells the Divorce Judge, "Your honour, I want to divorce my husband - - - he has been unfaithful to me." The Judge enquires, "Do you have any evidence, madam, to back up your allegation against your husband?" "Sure sir", she responded, "we have three children and not one of them looks like him!"

After chuckling over this joke, one also recognizes that some people just blame others even for their own follies. Some people become very defensive when an error is discovered. They either cover-up, make excuses or blame others. It is very likely that when such people were kids they were severely reprimanded, rather than advised or guided when they made mistakes. Or, they saw their parents frequently blaming, instead of helping, each other. Some de-motivated or selfish employees even get satisfaction if a co-worker receives 'hot words' from the boss. This syndrome is very unhealthy and dangerous, and the top management carries the primary responsibility for curing it.

I wish to refer to a profound quote on this sensitive subject:

> *"It has always been a mystery to me how men can feel themselves honored by the humiliation of their fellow beings"*
> *Mahatma Gandhi*

Sometimes there is a negative atmosphere in which people give excuses or pass on the blame, rather than fix the problem. People feel insecure and spread insecurity. They wonder when someone will stab them in the back or they feel the need to protect their 'back-sides'. The 'C.Y.A.' syndrome afflicts such an institution. People will be over careful to avoid mistakes instead of being productive and creative. I remember one of my senior colleagues in Grindlays Bank saying " the more I do, the more mistakes I'm likely to make. So, I play it safe and do as little as possible!" This tells us a few things:

1. The person is lazy.
2. He suffers from low motivation and poor self-esteem.
3. He does not enjoy his work.
4. The person is afraid of making mistakes, partly because of his own incompetence and partly in those pre-MBO days there was more reprimand for a mistake then praise for a job well done. The whole culture has changed in Grindlays since around 1973, as I have mentioned in the chapter on Corporate Culture.

In these days of delegation of authority and empowerment, it is important to ensure that the right people get the authority, and in the right doses. The degree of empowerment should be allocated based on job requirement and skills, experience, maturity and reliability of the person. This should be further backed by sound policies and procedures with a comprehensive internal audit system. In this way, the boss can more comfortably transfer power down the line and leverage his/her effectiveness.

Having said all this, the boss has to remain fully accountable for the performance of his company, department or team. He/She should not be a bloodhound, suspicious of the subordinates. However, he/she must be alert to 'smell' signs of trouble early on, to 'nip it in the bud'. One can't be a good delegator if one consequently wants to relax as a detached 'laissez-faire' manager. Delegate, but keep your finger on the pulse. Also, if a problem is detected, we should carefully analyze whether the cause is insufficient training, poor judgment, lack of coordination, defect in the machine or foul play. Either way, the leader will act quickly to minimize damage and take concrete steps to prevent recurrence. Foul play must not be tolerated.

If the persons involved in a problem just blame each other, we fall in the deep and dirty pit of "You did it"; "No, I didn't do it - he did it". We end up wasting time in morale lowering politics, instead of remedying the mistake, and moving forward.

Whichever way one looks at it, the boss has to take ultimate responsibility. Let me share with you my own case. I felt very honoured when Bank of America made me VP and Head of its New Delhi branch in 1981. Business prospects were positive and I had a bright bunch of young MBAs to support me. Within six months I was fortunate to win the largest single deposit in the bank's history in India. Along with the kudos came the feeling that I must lend the money at a high interest rate and maximise profit for my branch, rather than merely lend the funds to another branch, at a lower inter-branch rate.

It so happened that a fairly senior insurance executive who had a small loan account at our branch, even before my arrival, met me to say that he could introduce a large client of impeccable reputation. Being hungry to make large loans and assuming that a senior insurance officer would recommend only a creditworthy borrower, I agreed to meet with him. We met over lunch and the prospect gave me quite a few testimonials from large MNCs and major Indian companies, recommending him as a strong and reliable businessman. His 'audited' financial statements, seemed acceptable. He also presented his insurance policies, which showed high quality consumer products, and durables whose insured value was about four times the amount he wanted to borrow from us.

I was quite impressed and subsequently introduced him to two of my young credit/marketing officers. I requested my officers to analyze the proposal in the usual manner and to personally inspect the warehouses to check on the inventory, on which we would have a hypothecation (like a floating charge/lien). A few days later, based on the favourable reports and recommendations of the two officers, I approved the loan.

To cut a long story short, the loan went 'sour' in less than a year. We lost about half the principal amount after adjusting certain deposits and sales proceeds. Basically, the borrower was running a 'kiting' operation in collusion with the insurance guy. He had taken loans from seven banks by hypothecating the same inventories to them all.

One day the banks 'woke up' to their common problem and got together to sue the borrower. However, the case got 'bogged down' because he was able to flex political and perhaps financial muscle in the courts. (Indira Gandhi was India's Prime Minister in those days and this borrower had frequently boasted about his 'connections'.)

I had to write the 'Loan Loss Report'. It was quite tempting to blame my juniors. As I did my soul searching, I realized that all of us had been naive. When I initially told them that it looked like an interesting proposal, they probably took it as a signal that I was very keen to make the loan, and maybe their approach was more to 'please the Boss' with a quick 'yes' recommendation, rather than analyze the deal with healthy skepticism. I also should have realized that while these young officers were bright, they did not have sufficient experience to deal with such a racketeer. Also, with hindsight, I should have played a bigger role in studying the customer and his business in depth. Perhaps, I would have seen a red flag, if I had made more direct inquiries. It was clear to me that I could have done a better job, and I took responsibility in the report.

However, I felt depressed on how I could 'allow' such a silly loss to occur. This is when my boss showed leadership - he said, "Vipen, don't make such a mistake again and now be positive and think ahead. Hell, Bank of America can piss a million dollars in a day! This is a much smaller amount." This statement helped restore my confidence. Also, since I did not blame my subordinates, they did not feel betrayed by me and I did not have to carry the burden of moral guilt. I believe that I did not lose their respect and we continue to have good relations. In fact, one of them continues to prosper as a SVP at Bank of America.

As a result of this experience, I learnt a big lesson in risk assessment, but even a greater lesson in taking responsibility, and in integrity and leadership.

16

MOTIVATION

"Man does not live by bread alone,
but by faith, by admiration, by sympathy."

R. W. *Emerson*

I would describe the ability to motivate as the **art or skill** of **inspiring** and **enthusing** a person(s). To me, it also implies having an **interest** in that person and a **desire** to help that person improve in a general or specific way. That person could be one's child or subordinate, our companion, etc., or even oneself.

It has been said and written many, many times that a major attribute of a leader is the capacity and desire to motivate people in good times and in bad. It is, obviously, much easier to inspire people when business is booming and profits are rising, when salary raises and bonuses are high.

On the other hand, what do we do to motivate people when money is no longer a motivator (because of the law of diminishing returns) or when times are bad. Also, it is not easy to inspire an employee to produce more by offering more money when he is already burnt out and/or bored. It is also difficult for the boss to put on a happy face when the company is bleeding or when faced with defeat on the battlefield. However, it is in these kinds of situations where inspirational leadership becomes even more vital.

Recall the scene in Shakespeare's **Henry V,** when the English generals and soldiers are licking their wounds after being defeated in one of the battles against the French army. The English side is demoralized. The generals still see their king as a young inexperienced boy. Then, quite suddenly, through a stirring and passionate speech young King Henry arouses patriotism and re-kindles that fire in the hearts of his men. King Henry soon leads his renewed and motivated army of under-dogs to a decisive victory against heavy odds.

Today, a motivator or a motivational leader's characteristics will usually include the following features:
- Cares for his people
- Believes in his people
- Prefers to praise than to criticize
- Has the style of a coach, and even cheerleader
- Is fair in meting out rewards and punishment
- Takes great pride in the accomplishments of his people
- Is genuine in what he says
- Above all, leads by example

In most cases we hear or read about what the boss expects from his/her subordinates. Motivation and loyalty are **two-way** concepts, and all relationships have to have a two-way flow, otherwise problems will surface sooner or later. Therefore, in this chapter I have tried to compile a list of items on how a junior looks up to his/her senior for motivation:

WHAT THE JUNIOR EXPECTS OF THE SENIOR
- Show that you care for me.
- Give me as clear guidelines and goals as possible and let me get on with the job.
- Tell me how and where I fit in the organization (big picture).
- Give me necessary tools and authority to do my job well.
- Give me adequate time as well as 'space' to think and do my work.
- Praise me when I do a good job.
- Correct me when I am wrong – in private.

- Don't insult me – I am also a human being.
- Encourage and support me, especially when I am performing a difficult task.
- Make me feel like a member of the team.
- Involve me in decision making – I have some good ideas.
- Give me a reasonable idea of my career path.
- Give me regular training and development opportunities to improve myself and my career prospects.
- Reward me for superior performance and professional loyalty.

It is noteworthy that, if you praise the subordinate whenever he/she does a good job, this employee will accept your criticism or reprimand in the right spirit, when he/she has made a mistake. The subordinate will also view his superior as a 'fair boss'. On the other hand, if the boss only communicates criticisms when things go wrong, the employee feels that he/she is treated unfairly and becomes de-motivated.

I have listed here a few simple phrases to make employees feel good, feel inspired.

MOTIVATING PHRASES
- Thank you.
- Well done! Your work style reflects tremendous spirit.
- I trust you.
- I shall tell the boss that you are doing a fine job.
- Keep it up! You made a great contribution to the team.
- I value your advice.
- This is a tough, challenging task, but I know that I can count on you.
- You're on the right track – you have a great future in this company.
- Can I help you in any way?

I sincerely believe that there is great value in using such expressions **sincerely** and as **frequently** as possible. I'm sure that experienced people-oriented bosses can add many more inspirational phrases to this list.

I would like to inject a profound proverb here:

"They that value not praise, will never do anything worthy of praise."

SELF MOTIVATION

I believe that, ultimately, a successful person has to be largely self-motivated and self-inspired. We should not wait for others to motivate us. In fact, 'external' motivation cannot do much for us if we cannot 'lift' our own moral. External inspiration is most welcome as a reinforcement or supplement to our own up-beat attitudes.

While I was with Bank of America, the Country Head was David Artko, a highly cultured American with fine values and manners. He was truly people-oriented and it was a pleasure and honour to be his 'under-study'. His unforgettable sentence was, 'I know that you will be successful in your career because I see the self-starter in you.' He had done two things with these few words:
(i)   Made me feel good about myself. He had inspired me.
(ii) Reminded me of the importance of being and staying self-motivated.

This leads me to believe in the value and power of positive auto-suggestion which has been used to great advantage by champions in sports and other challenging pursuits.

Message:
Let's inspire ourselves and others.

17

THE ART OF REPRIMAND

"Corn is cleansed with wind, and the soul with chastening."
(Proverb)

At first glance, the title of this chapter may sound like artificial 'sugar-coating' when disciplining somebody. The idea here is to give the party at fault a clear message, without damaging his/her self-esteem and confidence, and encourage corrective action or positive behaviour, as the case may be.

We all make mistakes, otherwise we would be super-human. How a supervisor handles mistakes can have a great impact on employee morale, productivity and loyalty. We need wisdom, patience and balance, in good measure. Saying too much or bruising a personally sensitive 'nerve' will provoke an undesired response. Saying too little or too 'softly' may not induce sufficient response.

In old style hierarchical organizations, many employees would 'tremble' at the sight of a senior officer. People would try to cover up mistakes, thereby reducing or delaying chances for corrective action.

Let's imagine such a case/scene:

Boss screams to his secretary, "Tell that moron John to get his *a....* over here!" John comes in shivering "Yyyyes, Boss...."

The boss, without checking the cause of the error, "Do you realize what you have done? You are careless! I shall see that you don't get any bonus... Now get the hell out of my room!"

John whispers "Ssssorry", and he may even add "I wasn't the only one" or "Dick gave me the wrong part", and curses the boss under his breath as he exits. John also tells his friends how he was humiliated. Milder versions of this scenario take place in some companies, especially in developing countries, even today.

Now let's see how a people-oriented boss in a people-oriented organization would handle a similar error.

Boss to secretary, "Would you please ask John to come in."

John comes in and says, "Good morning, Mr. Brown." or "Hi, Jim."

The boss may not smile, but would avoid frowning too much and will reciprocate the greeting, and likely say, "John, as you know, we are working in a very sensitive area and we need excellence from everybody. In fact, I rely a lot on your experience and supervision to uphold our exacting standards. I heard about the production problem, and since it is your department, please tell me briefly what happened."

John answers Mr. Brown, "Like you said, this is a serious matter, I quickly analyzed the cause of the problem and it appears that my team received faulty parts. I take responsibility because I did not sufficiently explain the sensitivity of the parts to my people. The new machine was hurriedly assembled without checking the specs of the parts." The Boss says, "Please ensure this does not happen again. This costly error will make us all look bad. I shall also talk to the supplier to emphasize the importance of 100% conformity with our specs. I shall also get help to train our guys in quality management."

The boss concludes the meeting on a positive note by saying, "John, I have faith in your abilities." or "John, I know I can count on you to the correct the problem quickly." In certain cultures, the boss may also pat John on the shoulder, while saying this. Furthermore, if the situation so warrants, the boss may also add "…and John, if you and your team can produce the required quality on a sustained basis, we could talk about bonuses next time, rather than problems!"

John leaves the boss' office/room in a positive mood and will focus on improving quality, rather than bearing a grudge against his boss.

COMPARISON OF THE TWO STYLES

The first boss feels that his authority or power is exemplified or even amplified, if he insults the subordinate. This boss considers himself too busy to ask how or why the problem occurred. The subordinate thinks that the boss dislikes him and he in turn begins to dislike the boss. Bad morale and its implications are obvious.

The scenario is reflective of culture based on the defunct Theory X of Douglas McGregor, which basically says that man is generally lazy and unmotivated, and that he needs constant supervision and prodding. If people are treated like animals, as often was the case when cotton plantations thrived on slave labour, the poor workers had no real reason to be motivated. The only 'motivation' was fear of punishment by the overseer.

In the second scenario, the nature of the organization and the nature of the boss shows that people are valued and respected. The boss is doing his duty by (i) underlining the importance or sensitivity of the job; (ii) emphasizing the need for top quality work; (iii) showing his faith in the subordinate; (iv) inquiring about the cause of failure, instead of impulsively 'shooting his bolt'; (v) giving the subordinate a fair chance to explain the situation and propose corrective action; (vi) offering support through better procurement of parts; (vii) offering training in quality management, as well as a performance incentive.

This picture falls under McGregor's Theory Y and a lot more. This Theory says that man likes physical and mental activity. Man likes to create in some form or another. It is the quality of the work environment and treatment that can have a great influence on man's attitude towards work.

Here the subordinate does feel bad about his failure, but he does not 'lose face'. Also, there is no ill-will especially because the boss shares in the responsibility and shows support. The subordinate also gets motivated to solve the quality problem quickly and on a sustained basis because that achievement would lead to a promotion, bonus etc.

I would call the second example positive reprimand or counseling. Mistakes must not be taken lightly. They must be corrected in the best way possible. Here, a problem is not used as reason to 'attack' the person but as a basis for accepting responsibility, analyzing and solving problems, and as an opportunity for the boss to show that he/she cares for the company _and_ the employee. The boss has turned around this reprimand situation into an experience _of learning_ and development for the subordinate and has restored/enhanced his morale. The employee will likely focus on improving his performance and thereby please the fair-minded and positive boss. Any reasonable employee will not, under this scenario, develop a disliking towards the boss or use his/her energy negatively.

The scenarios may sound simplistic – I am aware that situations may be more complicated, especially when there are pre-conceived notions, prejudices or bad memories. However, there is a lot to be said for positive reprimand.

General Colin Powell is one of the best living exponents of disciplining people with the art of reprimand.

It is equally important to discern what kinds of mistakes should be reprimanded. Violations of the organization's principles and values must be dealt with firmly. Disciplinary issues and stupid behavior must be similarly addressed.

On the other hand, if people make mistakes while experimenting for innovation, they must be given positive strokes and encouragement to continue searching for new solutions and improvements. If the boss reprimands mistakes on the road to innovation and value creation, he/she will kill the creative spirit of his/her people. The leader realizes that such mistakes or even failures are necessary stepping stones to progress.

Note:
Inspired by the 'One Minute Reprimand' in 'One Minute Manager' an outstanding and still relevant book by Kenneth Blanchard PhD and Dr. Spencer Johnson M.D.

BUSINESS MINUS

PEOPLE = ZERO

৪৩৪৩ Part – C ৫৩৫৩
BUSINESS MINUS PEOPLE = ZERO

SYNOPSIS

18 People as Assets:
Physical assets are depreciating assets. Human beings, with good treatment and development opportunities, are appreciating assets.

19 Building Loyalty:
The traditional concept of loyalty is that the junior must be loyal to the superior officer and/or to the organization. Discussing the concept of two-way loyalty.

20 Women – The Still Under-Utilized Resource:
While women have greater opportunities today, there is still a lot to be done for the uplift of women.

21 "I did it all myself" (Really?!):
Bosses with big egos grab the credit when things are going well. We need to give credit where it belongs.

22 "I could have danced all night":
The message of the 'Pygmalion Effect' is demonstrated here.

23 Man vs Computer:
Emphasis that man is the original and ultimate software, without whom there can be no computer or computer software.

24 Personal Health and Fitness:
Health and fitness cannot be ignored. We commend companies that provide fitness and recreation facilities to employees.

25 Beware of Jealousy and Politics:

The danger of personal jealousies and politics. There is a need for tolerance and forgiveness.

26 How to 'Manage' the Boss:

I have stated that, first of all, the employee must be honest and diligent in dealings with the boss. By building credibility, the subordinate can influence the boss in a positive way, and win his/her support.

27 Fast Track Employees:

Fast track career programmes are commendable, but they should be fair and transparent. Also, such employees must not become elitist.

28 Teach'em Young! Teach'em Right!:

Highlights that good parenting and good early schooling can help make great future citizens, managers and leaders.

29 Job Security:

The importance of reasonable job security. Enlightened employers take positive steps in this area. It is difficult to guarantee jobs, but it is possible to assure employability. Employees should also take responsibility to develop themselves to protect and enhance their own careers.

30 Compensation and Reward:

Merit must be rewarded. But, avoid the feeling of the unfair and widening gap between the pay of top executives and the 'troops'.

31 Adaptability:

Need for people and organizations to be flexible and adaptable, especially in these rapidly changing times.

18

PEOPLE AS ASSETS

"... the real difference between success and failure in a corporation can very often be traced to the question of how well the organization brings out the great energies and talents of its people."

Thomas Watson, Jr
CEO of IBM
when IBM was consistently voted 'world's most admired corporation'.

These days, almost without exception, chairmen's speeches and annual reports of corporations mention that people are their most important assets. There is no debate against that. The debate is whether these proclamations are being put into practice. Also, it is quite interesting that the Balance Sheet of a company shows only Assets (we own) like land, buildings, plant & machinery, furniture & fixtures, computers, inventory, and receivables, which can be represented in pure accounting terms. Essentially, these are 'dead' assets without people.

To some extent, pre-operation expenses and development costs which may include cost of a training package, along with a sophisticated machine may be capitalized as intangible assets and be amortized. We may also argue that the human content (intellectual, labour) is included in the cost of hard assets. As a finance person I agree; but as an HR person and as a business manager, I wish that the all important human capital could be represented more directly. Perhaps, the personnel superiority of a company is reflected, to some extent, in its superior price-earning ratio or price to book value of its shares compared to those of peers.

Let's consider an example: Mr. Hot-Shot and Mr. Good-Shot perform exactly the same sales job in the same company. Both report to the same Sales Manager who treats them equally well. But Hot-Shot's sales performance is consistently 20% higher to his peer's. Other things remaining the same, Hot-Shot's superior performance would likely be the result of better aptitude and better attitude. In other words, the skills and the mental approach of a person are normally the main factors that distinguish one's performance.

Companies that recognize these factors, give great importance to them in selection and promotion. At the same time, the progressive company will have progressive training and development programmes that are linked to the career progression of the concerned employees or officers. Such training and development programmes of today's **learning organization** focus on improving aptitudes (skills) and attitudes (mindset) of its people to meet greater responsibilities and challenges. It needs to be emphasized that while 'technical' or 'operational' skills must be up-graded, as a person moves up the corporate ladder, greater attention must be paid to improving 'soft skills', especially leadership.

The time, money and energy invested by the individual, the educational institution or (learning) organization to increase relevant knowledge, skills and experience which in turn enhance the 'value' of the person, means generating **human capital**. Human capital has been generated one way or other from the beginning of history e.g. apprenticeship under the father or 'guru' who was an expert craftsman or hunter or farmer. Why, even the 'terrible' slave traders generated human capital by the special food and physical training they would provide gladiators in order to sell them for higher prices to the Roman warlords in years long bygone.

A cornerstone in the culture of today's best practice organization, which invariably is a learning organization, is its commitment to boost its human capital. Learning and growing is its way of life; it is just like 'second nature'.

I was in India for most of the period 1965 - 1983. During this time, India was turning very socialist. The country had not turned 'red' but became very 'dark pink'. Under Indira Gandhi's regime, we had to endure one of the highest income tax rates and other compulsory deductions so that there was little incentive for honest professionals to remain in India. This resulted in a huge and unprecedented brain-drain from India to the West, which continued well into the 1990s. In 1992, I read in the 'Arab News' that some American researchers had estimated that India had 'contributed' human capital worth $ 30 billion to USA since 1970. India's loss of human capital or 'brain-drain' was American's **brain gain** (here's a new, but easy, tongue-twister!).

Coming back to the corporate arena, I would like, with great admiration, to mention some fine examples of companies that successfully commit huge resources to increasing the value of their people: Citibank, Motorola (despite its recent setbacks), Microsoft, Shell, Unilever, Singapore Airlines, EDS, ABB and Toyota.

Having said all this, I have to admit that, so far, relatively few Asian corporations have made the transition to becoming real learning institutions. The reasons are fairly simple:
i)   Many of these companies are still controlled by the founders and/or their second generation, who attach greater importance to loyalty than building professional excellence.
ii) Whenever such rapidly growing groups needed a new skill, they just hired from the outside. There simply was no time or importance given to developing their own cadres. They did hire many bright junior locals, but there was insufficient attention given to developing them.

iii) Until the 'Asian Flu', more accurately the **Asian Calamity**, these conglomerates made easy or superior profits because of protected markets, natural resource advantages and cheap labour.

Consider this irony:
Many of these organizations happily spend $50 million on a hi-tech machine but are reluctant to spend even half a million dollars to train people who are involved in running the machine or marketing its products. They don't realize that a machine, even with good maintenance, is a **depreciating asset**, if nothing, due to obsolescence. On the contrary, a human being, especially in a learning organization is an **appreciating asset**.

I can say with a degree of pride that Sinar Mas Group, after initial years under the old business philosophy, began to change itself, especially since 1995. On the job training and under-study programmes have improved, and the Group has its own Management Development Centre which has a professional faculty headed by Prof. Teddy Pawitra, a leading academic, from the University of Tarumanegara which is arguably the most respected university in Indonesia. These factors will enable Sinar Mas to steadily reduce its reliance on expensive expatriate officers, without hurting performance.

Caltex is an enterprise which is jointly owned by Chevron and Texaco, and is a gigantic oil company in its own right. Caltex was a sponsor of the Asian Games held in Bangkok in the 4th quarter of 1998. Here is a quote of a recent Caltex advertisement supporting the Asian Games:

> *"There is no energy greater than that which drives the human spirit, to achieve perfection. If only for the moment. And remembered, forever. This December, the Asian Games tap the energies of Asian nations. Not just to see who wins, but to discover the best in all of us."*

This statement from a petroleum energy company **saluting the power of human energy,** is a profound reflection of the growing appreciation of **people as real assets** to create and activate 'physical assets'.

I would like to conclude this chapter by quoting the great visionary, steel magnate and philanthropist - Andrew Carnegie:

> *"You can take my ten best steel mills, but let me keep my ten best men - - - because these men will help me build even better mills."*

19

BUILDING LOYALTY

"The subjects' love is the king's lifeguard."
(Proverb)

I left Bank of America in 1983, essentially because of the relatively low salaries paid to 'locals' and the back-breaking, pocket draining income tax rates prevailing in India at that time. I was truly sorry to leave a fine institution that had developed me and had been kind to me despite the loan loss in New Delhi (see chapter titled: "The Buck Stops Here"). Moreover, it was because of fair treatment by my senior Bankamericans, I still have a definite loyalty to this institution, which I left over 15 years ago.

Throughout my professional career spanning over thirty-one years, I must have had about 15 direct bosses. During this period only two of them, on my very first day under them, respectively, said the same words in a grave tone to me, "Vipen, along with good work, I demand your <u>personal loyalty</u> to me." I tried to hide my surprise with a smile and my reply in both instances was something like, "I assure you of my professional support." (Both these bosses were bright and good at their jobs and I did not see any reason not to respect them.)

As I pondered over these 'demands', I realized that perhaps both these individuals were probably a bit insecure or that this was how their own bosses may have started out with them. Or, perhaps their alma maters had 'political' cultures wherein the boss started the relationship by demanding 'personal loyalty'.

I have always believed in respecting my bosses and supporting their professional goals as a team player. To me, personal loyalty in a corporate set-up only means:

> *I shall not stab you in the back or unnecessarily torpedo your proposal. However, if I disagree, I shall be respectfully candid. On the other hand, if yours is a good proposal, I shall support it in any way possible. In any event, I shall not take part in politics which is harmful to all concerned.*

Sometimes, when the subordinate wants to unduly please the boss or show undue personal loyalty, objectivity is lost, and necessary checks and balances get diluted.

I am referring this time to my loan loss experience in the chapter titled: "The Buck Stops Here". Now, with benefit of hindsight, perhaps my junior officers at Bank of America were trying to please me or show 'personal loyalty', or trying not hurt their boss' feelings, when they hurriedly recommended what turned out to be a bum loan, just because I had initially said that it looked like an interesting deal, before seeing any formal reports.

I have generally had a democratic and participative approach, but ever since that incident in New Delhi in 1982, I have become even more explicit in encouraging healthy dissent, with respect for the proponent (regardless of seniority).

Now let's consider loyalty in a corporate scene. In general, even today, many corporations, in varying degrees, believe in loyalty, as it was practiced in the days of monarchies and feudalism. The kings, maharajas, sultans and sheiks demanded, and at least, got apparent loyalty. Some of this was genuine loyalty because there was a common cause, e.g. 'expanding the empire', and where there was mutual trust. On the other hand, there was blind or superficial or slavish loyalty, based on fear of becoming an outcast, or even being beheaded as a traitor, in extreme cases. I would call that **'loyalty to royalty'**. Similarly, traditional or hierarchical companies have required, 'employees must be loyal'. There was an explicit or implicit demand for loyalty - virtually blind loyalty. As a matter of fact, several founders and at least their next generation gave great importance to this 'slavish loyalty', even from their senior executives. Salary raises and bonuses and promotions were more dependent on loyalty than on professional excellence. The top managers had little scope for practicing leadership. Until the 1960s many 'old school' businessmen in India employed _'munshis'_ who were confidants – cum – cashiers/accountants. These munshis could be recognized by their thick spectacles (mostly horn-rimmed), dhotis (male version of a cross between a 'saree' and 'sarong'). Their humble 'yes-man' appearance was a hallmark of loyalty, not infrequently superficial. These munshis were a breed apart, but their claim to fame certainly wasn't initiative or creativity. They just carried out directives of the owners without debating merits. Obviously, that kind of loyalty prevented 'direct stealing' but there was very little motivation for professional excellence. Business history is full of cases of bad mistakes and missed opportunities because of **yes-man loyalty**.

Fortunately, the corporate world has changed a lot in recent decades. Companies realize that they have to earn or win the loyalties of their people by being good employers and having shared values. Among the institutions that I have worked with, Bank of America is definitely a good example of being a winner of employee loyalty.

In my role as one the initiators and catalysts of culture change in Sinar Mas Group, one of my first initiatives was to re-define loyalty more as a professional partnership for which both owners/bosses on one hand, and employees on the other, are jointly responsible. I try to convince our people about the concept of **TWO-WAY LOYALTY** or two-way trust to make it clear that the company cannot expect genuine and professional loyalty if the company or top bosses did not create the right climate for people to feel comfortable and to thrive and enjoy their work on a long term basis.

I started to emphasize at different forums (see chapters on Motivation and Corporate Values) that we must make employees feel proud of being part of Sinar Mas. This would happen if the top brass **lived values** like integrity, respect, career development, competitive compensation, equity participation, promotion from within, fairness and openness in HR policies. I say that if (i) employees feel comfortable and enjoy coming to work; (ii) they are encouraged to experiment and be creative in an atmosphere where there is more reward for good work than punishment for innocent mistakes, we would automatically raise employee loyalty. In this process, employee loyalty naturally follows the loyalty and support demonstrated by the company, in the first place. In a corporation that earns the status of **preferred** or **coveted employer**, the employees do not have to be loyal - they naturally feel loyal and enjoy the pride of association. The simple philosophy stated in the Good Book "Do unto others as you would have them do unto you" is very applicable, *inter-alia*, for building loyalty.

Companies that have built up strong employee loyalty would include Hongkong and Shanghai Banking Corporation, Lincoln Electric Company, Royal Dutch/Shell, Microsoft, Nordstrom, ABB, Nestle, Southwest Airlines, Levi Straus, Bank of America (at least prior to merger with nations bank).

While realistic employees no longer expect guaranteed life-long employment even in Japan, good employees have the right to expect reasonable continuity and fair employment practices. Organizations which have 'employed' (gosh, pun again) **chain-saw tactics a la Dunlap,** have little right to expect (leave alone hope) for loyalty from their people.

I fully agree that in times of recession, some down-sizing is necessary. I also support the view that the persons who have to go through some nightmarish experiences or guilt, have to be given some reward to implement the mass termination of, otherwise, good employees in a decent and positive way. A fine example is Mr. Turnbull's handling of the staff reduction process at one of Procter & Gamble's plants in

Britain, as quoted by Charles E. Smith, in his refreshing book titled *"The Merlin Factor"*.

However, what I find hard to swallow, or stomach, is that some hatchet-men **cut** disproportionately high bonus cheques for themselves, while they **tear-up** the salary cheques of thousands of workers and managers.

20

WOMEN - - - THE STILL
UNDER-UTILIZED RESOURCE

"Woman enriches man's life with love and grace;
She deserves his respect, she deserves his praise!"

Great strides have been made in several countries in giving women better opportunities to advance into positions of authority and matching compensation. Sri Lanka, India, Pakistan, Britain, and Sweden have had women as heads of government (Sri Lanka still has, Indonesia is getting close and Myanmar almost did). Also, quite a few top MNCs have women in top echelons. Yet, we have to admit that while they represent approximately 50% of the world's population, and close to 50% of the workforce in certain countries, women probably enjoy only around 5% of the top positions - only 10% of their potential!

A lot has been said in all sorts of forums on the need for redress, but we still have a long way to go. The mind-set to accept lady bosses has been changed in many countries and a big improvement has been achieved in Financial Services, Marketing, Advertising, Communications and Public Relations. The trend is positive, but needs acceleration with a wider application covering more industries and more countries.

No manager or leader or workforce can afford to under-estimate or under-utilize this tremendous source of economic and social power.

Women politicians who have excelled in the twentieth century and deserve our admiration would include **Baroness Margaret Thatcher** and **Barbara Castle**.

Let me mention an exception - **Pauline Hanson** is unfortunately on the wrong track. After the last few Australian governments have made commendable progress in making the 'greatest island' home to a truly harmonious multicultural society, Ms. Hanson, through her 'One Nation Party' is trying to divide the country. Women need our support, but not this one, unless she turns a new leaf. Otherwise, I predict that she will go out like Enoch Powell did in Britain, because all the Aussies I know, without exception, have hearts as big as their island. If she continues to remain narrow-minded in a very broad-minded country, poor Pauline will be partying virtually alone on humble pie, before long.

A chapter about women would be incomplete and insipid if I made only a passing reference to **Baroness Margaret Thatcher**. The daughter of a grocer (also her first and biggest mentor), young Maggie graduated from Oxford and worked for a few years as a barrister. She had watched with deep regret, Britain lose economically, because Labor sponsored unions were 'bullying' management and lowering British productivity and profitability. She observed and analyzed the resultant drop in the value and importance of Sterling and the general loss of British prestige and influence in world affairs.

By this time she was convinced that her true 'calling' was in high level politics through the Conservative platform. She quickly moved up the party's ranks and became Britain's first woman Prime Minister in 1979. Her solid determination and leadership became evident very early. (i) She adopted a tight money policy and cut government expenditure. She took the big risk of curbing inflation, even if it initially hurt employment. (ii) She took a firm stance vis-à-vis the then aggressive Soviet Union which won her the accolade of 'Iron Lady'. (iii) She stuck her neck out to repulse Argentina's invasion from Britain's tiny Falkland Islands. This success raised Britain's morale and helped her to a landslide re-election victory. (iv) She reduced trade-union powers and defeated the coal miner's strike in 1984-85 to the relief of the majority of the population. (v) She succeeded to a great extent in making 'Britain a nation of shareholders' by reducing taxes and initiating privatization its huge state-own corporations. Examples are British Gas, British Telecom, British Petroleum, British Airways, British Airports Authority, etc., which have been generally good for the companies, employees and investing public.

It was her profound sense of history and diplomacy (Churchill-like, I guess) that made her convince other world leaders - President George Bush, President Mitterand and King Fahd to form a 'world coalition' to beat and expel the Iraqi invaders from Kuwait. She was, indeed, a major original sponsor of Operation Desert Shield. The (only) regret from her point of view that she 'poll taxed' herself out of the 'PMship', before she could directly relish the sweet victory of Operation Desert Storm. But no man or woman can take credit away from this leader, in this historic triumph for the free world.

There is no doubt that she had an autocratic style which inspired the comment that "the Iron Lady is the only 'man' in the British cabinet!". It was her obstinacy to impose the poll tax that eventually brought her down. But, while it is clear that she lacked flexibility, she had the 'guts' to stand by her principles, even if it meant losing her cherished prime ministership. The Baroness holds the record for being the longest continuous serving British Prime Minister and has left an indelible mark on modern Britain, with its prestige restored.

Baroness Thatcher is a fine symbol of the capabilities and achievements of the female version of our specie. I am convinced that there will be a much greater ratio of women in high places – government, business, military, etc. as the world is learning to de-stereotype the fair sex.

Note:
I had the great privilege to attend her dinner lecture in Jakarta arranged under the auspicies of 'Citibank Leadership Series', in 1996.

This important event was attended by top Indonesian government officials and businessmen – local and foreign.

An independent minded journalist asked her a 'sensitive' question about Soeharto's governing style. Being a gracious guest, her response was delicate, charming and non-offensive. The 'Iron Lady' had left her 'mask' at home! - - - and the audience had to 'read between the lines'.

Among leading women entrepreneurs, a name that really stands out, is **Anita Rodick**, the founder and CEO of Body Shop. Ms. Rodick has a tremendous business sense, coupled with a great feeling for animals and the environment. Traditional businessmen would say that it is difficult to make money if you give a lot of importance to ecology, animal rights, etc. Ms. Rodick has proved that if you address the social and ecological issues properly and build them sensibly into your business plan, you can make good profits on a sustained basis.

A few Asian women have distinguished themselves in business:

Khunying Chanut Piyaoui the visionary matriarch of the Dusit Thani Hotel group of Thailand. Through her tremendous leadership and vision, Dust Thani has become a well respected and recognized brand in South East Asia. She drew increased recognition in Europe after her company acquired the popular Kempinski chain that has its base in Germany, around 1996.

Sukmawati Widjaja, who is Vice Chairman of Sinar Mas Group, joined her father as she finished high school in Jakarta. For several years, Sukma was her father's right hand. Smart and quick to learn the job, she developed an excellent understanding of high finance and how to influence influential people. While Sukma is no longer involved directly in the day-to-day operations, she makes valuable contributions on corporate strategy and high level public relations. I must add that Sukma has a special gift in the HR side as well. She is able to attract good people, find the right positions for them, and keep them motivated. Furthermore, she has confidence, poise and personality that give her the ability to rub shoulders with CEOs of the world's top banks and heads of government, with relative ease.

Now, I wish to discuss a female leader, who was neither in business, nor in politics, but was respected and admired by businessmen and politicians alike, not to mention the poor masses who adored and worshipped her. In 1910, a teenage girl of Albanian origin comes to Calcutta, is shocked by the slums and poverty. This shock changes her life and gives hope to at least three generations of the really underprivileged in this historic city, which was the capital of British India until 1912.

One may just assume that **Mother Teresa** was a great missionary and a great social worker. These accolades are true, but form only part of the whole picture. In the context of the woman as a powerful, but under-utilized resource, let me also mention certain skills of this angelic, but dynamic, highly successful manager and leader:

- She had a great **vision** and **strategic planning capability**.
- She remained **committed** to her dream and created a world famous and respected institution - the **Missionaries of Charity**.
- She was a great **organizer** who was able to create a highly efficient and effective organization.
- She was a great **motivator**, who helped attract volunteers from all walks of life who would feel 'blessed' that they could serve under her.
- She displayed tremendous flexibility and **adaptability**.
- She had fantastic **marketing** skills. She was able to advertise her mission throughout the world and that helped in **fund-raising**.
- She had legendary **networking** skills.
- She practised fine **Human Resource Development** and **succession planning**, and groomed a very worthy successor to keep the flame glowing bright.
- She was **client-focused**, never forgetting that her job was to stay in touch with the poor, sick and orphaned and to help them with food, shelter, medical aid, education, and above all, **hope**.
- She became world famous and was honoured by monarchs and heads of government, but she never lost her **humility**.

- She **loved** and **cared** for her simple sari-clad (often bare-footed) nuns and helpers.
- She fostered **teamwork** among people of different backgrounds to serve the common goal.
- She **celebrated** success by **genuinely thanking** people who helped her great mission.
- She maintained the highest level of **faith** in God and her co-workers throughout her exemplary life.
- Her real power came from **moral authority** because she was doing the right things, in the right way for the right cause. This is the **essence of power through people and principles.**
- She is a **top example of leading by example.**

I am sure that I have still missed some important managerial attributes. In summary, all I now need to say that this woman was one of the most successful CEOs of this century, without even realising it. As businessmen and profit-oriented people, even if we ignore the charity aspects of this real and great legend, we can learn a great deal through this case of management by fully using HEAD, HEART and HANDS.

Coming to a few non-managerial spiritual aspects, Mother Teresa was a **saint** in her lifetime and in our lifetimes. Millions of people have been fortunate to see her and to be personally touched and blessed by her. There might be mystique or mystery about the 'achievements' of somebody who lived a millennium or two ago, because the historians might have been biased in recording or interpreting facts. Mother Teresa was <u>real</u>, as real can be - - - before our very eyes.

Whether the Vatican takes three years, thirty years or three hundred years to canonize her, Mother Teresa is already the **Saint of the Twentieth Century** and one of its **top managers**. I don't really know, but I wouldn't be surprised if the Pope may have asked her for her blessings.

This is also an opportune place to applaud another diminutive woman – **Master Cheng Yen**, a Buddhist nun whose Tzu Chi Foundation is doing an outstanding job of helping the helpless in about twenty eight countries. This great soul has won the trust, admiration and following of four million members, all doing voluntary service. Her foundation started modestly in Taiwan around thirty years ago, and is a living testimonial of a woman whose 'power' comes from love and care for the needy. Her principle is to give with 'compassion and wisdom', regardless of race, religion or nationality. A fine example is the food and medical aid provided by Tzu Chi volunteers, at great personal risk, to the weak and vulnerable folks in the midst of the civil war between rival Muslim factions in Afghanistan. Master Cheng Yen inspired these volunteers with her great spirit.

In my mind, Mother Teresa and Master Cheng Yen are dramatic exceptions to the title of this chapter. They rank among the most fully and beautifully utilized human resources in the world.

To close this chapter, I wish to salute the fair sex through a poem which I wrote at the time of the International Women's Conference in Beijing in 1995. (This poem was not formally published.)

TRIBUTE TO WOMEN

Man needs Woman since his very conception;
The Mother's value is truly beyond perception.

The Grandma's place is without compare;
Her heart is full of prayer, love and care.

The Aunt has an additional rewarding goal;
She frequently plays the "second mother" role.

Life is more bearable with the help of a Sister;
This is true for a Boy or a grown-up Mister.

What a great blessing to have a lovely Daughter;
Filling our hearts with joy and our lives with laughter.

Kindergarten is bare without a loving Teacher;
She shapes our minds and develops our future.

Woman's inspiration makes Man a champion;
Whether she's his Wife or his Companion.

Women like Joan of Arc color history books;
Admire their spirit --- not just their looks.

Women make good leaders - so let them grow;
Grow to top positions ---- including CEO!

Women's talents are more than domestics;
Let them flourish in military and in politics.

Woman enriches Man's life with love and grace;
She deserves his respect, she deserves his praise!

21

"I DID IT ALL MYSELF"
(REALLY?!)

"A man's praise is his own mouth stinks"

(Proverb)

My father was a diving champion and is still a big promoter of swimming. He has also been an avid moviegoer. My parents wanted me to become swimming champion and be a courageous kid who played by the rules. So my parents would take me to the cinema to see the original 'Tarzan' shows starring the Olympic champion and idol, Johny Weismuller.

Tarzan, a little 'white' boy, is the only survivor of a plane crash in the dense forest of Africa. He is fed and nurtured by apes. Later, he befriends more animals - 'Cheeta' the chimpanzee and 'Tantor' the elephant are his best friends. Eventually, our hero and protector of the forest and its inhabitants, finds his real mate - Jane, and they continue the good work, and so on.

While Tarzan, in his animal skin trunks, is clearly the hero of these interesting stories by Edgar Rice Boroughs, it is critical to recognize that he would not have survived more than a couple of days as a helpless babe, if the apes did not give him food, shelter, security and love. Later, when Tarzan is bigger and stronger, he still needs the support of many animals to fulfill his mission. He becomes <u>adept at networking</u>. Tarzan's long, loud, echoing call is his signal (and signature for recognition) to rally his friends against the transgressors.

The point that I am trying to extract from this story is that every person needs help, not only to survive in the forest or concrete jungle but also to progress and attain success. You cannot do it alone - that's for certain. I have come to believe that **'no man is an island'**. At the same time, a selfish or egoistic person loses popularity and may not be successful for long.

Let us take another example of a person who appears to be performing and succeeding on his own: Think about a champion boxer - Joe Louis the 'Brown Bomber' or Mohammed Ali who could 'float like a butterfly and sting like a bee'. I do not want to water-down the credit due to them but they did not earn those 'belts' and titles entirely on their own steam, as it may appear at first glance. They were without doubt, great champions. But, each of them had many <u>backers</u> in the form of coaches, sparring partners, advisors, promoters, etc., who helped these men achieve hero or even 'cult' status. Do you think they believe that they made it to the top single-handed?

Similarly, the monarch of a country or CEO of a corporation would be an ignorant egoist if he says that he can achieve anything worthwhile by himself.

It stands to reason that a leader minus followers is zero, impotent. The wise leader does not isolate himself/herself either mentally or physically. At the same time, people need some private time and space for thinking and rejuvenation. A certain amount of privacy is good for everyone but a leader will not cut-off links with his advisors and lieutenants. Great kings and empire builders of yesteryears maintain a fine balance - never under-estimating their people's skills and usefulness.

Today's leader may frequently try the 'Round Table' approach of the wise King Arthur, in order to encourage maximum participation of his 'knights'. This is not reduction of power or abdication - this is leveraging of his power for greater effect.

Message:

One can hardly consider oneself a leader without a strong following, which needs to be developed. In fact, the leader's power is magnified through the empowerment and participation of committed and competent people. The 'I am the lord of all I survey' attitude is naive, selfish, shortsighted, and self-defeating.

22

"I COULD HAVE DANCED ALL NIGHT"

"Praise youth and it will prosper"
(Proverb)

I am sure that most readers have seen the great musical (play and/or film) – **'My Fair Lady'**. Just recall the scene after Eliza Dolittle suddenly learns to speak English by correctly saying, with a clear accent and good pronunciation: "The rain in Spain stays mainly in the plain." Prof. Higgins who has been frustrated so far, cannot believe what he hears. Within seconds, Higgins tells Col. Pickering "By George she's got it!" Very soon these two English gentlemen and the flower-girl, Eliza, are celebrating. Eliza is ecstatic. She is looking beautiful, radiant and ecstatic, and she just cannot go to sleep. She sings: "I could have danced all night... I could have spread my wings, and said a thousand things...". Boy! Is she on a real 'high'! She continues singing even in bed. She is energized!

As realistic managers, we may discount a bit of the romantic scene and expression. But, business also has its romantic side (not flirtations with secretaries!). There is a great feeling of adventure when we develop a worthwhile vision and dream about the shape of our organization well into the twenty-first century.

Also, as people, all of us have experienced surges in our morale when we have triumphed at something meaningful or have been specially appreciated by our parents, teachers, or bosses. We are inspired to work late at night or spring out of bed early in the morning, because work has become more fun.

Such is the power of inspiration. Unfortunately, there are still many managers who do not exercise this power to motivate. Several managers still exert hierarchical power and order people around. They demand respect and realize mediocre results. The progressive manager or leader will respect his people and inspire and support them towards the shared goal. In this process, the leader naturally earns the respect and commitment of his team and achieves superior results.

Also recall a subsequent scene from the same play/movie: Eliza excels in her maiden appearance at the royal ball to felicitate the Queen of Transylvania. However, on returning home at Wimpole Street, the professor and the colonel are busy rejoicing, as if all the credit went all to the professor. Eliza feels ignored and belittled (ouch, pun again). This scene tells us that the owners or big bosses must not 'hog' all the credit. Give credit to the people who help you triumph. Even a 'common flower girl' blossoms into a lady if you treat her with respect.

There is a lot we can learn from the "Pygmalion Effect" - treating people well, training them nicely, and having faith that they will out-do themselves. Ultimately, this 'treatment' will help the boss approach the ideal of 'servant leadership'.

23

MAN vs COMPUTER

"Man is the brain behind the computer"

In recent years, there have been chess tournaments between computers and leading chess players. The battles that have attracted the most excitement and money have been the series of encounters sponsored by International Business Machines, featuring IBM's super computer - DEEP BLUE and the world's leading chess exponent - GARY KASPAROV.

In a few of these matches, Deep Blue defeated (a tired) Kasparov and the creators of the computer were jubilant because their machine had defeated the world champion. Many people congratulated the computerwallas. Think again, folks. Yes, Kasparov was defeated sometimes during that series. But, was Kasparov just humbled by a computer? This single man relied only on his own brain to win. On the other hand, the super-computer was built by pooling the brain power of many of the world's greatest brains in computing, supported by a highly potent chess programme which was created by the help of lots of chess champions. Deep Blue was armed with virtually all the tactical gambits and strategic moves by a multitude of chess virtuosos. In other words, one brilliant human brain was over-powered by the combined strength of many fine human brains - not just an electronic box! How would this computer be without the human input ... in <u>deep</u> trouble and 'feel' very <u>blue</u> in defeat.

A good manager or leader makes optimum use of his/her computers and machines but he/she makes sure that he/she motivates the people to build or create or use or maintain the hardware and software. The leader is always conscious that **people are the original and ultimate software**. In fact, nobody can dispute that man is the brain behind the computer. Accordingly, the leader will treat people with respect and appeal to their good senses.

As the great comedian and humanist, Bob Hope, said "The man who does not have charity in his heart has the worst kind of heart trouble." I am sure that good ol' Bob did not mean charity as just giving money. He meant it in a much wider sense. I wonder if Bob would have been so popular if he had been just an entertainer without that kind of heart.

24

PERSONAL HEALTH AND FITNESS

"Health and gaiety foster beauty"
"Health is not valued till sickness comes"
(Proverbs)

I am a great believer in the maxim: "healthy mind in a healthy body". These days, many large enlightened corporations have fitness facilities for their employees on their office premises. Some firms also have dieticians on their staff to advise people on what and how they should eat. A few companies also offer yoga and meditation classes. Several companies pay for memberships in country (golf) clubs or fitness/health clubs. These are all very commendable benefits, which make employees feel good, and the ultimate benefit is reaped by the institution. Some people enjoy sports like tennis, football, basketball and the like which bring out the competitive spirit, while developing team spirit and camaraderie.

Following in our family tradition, I habitually exercise in one form or another virtually everyday. I do a bit of yoga in the morning and end my work-day with an invigorating swim. The beneficial effect that underwater calmness and silence can have on one's mind is quite amazing. My muscles are stimulated, while work stress dissolves and evaporates, leaving my brain refreshed. I feel that this is an effective way to keep 'body and soul together'. I also absorb or catch a few good ideas in the swimming pool.

Anyway, to suit most personal preferences for fitness and recreation, I have the following poem for you.

FUN 'N' AND FITNESS

Swimming is the best exercise all-round;
While diving be sure you avoid the ground!

Tennis is a game of power, stamina and grace;
Takes years of practice to serve a frequent ace!

Soccer is a game for both young 'n' ol';
Use your feet and head, and score a goal!

Super sprinters are really hard to find;
True champions have a "one-track" mind!

Golf is a sport of tremendous co-ordination;
Whether driving or putting, use concentration!

Hockey is a game of skillful stick-work;
To win trophies it takes great team-work!

In cricket you try to hit the ball with a bat;
If you miss you're out and fielders say "Howzzat!".

In basketball you have to put the ball thru the cage;
If you miss the free-throw, your coach is in a rage!

Skiing, indeed is a pastime exhilarating;
Gliding on the snow and accelerating!

Sports and games make our lives stimulating;
Shaping our bodies and blood circulating!

Choose the activity that suits you. Just do not fall in the 'I don't have the time' trap. Like Nike says - just do it!

People can work harder for more years, if they remain healthy. Employers who understand and promote this simple paradigm will be rewarded by better long-term performance and commitment.

25

BEWARE OF
JEALOUSY AND POLITICS

"Resentment is like taking poison and
waiting for the other person to die."
Malachy McCourt

There is an old saying which goes something like this: "if there are two people stranded on a desert island they share **friendship**. But, if there is a third person, they share **politics**!"

In the dramatic play 'Othello', Shakespeare described jealousy as 'the green-eyed monster'. Jealousy or unreasonably coveting another's possession or position damages relationships, or at least prevents relationships from improving. The jealous person wastes a lot of time and mental energy just wanting what another has. Sometimes, it may only be a case of 'grass is greener on the other side', or, as an old Punjabi saying goes - 'the neighbour's wife always looks more attractive/sexy than one's own.'

Mind you, positive envy is okay - if we see certain good traits in a person, it is perfectly fine to emulate them. If we hear that somebody made it to the top of the organization very quickly, we may choose to react in different ways:

(i) We may jump to the (jealous) conclusion that he/she made it the 'wrong' way - favoritism, and/or even spread a rumour, or,

(ii) Congratulate the person sincerely, and even view the successful person as a role model and try to follow in his/her footsteps.

It is so important that we do not pre-judge people, especially negatively.

If one gets 'possessed' by the devil of jealousy and feels that the only way to get a promotion or similar reward is bringing the other guy down or look bad, things become dangerous. This obsession will often tempt one to entice a few supporters to form a gang. This bunch of people, instead of spending their work days productively and creatively, and building teamwork, with fair play, will then focus their faculties and efforts towards guerrilla warfare against the 'target'. Now, when the targeted person gets wind of the 'campaign', he/she could seek counsel and try to correct the situation. But, if the target reacts with a counter-attack, however subtle, the viscous political spiral gets bigger, to the detriment of all, including the institution.

Nobody would disagree that politics weakens, and sometimes destroys the organization. The point is, what can people and institutions do to throw 'Mr. Jealousy' and 'Mr. Politics' down the garbage shoot. (No recycling this time)

Mahatma Gandhi said, "I will not let anyone walk through my mind with their dirty feet."

As I have said or implied in so many chapters of this book, seniors must lead by example. There is no use if the corporate proclamations spurn politics, but some bosses are politicking for personal gain.

The organization should no doubt publish its values to encourage positive behaviour. However, it is equally important that the behaviour of the seniors must clearly demonstrate that their working style and working life is based on open competition and fair play.

Healthy dissent, sometimes behind closed (e.g. board room) doors, is desirable, in fact, essential to get views and recommendations from all angles. But, once a decision is made, even if not by unanimity, the seniors must present the decision with one face and one voice. However, if one boss whose 'idea' did not win, chooses to say, even in a whisper, to his people that the final decision is 'bad', he is laying the ground work for destructive politics. On the other hand, let's say that his idea 'lost' or was passed over, in favour of somebody else's proposal at the board meeting. Yet, he believes in being a good team player and conveys the decision in a positive manner to the team members whose proposal did not win. If some of those persons raise objections or point to the weakness in the 'approval', this senior should be able to say that all the pros and cons were duly debated by all members of the Board. He must convince the team that the decision is the best possible given the constraints, limitations, timing et cetera. He should also motivate them towards implementation of the decision. This is disciplined leadership.

Now, if it subsequently transpires that a key factor had been over-looked by the Board, there should be an open way to make a representation for fair consideration. Therefore, the policy of the organization and behaviour of the seniors should encourage free flow of ideas, even to modify a decision that was based on wrong or incomplete assumptions or inputs. Their positive style will reduce or pre-empt dissent and whispers (and secret hisses) that will ferment politics.

Therefore, the bosses have to take full responsibility for creating an atmosphere of transparency, fairness and trust. The culture should be such that we respect the person(s) sufficiently to avoid 'loss of face' feelings, even when that person's or group's proposal does not get the 'nod'. We already know that not everybody or every idea can be the winner. We also recognize that corporate resources are limited and have to be allocated to the best few projects or proposals.

It is the duty of the seniors to nurture a culture wherein enthusiastic and creative participation is the most important part of competition. Judging should be transparent and fair. It also has to be explained to the participants that there are no 'losers'. The non-winners will be able to observe where or how they fell short and gain experience on how to win next time.

Also, if an organization is infected with politics, good employees get frustrated and lose their initiative. Some will unnecessarily face road-blocks or bottle-necks. Still some others will feel insecure and worry when they are 'forced to take sides'. What a mess! Everybody suffers! Many good ones will leave.

Just visualize the human body - we have various organs and systems that work in harmony. Now, if one part, say a foot gets infected, the whole body's temperature rises to fight the infection. In our context, the entire organization should be alert to unitedly fight the scourge of politics. If the infection in the foot is acute, we may use antibiotics against the harmful germs. Similarly, the appropriate person(s) should issue strong warnings to the offender. If unfortunately, the harmful germs are not controlled, a decision may be taken to stop the gangrene from affecting the whole body by amputating the foot. Similarly, if the offending party continues in the mean and unhealthy way, the appropriate person(s) has to stop the political poison from spreading and hurting the whole institution. The foul element has to be fired.

Let us now ponder for a while on **apology** and **forgiveness**. If I had made a mistake or said something that hurt one of my colleagues, I should have the courage, humility and sincerity to apologize. My tone should be of genuine regret, for the inconvenience or emotional injury caused by my action or behaviour, and include an assurance that this would not happen again. On the other side of the coin, the affected person should also be gracious to accept the apology sincerely - - - forgiveness must also be genuine. If either apology or forgiveness, or both, are not earnest, there will be no real improvement in the relationship or healing between the two parties. Over a period of time, the relationship can, in fact, deteriorate to the detriment of the persons and the company. The corporate culture should be such that people do not have to suffer undue 'heart-burn' to apologize, because the other person has the heart to forgive quickly and sincerely, for the benefit of their relationship and their institution. Senior officers have to set the example, as usual. I recall a profound proverb on forgiveness:

"The noblest vengeance is to forgive."

I realize that to create and support such a spirit and culture is not easy. One of our main challenges is very much so. Also, we have to emphasize that the 'enemy' is outside, not inside, the corporation.

I feel that this is the appropriate place to quote one of the great brains of the late 19th and early 20th century, George Bernard Shaw:

"Treat your friend as someone who'll one day become your enemy. An enemy is someone who'll one day become your friend."

There is a great lesson for us in these words, provided by a man with profound perception, a fine sense of values and a beautiful way of expressing himself. I read this quote when I was about fifteen, and memorised it!

Let me quote another great Irish writer who laments the abuse of religion as a political weapon:

'We have just enough religion to make us hate, but not enough to make us love one another."

Jonathan Swift

As a realist, I really cannot disagree with Swift because of what is still happening in the Middle East, former Yugoslavia, Kashmir, Afghanistan, Central Africa, etc. However as a hard-boiled optimist, I believe that there is enough goodwill and international conscience that these situations will improve, albeit gradually. Although I wish it would be a lot <u>swifter</u>. In any event, when I observe more and more young people of various ethnic and religious backgrounds, learning together and playing on the same teams, in internationally oriented schools and universities, I feel that there is hope for peaceful co-existence. I cannot help believing that our children and our children's children will make the world a better place.

Message:

It is people who create politics <u>and</u> people who can eliminate/pre-empt politics. Concepts like shared vision, unity of purpose, fairness and trust, backed by model leadership can keep the organization devoid of harmful politics, and therefore, stronger and 'richer' in every sense of the word. The attitude of I'm OK - You're OK - We're OK must be 'cultivated' and 'internalized' throughout the system.

In the long run, we would be well guided by the old proverb:

"Jealousy eats nothing but its own heart."

26

HOW TO 'MANAGE' THE BOSS

"Good counsel has no price"

(Proverb)

For me, managing the boss is one of the most difficult and important concepts to write about. In fact, I have hardly read any specific literature on this topic.

I believe that the trick lies mainly in how the subordinate, at any given level, performs and behaves, versus the expectations of the boss. This will frequently determine how the boss treats, and responds to the subordinate.

Suppose the subordinate asks the question, 'how do I manage the boss so that he/she appreciates me?' Perhaps the subordinate should consider the following tips, which are largely based on my experience and observation:

1. You should start by focusing on the targets agreed with the boss and achieve them to the best of your ability.

2. You should keep the boss informed of progress, especially of high impact goals, which are more important to the boss.

3. Make sure that you meet deadlines.

4.   Your presentations should be accurate, crisp, and to the point, as well as interesting, in relation to the objectives.

5.   If you have achieved your targets, 'stretch' yourself to higher levels.

6.   If you have achieved your targets or are progressing well, perhaps you may take on a new project or task, which is important to the company and boss. This is a case of going beyond the call of duty. Such initiatives will score points for you.

7.   When faced with a problem, don't just 'dump' it on the boss' lap. Mention the problem and say how you have tried to solve it; or propose alternative solutions and implications to make it easier for the boss to advise or decide.

8.   Do make proposals for improvements and innovations, but avoid half-baked ideas which waste the boss' time.

9.   When the boss is under pressure, ask how you can help.

10. Your behaviour should be such that you earn the boss' trust and give him the feeling that you trust him as well.

11. Respect the boss. However, there should be no need to fear him when you have done nothing wrong.

12. Don't be afraid to give contrary opinions as long as your logic is sound and your expression is respectful. A good boss will like you for this.

13. Don't speak ill of others in front of the boss. If you do, the boss may wonder how you speak of him behind his back. There may be loss of trust.

14. Definitely do not run-down or ridicule your boss in gossip or other loose talk.

15. If the boss is not treating you fairly, first try to analyze the situation and see if you can take any corrective measures from your own side. If you are sure that the boss is acting wrongly, try to approach him in a respectful way. Explain the situation and ask for his understanding. If things do not improve and your morale and performance are being hurt, seek help from the head of the Human Resource Department.

16. If the boss has forgotten to praise you, do not be disheartened. He may be pre-occupied with pressing issues. Moreover, it is good to show that you are self-motivated and don't crave for praise.

17. Some bosses don't praise frequently, especially in Asia, because they believe that such gestures may 'spoil' the subordinate. Here, take satisfaction that he/she is the same with others.

18. Sometimes the boss may be insecure because his own boss has been hard on him. If you sense this, work in a way that supports him and lightens his burden.

19. As far as possible, help your boss to look good.

20. In cases where the boss is unnecessarily rude or negative towards you, stay focused on your work and ask some mature confidant for help. Don't neglect your work or that could justify the boss' negative attitude. Just stay out of his way until you have achieved a goal dear to him.

21. Do not expect the boss to be perfect, just as you expect him to forgive your own imperfections.

22. A boss, like any human being, likes praise, especially when he/she has achieved something worthwhile. By all means, praise and congratulate him. However, false flattery must be shunned; there may be a short-term gain but he/she will see through you, and respect you less. Please see chapter titled 'ENGULFED IN WAR' for an example of how I was able to persuade my Saudi boss to grant a war or hardship allowance to our staff during Operation Dessert Storm/Dessert Shield. While writing that chapter, I realized that I had unwittingly managed my boss.

23. If the boss is about to do something illegal or unethical, politely draw his attention to the consequential risk. If he persists, distance yourself from that action. Also, depending on circumstances and the nature of the risk for the institution, it maybe necessary to report the problem to a higher authority. Here, it is necessary to distinguish between personal loyalty and friendship, vis-à-vis professional integrity and ethics. These are very important aspects to human relationships. True friendship includes proper support and honest advice. If the wrong-doer ignores your advice, do not think that you are being loyal or sincere by participating or helping in a cover-up. Beware of becoming an accomplice.

24. If the boss directs you to convey 'bad news' (e.g. reduced benefits) to your team or subordinates, do not try the short-term populist tactic of trying to look good, while making the boss look bad. It behoves you to preface the message with the background circumstances and explain sincerely that it was a well thought out corporate or departmental decision. Give comfort to your subordinates that your boss also regrets that some people would get hurt, but that he will be humane and fair to minimize the pain for the persons affected.

25. Avoid losing your temper against the boss, as far as possible. Let me tell you about my folly on this topic:

    I was about twenty-seven years old, and it was the peak of the Delhi summer. The bank was dusty and there was no air-conditioning due to major renovation work of our premises. My boss rudely shouted at me (now for the third time) in front of my subordinates. I felt insulted and shouted back in a reflex action, and without thinking. I should have realized that he was under pressure and he was suffering from withdrawal symptoms because he had just stopped smoking (from forty cigarettes a day). To this day, I feel that I should have controlled myself, especially since he was twenty years older than I, and he was basically a good man at heart. I had managed myself poorly, and consequently managed my boss badly, because my bad behaviour only made him more resentful. I should have been sensible enough to hold my temper even though I was wrongly reprimanded. I should have backed off and subsequently discussed the issue with him in private. At that time, I had not even heard of Stephen Covey and did not have the benefit of his advice – *'first understand and then be understood'*.

I sincerely believe that good performance and genuine behavior by the subordinate will normally bring out the best in the boss. In essence, **managing the boss, to me, means how we manage ourselves vis-à-vis the boss.**

We should keep in mind that nobody is 'whole'. We must not focus on or take delight in magnifying the boss' weaknesses or skill gaps. On the contrary, we must help to fill in the gaps or shortfalls. And, to the extent we 'encourage' the boss to depend on us, to that extent we manage the boss in a positive way.

Let me put it in another way: we should remember that if we want to manage the boss' performance for the general good of the department or company, which includes ourselves, we first have to make sure that we ourselves turn in top quality performance. After all, in the main, the boss' performance is the sum of the parts or aggregate results of his subordinates. Therefore, it should be clear that **real control comes not by exercising control but by top performance, sincere behaviour and proving to the boss that we are reliable and trustworthy.**

I have to concede that it is generally easier to give counter opinions to a professional boss than a boss who is also the owner. However, I can say that when I followed the above-mentioned guidelines, most owner-bosses were reasonable, in fact appreciative. I still feel that this is an area wherein I have to improve significantly. I find that if I make my case or counterpoint with emphasis (assertiveness), I could be seen as arrogant. On the other hand, if I do the same softly to appear humble, the point may not be taken seriously. Also, I have to learn when to make my case, with some bosses, because their responses depend on their prevailing states of mind, especially in these days of monumental pressures. I have also learnt (slowly), when to back-off and come back to present the idea in a different way, on a better occasion.

In any event, if despite your best efforts, the boss remains negative, hope for him/her to be transferred or seek a transfer for yourself. Also remember, that patience can help in most situations because life is a series of transitions. In any case, don't let the negative boss treat you like a slave or puppet or whipping boy. Do not lose your dignity, your self-esteem. Also, don't confuse the concept of 'yes-man' with professional loyalty. This means that you will sincerely support the boss' decisions and efforts, provided they do not go against the corporation's shared values and applicable laws.

Overall, by doing and saying the right things with commitment and sincerity, you have a far better framework and greater hope to 'manage' the boss for the general good. Like I mentioned earlier, this is not an easy concept to explain, but I hope that my readers get a feel for it and find it useful.

GOOD LUCK!!

27

FAST-TRACK EMPLOYEES

"Challenge brings experience and experience brings wisdom"
(Proverb)

Many quality corporations have accelerated training and career development or fast-track programmes for high potential people. This is a good concept - good for the company and good for the deserving employee.

Sometimes, other employees feel let-down and discriminated. Therefore, it is critical that the fast-track programme is properly communicated. The programme and its criteria should be fair, transparent and open. In general, management should be able to reasonably defend its decision to admit or not to admit a candidate as a fast-tracker.

Morale problems can also surface if a fast-tracker behaves in an elitist or arrogant manner, or has leap-frogged over a better candidate because of 'connections'. Remember the Bendix - Mary Cunningham saga?

Moreover, the fast-tracker should be mentored and challenged and guided to ensure his/her progress versus the targets and career plan. The candidate, whether an MBA or a young high potential officer, should be aware that his/her privileged career path has to be deserved consistently or the aspirations maybe 'off-track'. They must realize that this accelerated programme is a privilege and not a right. The high potential person should also be able to take on more load or pressure than others. Care should be taken to motivate such employees but not pamper them. If we treat them as 'anointed' prima doñas, we shall be doing them and the company a disservice. Similarly, if we handle them with kid gloves, they will not mature sufficiently. The Human Resource Department has a major role to play in the entire programme.

Actually, I see such schemes in the light of athletics - not a 100-metre dash, but a **marathon race, set in stages**. The length of the course should be the same from management trainee (entry) level to the top office. Fast-track should mean that the more talented candidates, provided they maintain their required progress in learning and performance, would have shorter stops at each stage. There should be no unfair criteria, or unfair interpretation/implementation thereof, that gives undue advantage to a preferred candidate (like performance enhancement drugs in sports). Similarly, no qualified candidate should feel handicapped. Also, it is better not to skip any stage except in highly exceptional cases. Eventually, it is hoped that the fast-tracker will compete against himself/herself.

There is an old Urdu '*sher*' (couplet) which says: "Henna leaves (which are dark green) give forth their beautiful (orange) color after being well-ground on the grindstone - - - and man comes to his senses (gains wisdom) after experiencing the grindstone of life."

Drawing on the lesson of this couplet, I feel that the speed of the career progression must be realistically tailored to ensure that the still-developing fast-tracker does not reach his/her level of incompetence pre-maturely.

Let us take a mountaineering example:

Supposing a person with insufficient climbing skills and experience is over-ambitious and impatient, he may reach the summit of Mount Everest by helicopter. He can have himself photographed in full mountaineering livery and boast success to his friends. However, he knows that his success is hollow and will always feel guilty and lack confidence in the company of accomplished mountaineers, real experts. Also, once people come to know that he did not actually climb up the peak the hard way, they will stop trusting and respecting him. He will be treated with suspicion like an 'outsider'. Similar would be the fate of a person who does not deserve to jump up to the top echelons of the organization, but gets there by unfair means.

Like any HR policy, fast-track programmes must be implemented sensibly and fairly. This is indeed a great way to identify and develop future leaders, if done correctly.

28

TEACH'EM YOUNG!
TEACH'EM RIGHT!

"Child is father of the man"
William Wordsworth

In the last chapter, I wrote about fast-trackers. Subsequently, two questions came to my mind. Who helps to put youngsters on the fast-track? How do we help the head-start process <u>with</u> values? Even born leaders need nurturing, education and mentoring. I think that we all agree that of the answer lies in good **parenting** and good **schooling**, especially in the tender years.

During the earlier years of my wife, Kuko's teaching career, she mostly taught eight to twelve year old students. When we moved to Bahrain, in 1983, Kuko reluctantly agreed to teach in first grade. However, within a few weeks in the job she told me that she found it even more satisfying to teach five to six year olds because she could see the dramatic speed of child development at that age. Subsequently, when we moved to Indonesia, Kuko was very happy to further 'demote' herself to kindergarten, where she found still greater job enrichment and enjoyment. I remember her telling me that human beings learn almost 80% of their lifetime knowledge during the first five to six years of their lives. In the anthology of interesting experiences, called CHICKEN SOUP FOR THE SOUL, there is a profound contribution by Robert Fulghum titled '**All I Ever Really Needed To Know, I Learned in Kindergarten**'. In this two-page piece, he tells us in a most concise and eye-opening manner, the wisdom he learned in and near the nursery sandbox - sharing, fair play, neatness, the arts; balanced diet and balanced life, which includes rest periods. He also learned the fundamentals of plant and animal life and the all important attribute of learning by **looking**. All this was 'absorbed' and learnt in an atmosphere of **love**, which perhaps, is the most important feature of a good nursery school.

In 1996, Kuko joined a truly fine pre-school called **Kinderland**, promoted by a highly cultured couple, Seemun Adijanto and her husband Dr. Suparno, that strongly supports education. One day, Kuko asked me to write a **school song** for Kinderland. I hesitated at first, because although I had written a few poems, I had never written a song for an institution. Anyway, I promised to give it a shot, trying to be a 'supportive' spouse.

I started to focus on little kids of about twenty nationalities, in this beautiful pre-school, receiving the **foundations of education** – not just a-b-c or 1-2-3. I also pondered over love, discipline, respect and similar values that the world's future citizens and leaders would need. I went to sleep with these engaging thoughts - - - and the next morning's gentle sunrays woke me with the following lyrics:

THE KINDERLAND SONG *(in Jakarta)*

Come, do come, and sing along,
Join the chorus of our school song.

This is the place for fun while learning.
This is the place for fun while growing.

We're learning more than the alphabet —
Learning to share and show respect.

We're also learning right from wrong
Even while we're singing our song.

We are happy children from many a land
We are the smiling faces of Kinderland,
Of Kinderland - - - of Kinder L-A-N-D...**KINDERLAND!!**

Fortunately, Kuko and Seemun liked the lyrics and one of the teachers composed the music for this little school anthem.

29

JOB SECURITY

"The future belongs to those who prepare for it"
R. W. Emerson

"Job security depends on the quality of the employer and employee"

In these days of globalization and de-regulation, competition has soared dramatically. Many industries or companies that cannot innovate sufficiently, strive to protect their margins by resorting to cost-cutting programmes. Such processes invariably include large redundancies and terminations. The person leading the termination is often described by employees as the 'hatchet-man' when they are 'polite'.

Massive severance is painful for the corporation and employees, as well as the community in the case of a dominant organization going through the exercise. People get 'rationalized' or 're-engineered' out of their livelihoods. In most western countries, such terminated employees at least have the 'safety-net' of social security/welfare.

However, in most other countries terminated employees do not have this luxury and generally end up doing much lower grade jobs. This prevailing epidemic of the Asian Flu (flu is a very mild expression this time - we call the crisis a lethal combination of a major earthquake, volcano and typhoon) has devastated Indonesia the most. It is really depressing to see the sudden surge of beggars on the streets. In addition, a huge number of expatriates have lost their jobs because they have suddenly become too expensive. (Some have also left because of the insecure feeling of the terrible May, 1998 riots, and have to find jobs in other countries, which is not easy at this time.)

Whichever way one looks at it, job security has always been a major factor in the lives of people. However, it is obvious that the cozy days of protected markets and exclusive licenses/franchises are over. Even government jobs - civil service or military - cannot guarantee long term employment in many countries because of pressures to reduce budget deficits. Reliance on people will continue to be reduced due to office automation and deployment of advanced remote-controlled weapons systems. Even one of the cornerstones of Japanese society, 'life-time employment', is crumbling.

Most people would agree that private sector enterprises are no longer in a position to assure job security, even implicitly. We all have to be aware that sustained, long-term profits are the only guarantee for employment - that too for employees who meet the ever rising standards.

Given the need to down-size, what can a socially conscious, responsible institution do to mitigate the pain of unemployment? Enlightened companies are endeavouring to help and enhance the 'employability' of their people. This concept means that most employees will be given comprehensive and progressive training and development opportunities not only to move up the company's own corporate ladder, but also to broaden their skills to make them more employable even in other industries when bad times come. Some fine employers that have to down-size, arrange and pay for special courses to re-train exiting employees. Quite a few of these organizations also help departing workers by using their services on a part-time contractor basis. Such institutions may also issue letters of recommendations, and in deserving cases, pro-actively use some influence with recruitment firms and important business associates to find suitable positions.

Such corporations are deemed as more desirable employers. They would normally attract better talent and earn more loyalty from their people.

30

COMPENSATION AND REWARD

"If you pay peanuts, you get monkeys"
(Proverb)

Compensation and reward policies are one of the major concerns of both employees and employers. The tussle will never end, but both parties have the responsibility to ensure that their differences do not get out of hand.

It is generally gratifying to observe that trade unions have become more reasonable in several countries. France is one of the exceptions among the prosperous countries, but things will change when realities, like loss of competitiveness, become clearer.

Meanwhile, it is disconcerting to note that the gap between the CEO's package and that of the lowest level employee in a given company has increased exponentially. I am all for higher component of variable pay. I am all for granting entrepreneurial type incentives to encourage top executives to boost the value of the corporation (not just boost the share price during 'bonus periods'). Stock options and special bonuses are all fine. But don't some of these high flying big boys feel a little guilty on the over-loaded pay-reward packages they write for themselves and have approved by their hand-picked buddies on the Board?

They are creating much wider, gaping compensation gaps! Don't they realize that the employees would get the impression that the **'top dogs'** are getting too greedy and grabbing outrageously large bones. This feeling gets even worse when other good people get 'chain-sawed' in the name of stockholder value, and because the CEO wants to get rich quick. Moreover, in the event of a take-over, the CEO must also have a golden parachute all ready to open, while the humble 'pawns' are given a few leaky life-boats!

Isn't this the wrong way to motivate people? Is this the way to build loyalty? We all agree that compensation is an important issue. But are we doing enough to nurture long-term excellence, and durable and genuine professional loyalty?

In general terms, compensation should be fair and competitive with peer companies. The 3 Ps of **Position, Performance**, and **Person** are a good guide. Compensation should be related to the position, rank or title. Compensation and reward should also be based on the performance of the person. Moreover, the special skills, contribution and potential of the person should also be recognized in the overall package. This is particularly vital to attract and retain unique and creative people.

Just like a very hungry person will think about food instead of concentrating on work, an employee who genuinely feels under-paid, will think more about money than the job. On the other hand, if my salary is doubled (ha, ha!), I might be motivated to work longer hours up to a limit. But the double pay cannot suddenly make me more creative, if I am not that kind of person or because the working conditions are not conducive to creativity. Meanwhile, there is growing evidence that for highly creative people, money is not much of a motivator once the main needs are taken care of.

As I see it, the 'secret' therefore is to pay well on the broad lines mentioned earlier <u>and</u> to create an environment wherein people enjoy working. It is when people are having fun that they worry less about money. Working conditions and incentives should encourage positive ambition, not greed.

When it comes to annual salary raises and bonuses, it is a rule of thumb in many companies to use the 'Bell Curve' method. Here the top 10-15% get high rewards, the bottom 10-15% get little or nothing and the bulk of the employees get lumped into an 'average' reward category. It is a 'convenient' way to administer salaries. But is it the leader's job to do things conveniently or to inspire the right people, and motivate more people to improve? The Bell Curve method, by definition, automatically puts too many employees into the mediocre bracket. If the vast majority gets a mediocre raise or bonus, their performance will also become mediocre before long. Therefore, management has to reshape the curve or policy in a way that inspires continuing improvement towards (the moving target of) excellence.

Generally, there is a 'point' in most people's compensation (subject to a fairly wide range) after which the law of diminishing returns begins to apply. After this point, reduction in the compensation may act as a de-motivator, but additional money does not do much on the positive side. Moreover, we find that the bright, ambitious, self-starters, after that point of monetary security/satisfaction, are really motivated much more by meaningful challenges, recognition and career advancement. These are issues that make them feel good about themselves and they can see that they are progressing towards their cherished dream or self-actualization.

A company that does not pay high salaries, and yet makes its employees feel good, is **Walt Disney**, especially at its highly popular and well managed theme parks. Disney has created a tremendous environment - physical, technological and emotional - wherein its people feel good just to work in its 'magic kingdoms'. These employees enjoy being happy and enthusiastic hosts to happy and enthusiastic visitors of all ages, nations, religions, and races - - - "it's a small world, after all!"

31

ADAPTABILITY

"Experience teaches us that those who do not adapt to changing trends and environments can at best look back at their 'glorious pasts'. They really do not have much of a future."

The leading firm of business consultants, Booz·Allen & Hamilton, published in 1998, a fine book titled "Thought Leaders", based on insights of leading lights in the business and academic world. In this book, Professor **Charles Handy** of the London Business School very appropriately said " - - - life is understood backwards, but unfortunately it has to be lived forward." He was talking about the 'Federal Model' to meet the challenges in the Information Age, vis-à-vis the old models which were developed by engineers in the Machine Age of the bygone era.

The 'Round-Table' association which has world-wide membership, has a nice crisp motto - "ADOPT, ADAPT, IMPROVE". In this chapter, I wish to focus on the importance of adaptability from the personal and institutional viewpoint. The way I see it, 'adapt' is the key word of the three. I feel that if one is adaptable, then there is a far greater chance to 'adopt' good principles and concepts and to 'improve' in general or in specific areas. In other words, when an organization is open-minded and flexible, i.e. adaptable, it should be easier for it to adopt and improve for its long-term viability.

Technology and lifestyles have tremendous impact on each other and on the business environment. Furthermore, political landscapes continue to change in many countries, which will affect their business climates and lifestyles. The successful people and organizations will be those who will be able to change or even lead change, without compromising time-honoured principles and values. Experience teaches us that those who do not adapt to changing trends and environments can at best look back at their 'glorious pasts'. They really do not have much of a future.

Now, I wish to talk about adaptability in different situations:

INDONESIAN SCENE
(Entering 'Era Reformasi')

Until mid 1997, Indonesia was one of the favourite emerging markets for investors from many countries. Indonesians were proud that in 25 years their per capita income had rocketed from less than $100 to $1,000 in mid 1997. Frequently, expatriates who initially came here on short postings, would fall in love with this country. Indonesia's interesting cultures, religious tolerance, friendly attitude towards expatriates, moderate climate, scenic beauty, as well as cheap and respectful domestic servants would charm them into extending their assignments and even settling down here.

Indonesians have an interesting habit of abbreviating names and phrases. When the crisis started, the initial focus was on the monetary aspects and they coined the expression **'krismon'** for *krisis moneter.* Within a few months, people realized the magnitude of the problem and began to accuse Soeharto and his inner circle of corruption, collusion, and nepotism, locally referred to as ***Korupsi, Kolusi dan Nepotisme (KKN).*** Therefore, the situation also reflected an enormous political problem which resulted in sky-rocketing prices of basic foods, massive unemployment and severe discontent. All this culminated in ugly riots and resignation of Soeharto in May 1998. The essence of this all encompassing crisis was captured in the new piece of vocabulary, **'kristal'** for *krisis total.* I would like to suggest one more acronym to my Indonesian friends – **'kristik'** for _Krisis Politik_, which, without apologies to Saddam Hussein, is the **'mother of all crisis'** in Indonesia.

By September, 1998, the Indonesian Rupiah had lost around 80% of its value compared to June, 1997. In the meantime, the Jakarta Stock Exchange's market capitalization has fallen to a mere 10% in dollar terms.

It is especially in this crisis situation, that past successes or strengths, particularly which were not genuinely attained by certain major groups, are no guarantee for future survival or progress. On the contrary, the easy profits made during the previous era made some groups complacent and even arrogant. If this kind of company does not adapt, it would soon be crumbling like the proverbial 'house of cards'.

History tells us that in certain situations, it is not enough to be merely big and strong. This is the time for survival of the fittest, which includes adaptability. Companies who did not over-extend themselves and have good reserves or who are in export-oriented business will escape with bruises and burns and eventually emerge stronger. At the same time, companies have to be open-minded to understand the new realities, i.e. new challenges and opportunities, and to adapt their business styles, structures and processes accordingly.

On the other hand, some companies which still have financial viability and are well positioned, are learning to adapt to the new political and business environment. Sensible companies will find cheaper and better ways of doing things, slashing wasteful spending. Wise companies will not indiscriminately fire all expatriates. They should re-assess the value of all officers in relation to their cost to the company, and make fair settlements with those who are no longer needed. Smart companies and people will divest non-core assets, especially those which were bought or built for image purposes. Sinar Mas is meeting this challenge by reviewing its investments, activities, systems, people and corporate culture to ensure that it emerges as a much finer and stronger organisation that can better weather storms, and at the same time, better capitalize on new opportunities. It is a tough battle, but highly worthwhile.

It was disappointing and sad that some business magnates continued to be in a state of denial and did not realize that ego and prestige cannot be deposited in the bank. In fact, I sincerely believe that their image and reputation would be better served if they sincerely and honourably settle their debts, rather than hope for some easy way out. On the other hand, companies with genuine problems deserve softer treatment by their bankers, especially if there is hope for revival. The situation calls for integrity on the part of the borrowers and a balance of reality and patience on the part of the lenders.

Similarly, employees must also realize that it is extremely difficult for employers to boost their salaries to the full extent of inflation in cost of living. Both employers and employees are being put to the test of sharing a more difficult business climate and have to support each other during this unprecedented crisis. The pain has to be shared by sacrifices on both sides. This is the time to hold hands.

At this stage, it is useful to discuss a really disheartening and discouraging industrial relations incident. In August, 1998, a well-established synthetics/textiles company outside Jakarta could not settle amiably with its workers. It is difficult to expect workers who cannot even feed themselves and their families to be efficient and disciplined. The workers union initially demanded a raise equivalent of $12 per month. The company's attitude was quite inflexible and its counter-offer was a mere $2.5, which inflamed the hungry workers. The talks broke-down and some of the irate workers set ablaze about thirty-six cars and nine rooms. Over seventy executives and their families had to be temporarily evacuated to Jakarta. Traditionally, trade unions were controlled by the apex union called SPSI - *Serikat Pekerja Seluruh Indonesia* (Labor Union of Indonesia) which was ultimately controlled by the then Soeharto government. Also, in the so-called good old days, an owner could 'buy protection' and workers were at the mercy at the owner's whims on compensation and working conditions. Connections and 'fees' would help to control the unions. Furthermore, the army and/or police would intervene on behalf of the owner, as and when required. This kind of protection is no longer 'reliable' in the old sense.

Soon after the above-mentioned arson, the owner agreed to a 'higher' raise of around $9 per month. While things are back to normal, a dangerous precedent has been established, especially in the post-Soeharto era, with reduced control over strikes and related actions. Workers now feel more confident that they can resort to violence, arson, etc. or threaten such action to have their demands met. Employers have to adapt to such situations and emerge as happy survivors in the long run. They have to be proactive on staff welfare and industrial relations to pre-empt future labour-related disasters.

My objective of giving this example is not to criticize any specific company. My aim is to draw attention to corporate policies and practices, and honestly test which need to be 'buried' and which new ones need to be adapted or adopted to make the organisation genuinely better, more competitive and more viable.

In any event, employers have to be humane and listen to their conscience, when an extra 30 to 50 cents per day can help satisfy basic hunger of their own productive workers. This little cost does not hurt corporate profits. On the contrary, it should be seen as an investment to win worker loyalty during these traumatic times. At the same time, labour unions must not exploit their new-found freedom and demand unrealistic raises, which eventually can backfire on workers, especially if the company is already on the verge of bankruptcy. In other words, both sides have to adapt and co-exist cordially for mutual benefit. It is sincerely hoped that both groups remember that they are the most important co-stakeholders in the enterprise.

It must be recognized that some of the reform measures are beginning to show results. From just three parties in the previous era, there are

48 registered and active parties today. This is the other extreme, and some polarization is desirable. Since the second half of 1998, we do see signs of freedom of the press. Monopolies of certain privileged groups have been dismantled. Privatization of some state owned/controlled companies have been initiated, although the speed needs to be accelerated. There is talk of making the Police a little more independent of the Armed Forces. Furthermore, the government is apparently making a sincere attempt to work out a plan for independence or significant autonomy for the former Portuguese colony of Timor. A referendum is due in August, 1999.

Indonesia has tremendous natural resources, a sizable domestic population and market, popular tourist resorts for recreation and rich cultural exposure - - - the right ingredients. Only political stability and professionalism are now required to complete the magic formula for attracting a new flood of foreign investment. Perhaps, my affection for this wonderful country makes me feel somewhat optimistic about Indonesia's future.

PHILIPPINE EXAMPLE
(Consolidating gains)

A great example of a fine organization in the emerging markets is **Ayala Corporation**, headquartered in Manila. Ayala was founded over one hundred and sixty years ago, and remains a family-controlled organization to this day. How did the Ayalas survive, indeed flourish, under so many regimes? The Philippines have had their ups and downs under Spanish colonization, American control, World War II, post-independence chaos, martial law and oppressive regime under Ferdinand Marcos, followed by Cory Aquino's People's Power and recovery under Fidel Ramos.

I believe that this institution has continued to thrive because of **vision, and adaptability to new realities, without compromising its basic beliefs and values**. This corporation, now under the fifth/sixth generations since the founding Ayala, has resisted short-term temptations if they were to hurt its image or long-term viability. They have diversified sensibly and have given considerable authority to hand-picked and well-nurtured professionals to head their operating units. These executives are respected and well rewarded consistently by the Ayalas.

INDIAN EXAMPLE

(Democratic principles but lacking principled democrats)

Now, I wish to discuss adaptation or lack of it when government ideologies change or when a new political wind blows through a country. India, under Nehru, chose the centrally planned economy model which he thought was good for a highly populous and poor, newly independent country. After all, on the face of it, Soviet Russia seemed to be doing well. China, then considered a dear brother by India, not just good neighbour, was also on the same track.

Along with this central control on major economic activity, came the notorious 'LICENSE RAJ' which favoured a few already rich conglomerates and government 'undertakings'. Sorry to digress a bit, but I need to make a side remark here: The creators and preservers of public-owned corporations may have displayed unconscious foresight in calling each of these high cost and mostly poor performing companies 'Government of India Undertakings'. Now, nearly all of these undertakings need undertakers!

With the dismantling of the License Raj since the early 1990s, most of the 'privileged ones' have found it difficult to adapt to this new era of de-regulation. The sad part is that instead of trying to improve their styles, systems and technologies, they are spending a lot of their energies in building obstacles for (foreign) competitors to the detriment of the Indian consumer and in violation of the spirit of the World Trade Organization (WTO). In my banking days in the 1970s and 1980s, I considered it a privilege to be acquainted with the Birlas,

Thapars, Singhanias, Modis, DCM/Srirams, etc. They had all been good clients and gracious hosts to me. Therefore, I was rather surprised and disappointed that some people worked harder to upset Sinar Mas' $280 million paper project in Maharashtra, than to improve their own quality, efficiency and competitiveness. I sincerely hope that all players play fair. India is a growing market; let us all compete in the tradition of gallantry. On the other hand, it is gratifying to see many professionals turn into entrepreneurs and win kudos for themselves and the country. Some examples are **Infosys**, founded by Narayan Murthy; **Hindustan Computers/NIIT**, headed by Shiv Nadar; **HDFC Bank** headed by Deepak Parekh. It is noteworthy that Murthy and Nadar have made millionaires out of many of their colleagues. This is something that the old business houses need to learn, if they want to win real loyalty and commitment of their managers and encourage creativity.

AMERICAN AUTOMOBILE INDUSTRY
(Humming along after bumpy rides)

America was and is the world leader in the automobile industry. The 'big three' - General Motors, Ford and Chrysler, were naturally very proud of their achievements and generally good profits until the oil crunch around 1974. The oversized gas-guzzlers were no longer attractive, but the Detroit kings took their own sweet time to change. That complacent attitude give a tremendous 'opening' to the likes of Toyota and Honda, not to mention a few European brands.

Instead of quickly adapting to the new realities and also learning how to export to Japan, Detroit's 'Chief Driving Officers' complained about the Japan's trade barriers. While there was indeed some legitimacy in that protest, the Americans also underlined that Japanese refused to buy Detroit's left-hand drive cars! This was a combination of ignorance and arrogance on the American side. (Their rationale: After all, if Japanese could conform to American standards, for American customers, why shouldn't the Japanese adapt to American standards also in Japan? - - - come again!)

In short, the American car makers scored low on adaptability. They were becoming part of the 'rust belt'. Eventually, after taking several years of losing market share and profits, there was a clear recovery. Detroit's pistons (cagers and car makers alike) were pumped up again. They all, especially Chrysler under Lee Iacocca, reinvented its cars and the car assembly business. GM, in fact, took the radical step of creating a new legal entity called SATURN, so that it would not be in any way 'contaminated' with the old habits and union problems of the main GM. American car manufacturers were slow to adapt but we must credit them with their eventual dramatic recovery in profits and pride. Sometimes we have to pay a high price to learn.

JAPANESE SITUATION
(Reforming and consolidating)

After World War II and the end of the American Occupation of Japan, there was this 'cozy and comfortable relationship' between the Liberal Democrat Party (LDP) and Japanese business, which led to the phrase: JAPAN INC. This concept worked very well for a couple of decades. They agreed that since Japan had little natural resources, and they had disciplined and skilled labour, the engine for economic growth and power would be exports, especially since the Yen was so cheap at around $1 = ¥ 300, even in the mid 1970s. Their 'secret' was to sell locally manufactured goods at extra high prices in Japan, and use these extra profits to subsidise their exports to U.S., Europe and the rest of the world at very low prices. The poor Japanese customer had no choice because it was: (a) patriotic to 'buy Japanese' and (b) imported goods were expensive due to the high import tariffs and local mark-ups.

As a result of their wonderful formula, Japanese foreign exchange reserves swelled to hundreds of billions of dollars and Japan became the world's largest creditor. Meanwhile, the Americans saw their markets being taken over at home and overseas by their Japanese competitors. Since, the Americans could not adjust their own cost structures and production efficiencies fast enough, they chose the financial and political method of 'talking-down the Dollar'. As a result of this, and some help of Bank of Japan and certain other Central Banks, in a matter of a few years, the Dollar weakened to as low as ¥ 80 around 1996. By then, it was clear to the Japanese that they had become an extremely high cost economy. They had also boosted their real estate prices to the most exorbitant levels and the Dow Nikkei Index crossed the 40,000 mark in 1995. It is alleged that the 'Yakuza' (Japanese Mafia) played a major role in inflating the bubble. Since then, the bubble burst like bubble gum on the faces of many big punters. The Nikkei has plummeted, year after year, to around 13,000 in 1997-98. At the time of writing, with the Yen around 120 to the Dollar, the Nikkei has improved to 17,000.

The Japanese company that stands out for adaptability, amongst other achievements, is **Toyota**. It has been able to improve its own productions efficiencies through better training; automation, including, robotics; better dealership arrangements; efficient overseas assembly plants and partnership style outsourcing. The great standards set by Toyoda-san have been further improved by 'Team Toyota' that says 'our high standards are yours' to its worldwide clientele. And, don't forget the LEXUS, which is a competitively priced example of luxury on wheels and has forced Mercedes and BMW to re-engineer their production processes, to become more cost efficient.

On the other hand, Japan's number two ranked auto maker – Nissan – which is wilting under a heavy debt burden, has swallowed its pride and accepted Renault of France as its controlling shareholder.

The great Sogo Soshas (Trading Companies) have also made significant changes. Instead of concentrating on traditional trading, they have made bold equity investments with leading companies in many countries in all continents (excluding the home of the tuxedo-clad penguins), especially in South East Asia. Some of these Sogo Shoshas are showing great agility and flexibility and they have implemented strategic alliances after carefully selecting their partners. They are willing to inject not only equity, but also arrange and guarantee relatively low-cost financing, for a competitive fee. Such financing is available for pre and post shipment use for export-oriented companies in South East Asia. Also, in special cases where their partners have competitive advantage, (added value, resource based business) these Japanese companies are arranging terms loans with options to convert to equity. This flexible financing approach, together with pursuit of 'trading rights' will strengthen the Sogo Shoshas. In this area, Nissho Iwai, Itochu, Mitsubishi, Marubeni, Mitsui and Sumitomo have shown great initiative and are expanding their alliances with select reliable companies in the ASEAN Region, to mutual advantage. Notwithstanding the current Asian crisis, I believe that those investments which were based on sound fundamentals, will do well. In fact, Japan Exim Bank's special fund (e.g. Miyazawa Plan) allocations are partly intended to support Japanese manufacturing joint ventures in Indonesia and neighbouring countries.

Major consolidations are also taking place. Following the merger of Japanese paper giant company Honshu Seishi with Sin-Oji in 1996 to form 'Oji Seishi' and become the world's 3rd ranked paper company, the oil giant, Mitsubishi Oil and Nippon Oil announced merger plan in October 1998. In November 1998, Dai-Ichi Kangyo Bank and Fuji Bank announced that they are combining forces in their trust banking business. We can be sure that more consolidations and alliances amongst Japanese institutions will follow. At the same time, we are witnessing that the Presidents/CEOs of many traditional Japanese companies have been changed since late 1998, to usher in new management styles to meet new challenges.

The one area where the, otherwise foresighted Japanese have been in a virtual home-made strait-jacket, has been their banking sector. They did not learn from the mistakes of the go-go days of American banks, and made a plethora of bad loans. Many of the bad loans were to 'friends' who were speculating in the over-heated real estate game and bloatedstock market. The bubble burst in 1995, but the banks with the tacit approval of their 'friends' in the Central Bank (BOJ) and Ministry of Finance (MOF), did not take adequate steps to secure or recover the loans. Worse still, they did not recognize their losses for about three to four years. In other words, there was a concerted cover-up or state of denial while the whole world was yelling 'watch out' and waving red flags. Anyway, under the new Obuchi-led government, with Miyazawa as Finance Minister, the reality has finally been accepted. Many of the banks, which rank among the world's largest on the basis of gross assets (not net assets or net equity) will shrink dramatically and will have to accept government 'rescue funds' against tough conditions, including firing many 'involved' managers. Also Long Term Credit Bank (LTCB) and Nippon Credit have been nationalized. They will be sold after certain criteria are achieved, probably to foreign institutions.

It must be acknowledged and appreciated the certain Japanese newer and technology based companies have been very adaptable, agile and nimble e.g. Sony, Nintendo, Softbank. The world is witnessing how Japan's financial sector and the traditional companies, which have been much slower to change, are paying the price of their old styles or 'sins' and adapting to new accountability and re-structuring, as I write these paragraphs. The ultimate price is being paid by the Japanese taxpayers and those who have and will lose their livelihoods. These are historic lessons in (1) adaptability and (2) doing business in a professional manner, in the first place.

The great behemoths of Japan can learn from the great SUMO-WRESTLERS of their country. The Sumos are huge and heavy human giants. But, they are guided by tremendous discipline and self-control - - - and what finally counts in the sumo ring (or market place) — strength, matched with speed and agility - - - and keeping the fans (consumers) excited.

Japan has many brilliant minds and many, many people who are hard working, skilled and resilient. Japan is capable of great sacrifices, compared to many other countries. They have the spirit. The big nationwide adaptation process has started. Japan, as the world's second largest economy and the biggest creditor-cum-engine of the Asian economic landscape has begun to gather steam again, slowly but surely. I am of the firm belief that the Japanese locomotive will be pulling out of the stagnant or 'stationary station' fairly soon and will pull along the other Asian wagons with it, at a decent clip. Putting it in another way, I am confident that **The Land of The Rising Sun** will reform and restructure itself, and usher a new dawn over Asia, which will have a tonic effect over the rest of the world.

SITUATION à la FRANCE

(Wanted: sensible restructuring. Union 'excesses' will eventually hurt union members and 'welfare')

France has the world's fourth largest economy. French 'class' and tradition are the envy of many countries. Ladies want to look 'chic' with French beauty products. Men get high when they get a whiff of a woman's **Channel** or **Hermés** *'parfum'*, as they walk past in style. French cuisine, and cheese and wines and confectionery are legendary. The French have also a high place in high-technology, as they have had in *'haute couture'*.

But, how is the French nation, as a whole, coping? **Alcatel**, the telecommunication equipment giant went through a painful restructuring and embarrassing CEO scandal a few years ago, to emerge as a streamlined powerhouse and global competitor. The **TVG** train, which speeds like a comfortable airplane on tracks, is a marvel of French engineering. **Accor**, the hotel group and its smaller rival **Club-Med** have also become more efficient and are regaining profitability. The great retailers like **Promodès**, **Carrefour**, and **Pinault Printemps-Redoute** have each made a fine art of reaching out to their customers. In other words, the above examples show good adaptability as well as pioneering in certain retailing concepts.

Sinar Mas is a proud partner of Promodès in Indonesia. The first **CONTINENT** brand hyper-market in Jakarta opened in October 1998 and the second in March 1999, replacing Wal-Mart as the anchor tenant. Our French friends running CONTINENT have spent a great deal of time trying to understand the Indonesian consumer and local business conditions. Here, I must add that the talented Peter Ong (Managing Director of our Edible Oil Refining and Consumer Business and his very able right-hand person – Pudji Nurutami – played a very laudable role in guiding our French counterparts. As a result, over 90% of the stock keeping units (SKUs) are Indonesian products, meaning that the French discount format has been tailored (adapted) to suit Indonesian conditions. They also see themselves as long term players and have chosen to stay while certain American and Thai competitors packed-up and left, or did not open because of the May 1998 riots and continuing political uncertainty. Furthermore, we should give Promodès credit for wanting to expand quite aggressively during these 'interesting times' and even increase its equity stake in Indonesia.

Sometime back in 1996, Franky, Peter Ong and I were to visit Paris and we were told to delay our trip by a week because of the rail strike. On another occasion, we had to alter our flights due to an Air France strike. Then, in 1997, there was a truckers' strike. I also recall the French fishermen's violent strike to prevent import of cheaper fish from other countries. I and many others were **dumbstruck** by these **strikes**. I feel that the French people have to get together and try to strike this five-letter 's'-word out of their dictionaries. Seriously, the French unions are entitled to the right strike but, *Monsieurs* don't hold the entire country to ransom. Also, France will lose its competitive advantage because of its high cost structure, which will eventually hurt the striking workers.

National pride is a great thing and I wish my Indian compatriots learnt a bit from '*nos amis Français*', on this subject. However, many traditional French people, businessmen included, still hope to do big business the old way i.e. rejecting concepts American, as a 'contamination' of their beautiful culture. They should see that the world is changing, although not necessarily for the better, in every case. For example, many restaurants still want to serve food the good old French way, with five to seven courses, very relaxed with matching wines, exotic *fromages*, *petite fours*, cognac, etc. etc. That is always a most delectable and delightful experience for the guest, especially. It is also a pretty expensive experience for the host. Yet, the prestigious three star members of '*La Chaine Rotiserie*' and similar *chef* guilds do not make that much money these days, to match their prestige.

Today, big money is made by running fast-food chains like McDonalds, Kentucky Fried Chicken, Burger King. Their service is quick and the price is right. Their quality is not worth writing home about. But low cost, convenience and speed form the 'name of the game' these days for mass marketing. Instead of condemning these American ideas, the French should themselves learn the magic of franchising and standardizing of their processes and products, and purveying them with French fast-food elegance. *Mon cher amis*, you cannot go against the trend unless you are satisfied with 'boutique-size' profits. By all means, keep your boutiques and specialty restaurants also and treat them like **gastronomic temples** to perpetuate beautiful French tradition. However, to make big money the modern way, learn from your great discount stores - *hyper-marchés, s'il vous plait*. I think a simple analogy will help: **Mercedes** is arguably one of the best cars in the world and a source of German pride. But, **Toyota** makes more money than Mercedes. This is because Toyota covered the mid-price market very well and graduated to its up-market Lexus, to compete in the luxury car market. Daimler-Benz has prestige, but Toyota being the more adaptable, is the more profitable. Having said that, Daimler and BMW are adapting themselves by introducing smaller and cheaper cars to win a wider range of customers.

Talking about successfully broadening of customer base, **L'oreal** has been able to combine the best of French exclusivity with mass marketing by creating or acquiring three, four and five-star brands. L'oreal now has a wide range of products and brands to be a very successful long-term player in beauty products, cosmetics, skin-care, fragrances, etc. Similarly, **Danone** has grown very successfully into a multi-brand packaged foods company with manufacturing operations in about twenty countries. Danone recognizes the importance of 'local flavouring' (adapting) with western production and marketing techniques.

You can choose how exclusive you want to be. Remember, if you are too exclusive only the few rich aristocrats will come to you. That's fine, if that's your ambition. But, just keep in mind that having only exclusive products excludes many potential clients and profits. Also remember, that in these very competitive times and in periods of recession, the high-end shops and brands are first ones to get hurt. Just observe how adaptable your countrymen in your famous **French Foreign Legion** are. You can learn from your 'legionaires', and match the Americans at their 'FF' (I only mean fast- food) game.

It appears that the French have started a few exciting fast food brands – **'Au Bon Pain'**, **'Deli de France'**. This is a welcome change for people who wish to also have non-American foods at fast-food prices. The French adaptation is taking place, and should help preserve and spread your French culture, and boost profit, at the same time.

As mentioned earlier in this chapter, and the chapter titled "Change - - - And Coping with Change", there is really no choice. However, we do not have to 'ape' or blindly copy others. We have to use our unique local or traditional strengths in new ways, in an increasingly cost and speed conscious world. Nirula's, a small but successful fast-food chain which started in Delhi in the early 1980s and sells American, Italian, North and South Indian foods, ice creams and sodas, has been able to stand firm against the American big brand invasion. Maybe, the

Americans can learn a thing or two from Lalit Nirula, its founder and CEO.

ADAPTING BY REINVENTING CORE BUSINESS

Another example of adaptability is changing to meet new economic situations, life style trends and opportunities. It will sound really curious that **Nokia**, the most famous company and brand of Finland, started as and remained a pulp & paper company for many decades. Then, in the late 1980s, its management observed the growing competitive advantage of pulp and paper companies in Brazil and Indonesia. Moreover, the main growth markets for its product were no longer in its hinterland. They felt that their long-term viability would be better served by becoming a technology company. Furthermore, they wanted to be not just a great Finnish company but a global player. With these thoughts, their crystal ball revealed the coming boom in wireless telecommunications - mobile cellular phones and satellite phones. They disposed of the traditional business and jumped, with both feet, into manufacture of these mobile phones, giving established companies like Motorola, NEC, LM Ericsson a run for their money. This is a case of a company completely re-inventing its very core business, leave alone re-engineering its organization and processes.

Another fine case evolving before our very eyes is the metamorphosis of **Monsanto** from a chemical company into a **life sciences company**. Monsanto has divested itself of several traditional chemical businesses and is concentrating its resources and energy to engineer and develop radically new products with the **engine of hi-tech genomics** and related applications.

In order to accelerate the pace of commercial development, Monsanto has invested over $3.5 billion buying about ten strategic biotech companies since 1993. Wall Street has enthusiastically cheered the new Monsanto.

The message is clear: We have to adapt on a continuing basis, but while we must change frequently, we must not give up our ethical values. Therefore, I would like to end this segment by quoting Thomas Watson Jr., who made IBM a truly great corporation:

> *"I firmly believe that any organization, in order to survive and achieve success, must have a sound set of beliefs on which it premises all its policies and actions.*
>
> *Next, I believe that the most important single factor in corporate success is faithful adherence to those beliefs.*
>
> *And finally, I believe if an organization is to meet the challenges of a changing world, it must be prepared to change everything about itself except those beliefs (values) as it moves through corporate life."*

PERSONAL ADAPTABILITY

So far, I have discussed adaptability only in the context of countries and institutions. Now, I wish to touch upon personal adaptability, making myself the guinea pig.

My first school was Church Park Convent, which was co-ed only till the age of ten, when boys 'graduated' to (big) boys' schools. The female teachers and nuns (mostly Irish nuns in those days) loved and enjoyed us children. They called our boyish pranks 'cute' or 'sweet'. We were 'the Clowns of God' (as Morris West wrote in his great novel about a Pope), to these loving teachers and nuns ('nun nicer').

As mentioned elsewhere in this book, my parents sent us and frequently accompanied us to films like Tarzan, Robin Hood, Rob Roy, etc., and as we grew a little order, to epics like Ten Commandments and Ben Hur. I soon began to understand that might isn't right and that might must be used for the right. I also became a sub-conscious advocate for the under-dog at school.

When I moved, from the Convent, to the all-male Madras Christian College School (MCC), I was in for my first but huge culture shock. First of all, what was 'how cute' to my former doting female teachers, became 'how dare?' to my new male teachers. Remember, Frauline Maria in the popular musical 'Sound of Music'? The tough hearted nun called her a **devil**, while the Mother Superior called her an **'angel'**. Well it took a few years for our Headmaster to convince the junior masters that there just might be a latent angel lurking in boys like me! Another problem for us boys was that some of the parochial masters were prejudiced against us 'convent boys' because we spoke English with a better accent and were, therefore, deemed arrogant.

Also, in a boys' school like MCC, you could become a hero among the boys if you did something naughty or defied the 'less important' master. At that awkward age, having been influenced by Robin Hood and Rob Roy to support the under-dog, I was ready to attempt heroism. So, on one occasion, when I observed that an innocent boy was being physically punished, I could not control myself and made a plaintive appeal to the master "Sir, you're punishing an innocent boy." As a result of this utterance by me, a self-appointed, ten-year old defence lawyer, I ended up receiving the heavy gavel on my then tender head, which still has a few bumps. (This Robin should have kept his hood on to protect his head!)

I only wish that I had learned quickly and adapted after the first blow to the head. But, something very similar happened a few months later, and the dummy in me thought that the master would believe me at least on the second similar incident. However, I inflamed him even more. As a result I had to learn another painful (non-academic) lesson.

I finally learnt that the trick and fun in this tough boys' school lay in being naughty and not getting caught; or better still, getting the other student, outside your own 'ring' or gang into a fix.

I hope that even with this kiddish example, I have been able to establish that we cannot ignore the culture of the institution, at any stage. I certainly was a victim (not all-together innocent, mind you) of culture shock, well before my adolescence. The point is that every organisation is different in its culture and two things are required to ensure smooth culture assimilation: (a) adaptability of the individual and (b) the pro-active nature, or rather <u>culture</u>, of the organisation must be such that it welcomes new members. This can be achieved through presentations during the (campus) recruitment process and subsequent induction and orientation programmes.

Notes:

While MCC produced some naughty boys like me, it also produced many fine citizens, who are successful in business, hi-tech industry, military and civil service. I am also pleased to say that Mr. P. Chidambram, who has been Indian's Commerce Minister and Finance Minister, under two different political banners, was one year my senior in this great school. I personally believe that Chidrambran has the potential of becoming a good Prime Minister, if India's parochial and greedy politics would change. Can you image a culture change in India's political scene? Very difficult, but very much needed.

ಹಹ **PART D** ಲಿಲಿ

WHISPERS

IN MY HEART

WHISPERS IN MY HEART

SYNOPSIS

32 The Power of Humour:

It is heartening that more people are appreciating the value of humour in personal interaction and in the institutional context. I have proposed creation of a hypothetical franchised 'Laughter Club'.

33 Citizen of the Planet:

Although I am an Indian national, I feel for the planet and its inhabitants. I want to feel like a citizen of a border-less world, where we grant permanent, multiple-entry visas of love to everybody.

34 Character Counts:

I have tried to paint the difference between personality and character. I have given examples of key attributes of character and then compared famous persons vis-à-vis their personality and character.

35 Man and Environment:

Man is the biggest polluter of the environment. Man has the capability of improving the environment. It is a matter of awareness and attitude. Fortunately, through the efforts of responsible NGOs, there is hope. I have included two short stories on this subject.

36 Engulfed in War:

Personal experiences of my wife and myself while we were in Daharan, from where the air war was launched by the Allies against Iraq in 1990-91. I have mentioned important conversations with my boss, regarding staff welfare, during 'Operation Desert Storm'.

37 Go! Fly a Kite!:

I have used the kite-flying hobby as an example for balance, control and flexibility in a management context.

38 Success and Morality:

I talked about my father's advice on the eve of starting my first job. I have mentioned the moral decline in India after Prime Minister Nehru. Shed light on companies that make money through harmful products, like cigarettes, and the need for phasing out such businesses in a fair, sensible way.

39 Learning from Flowers:

Flowers provide us beauty and fragrance, then give forth seeds for the future and willingly wilt and go back into Mother Earth. Similarly, leaders should also nourish people in their organization, achieve important goals, and gracefully exit after developing good successors.

40 Patience, but not Complacence:

I have mentioned the speed of change that has taken place in the 20th century, and people getting used to instant gratification. We need to have 'positive patience' or a sense of urgency, balanced with a reasonable level of tolerance.

41 Corporate Prayer:

I believe in prayer. I have concluded the book with a little prayer on behalf of the corporation. I hope that this prayer captures the essence of this book.

32

THE POWER OF HUMOUR

*"After God created the world, he made man and woman.
Then, to keep the whole thing from collapsing,
He invented humor."*

Mack McGinnis

Most readers would have read at least a few issues of the **Reader's Digest** - the world's most popular monthly. It contains skillfully condensed articles on politics, economics, social issues, the environment, science, etc. An additional attraction is the space it devotes to humour - 'Laughter, the Best Medicine', 'Humor in Uniform', 'Life's like that', etc., plus witty sayings and anecdotes at the end of some articles. There must be a good reason for the editors to give such weightage to humour.

A lot of people take life too seriously, they do not find the time to smile or laugh. They get dominated by deadlines and targets. They eat, drink, sleep, *work, work, work.* As a result, they miss out on many good things in life. They get stressed and pass on the stress to their co-workers and family members. Health problems surface in many cases. In some instances, people become dependent on 'scotch on the rocks' and their marriages end up likewise. Many careers are hit by early burnout. What a *flaming* pity!

Towards the end of one of my interviews for joining Grindlays Bank, a senior Irish officer said to me, "Young Kapur, be aware that many jobs in the bank are tedious and boring - be sure you don't lose your sense of humour - - - humour will keep you going." I guess I took his advice on humour quite 'seriously'! What an insightful piece of advice.

When two people have a tiff, a nice humorous remark by one can sometimes act as a soothing balm on the injured feelings of the other person, and before long, both parties could well be laughing as if nothing unpleasant happened just moments earlier. A humorous person is generally very popular. e.g. Ronald Reagan. People enjoy his/her company. Such a person is able to captivate the attention of the audience.

Let's read one of **Mahatma Gandhi's** candid statements:
"If I had no sense of humor, I should long ago have committed suicide."

Just imagine the uphill challenges he faced. Long periods of fasting and strenuous 'Salt Marches' and the like took their toll. He was thrown into jail many times because of his determined (but peaceful) marches and demonstrations for India's independence. He even had to make peace between rival factions among his own followers because they were from different religions or had very different priorities. He had to keep pressure on the British rulers and yet remain on friendly terms with them to keep on track, negotiations for a peaceful independence for India. For those who have read about this patriotic saint or have seen the Oscar winning film – 'GANDHI', you would have noted that this frail looking, scantily dressed individual had a fine sense of humour. This not only helped him maintain his sanity and continue persevering but also acted as a friendly weapon to 'disarm' his British opponents.

Now please consider this saying by Commander-in-Chief of the Allied Forces during World War II and former President of The United States, **Dwight (Ike) Eisenhower.**

"A sense of humor is part of the art of leadership, of getting along with people, of getting things done."

This inspiring leader who led by example, tells us that a leader also uses humour to be endeared to his people and to win their support. A leader also looks confident, even in times of crises, if he can exercise wit correctly. This in turn lifts the morale of the troops and public at large. Furthermore, a leader with humorous charm is often accepted as 'one of us', despite his exalted position.

Alan Simpson wrote:
"Humor is my sword and my shield. --- "

This is a witty and powerful statement. Humour reduces tension when things are going nowhere in a discussion. A smile or laugh can change the mood and give people time to 're-group' and try again. Humour opens doors, if we use it properly. We can use the sword of wit to catch our opponent offguard, especially in a political debate. On the other hand, if a person verbally attacks us, we would usually be better off using the 'shield' of humour to deflect the attack, rather than hit back and enlarge the battle or spoil a relationship.

A sense of humour is not just being able to crack jokes or tell funny stories. It is also the ability to say something witty at the right time. It is equally important to see the lighter side of life even in tough situations and when we are the under-dogs. Moreover, it is no less important to appreciate humour when displayed by people around us.

Without further ado, I offer readers a little article of mine which was published in the Asian Wall Street Journal of March 17, 1998.

CONFESSIONS OF A "DAFFYNITIONIST"*

A person generally subscribes to The Asian Wall Street Journal for 'serious' subjects like stock quotes, economics and politics. That said, even serious readers need to take a few minutes off to relax, smile and maybe even have a hearty laugh. That's where I come in. For you see, I am an aspiring writer of "daffynitions", those clever (and hopefully amusing) little definitions you find at the bottom of this page in the 'Pepper … and Salt' column, or, as the journal's editors call it, 'Peps'.

I have always enjoyed jokes and gags and have long been fascinated by writings that are creative and witty. I first came across daffynitions, or "deft definitions" as they were then called, in the Reader's Digest while I was just a schoolboy. I was intrigued as to how people could look differently and creatively at words, adding colour and clarity and wit in the process. Thus began my romance with language.

After years of toying with words, I have now reached the point where I actually begin to feel inadequate or dull if I experience a long lull without writing something funny. Daffynition ideas can come at any time, often in spurts. Therefore, it is that my mental antenna should be on at all times. The whole process is really quite simple: I observe a situation or read a word and presto! Its daffynition is born. I have to admit that some ideas have been delivered in the private comfort of the bathroom or while stuck in a traffic jam. I am often struck with a daffynition idea in the middle of the night when I am semi-asleep. But, alas, at least half of these ideas are lost because I did not write them down and forgot them by the morning.

My wife says that I even speak daffynitions while sleeping, often leaving her unable to sleep for her own laughter. But in order to understand the world of a daffynitionist, one has to understand how a daffynition is born.

A few weeks ago, for example, I was quite astounded with the variety of definitions that could flow from one's mind based on the expression - 'matter of fact'. I first heard myself saying **cellulite is a matter of fat** and suddenly a string of rhyming definitions flooded my mind, namely: **ALLIANCE: a matter of pact; DRAMA: a matter of act; DIPLOMACY: a matter of tact; MILK: a matter of lact.**

Sometimes a daffynition is triggered by a more serious occasion. Some months ago, I was reading about the summit meeting between President Clinton and President Jiang Zemin and began ruminating on their 'special summit dinner'. In a matter of seconds, it came to me, **SUMMIT DINNERS: peace-meal.**

Television is of course, a constant source of inspiration. About a year ago I was watching a not-so-interesting talk show, and out comes a new daffynition **"TALK SHOW: Yappy Hour"**. Similarly, one day I was watching a basketball game while just happened ---- be blessed by beautiful cheerleaders. After the game, I switched to another channel where Saddam Hussein was shown presiding over his cabinet. Pop! The idea came **DICTATOR: Fear Leader.**

Sometimes the inspiration is a bit more highbrow. A while back, I was in an art gallery where I saw an impressionist painting of a corn field with a scarecrow in the middle, resulting in **"SCARECROW: corn man"**. Even the world of finance can spur me on. The other day I was watching *Money Line* which showed brokers yelling from the floor of the Chicago Mercantile Exchange. Voila! Out came another definition: **COMMODITY EXCHANGE: hoarse trading.**

Of course, there is no end to the member of daffynitions friends and relatives can inspire. On one occasion, a friend of mine said that he could not join us for dinner because of acute tonsillitis. I advised him to go for a **TONSIL EXAMINATION or peep-throat.**

Several years ago, friends of ours adopted a baby from an institution in Calcutta. While sharing their joy, I couldn't help thinking **ADOPTION CENTRE: stork exchange.** Once, I was observing our gardener while he was trimming our hedge. Result - - - **GARDENER: sheerholder**. By the way, the movie "*American Gigolo*" inspired this little gem - **GIGOLO: Feemale**.

As you can see, I frequently find myself in a daffynition state of mind. But that is not to say that, I don't enjoy a good old-fashioned *pun* every now and then, especially when it comes to politics. In the early part of the last US presidential campaign, I scribbled: "I wonder if the Clintons enjoy **Whitewater Rafting**." Subsequently, about a month before that election I wrote, "The Republican campaign appears to be in the **Dole-drums**." As you can see, I am neither Democrat nor Republican - just a non-aligned Indian, giving balanced (as in budget) doses of **Pepper ... and Salt** to both parties. I do hope that these lines will spark some bi-partisan chuckles!

&c&c&c&c

I recall an old friend of mine who was an ardent subscriber to PLAYBOY magazine. When I teased him about his addiction to this 'skin-mag', he retorted, "I buy it mainly for the party jokes and cartoons!" I hasten to urge the beautiful playmates and bunnies not to be too upset because he was at least half-lying. Anyway, this underscores the need for PLAYBOY to include humour to improve its image, and broaden its readership. This is a case of using humour as a marketing tool. No wonder, most newspapers have a comic section.

Doctor Michael Titze, a German psychotherapist, organized an international congress in Basle, Switzerland in October 1998, to explore further the **'science of laughter'**. Medical research has revealed the healing power of laughing. Laughter itself has become a therapy because it relaxes us, eases stress, lowers blood pressure, improves circulation and, helps the immune and digestive systems.

For those who rely on statistics, I read that a child laughs on an average, three hundred times a day, while an adult does so only fifteen times. Wow! There is scope to improve by a factor of twenty! Let's learn this valuable art from our little ones.

India could well claim the distinction of being the first country to have (informal) 'laughter clubs'. In the last two to three decades, many people in several towns gather early in the mornings at public parks just to have some hearty guffaws. They are convinced about the mental and physiological benefits of laughing and feel that this is a perfect way to start their days. These associations were started by retired people, but the giggly contagion has spread to youngsters as well.

I dream of various things I would do when I 'retire' back to India. I'll let you, my special readers, into a little secret: Since franchising is so popular these days and is a growth industry in itself, I plan to create a franchise called '***Guffaw Group.com***'*, (incorporated with unlimited viability in **Cooked Islands**). Then, I'll use the financial advisory and underwriting services of one of the **Barely Stern** guys, who's too good to be **sacked by Goldman**, to help me have a **Paineless IPO** with all the **Webbers** of the world's first **'laughing stock'**. For a little more fun, or pun, the smart people at **Wit Capital** could humour their online clients to subscribe. They will shortly be starting *undue diligence* to establish my **fidelity**. Meanwhile, I am seeking assistance from one of my **brothers**, who is not a **layman** in strange IPOs. Also, I am requesting **Warren** to **buffet** any *'vulture capitalists'* that come in my way. (Please keep all this under wraps, otherwise we'll get into trouble under *section 144 of SEC de-regulations*). I hope to work **merrily** even if they **lynch** my IPO.

President Clinton has been a very successful president. He is brilliant in many respects, but this is obviously tempered by his irrepressible 'centre of attraction'. Moreover, his great charisma made him an attractive target to women, seeking a 'glamorous kill', just like many

---

* Here .com stands for comedy, silly!

males aim for glamorous ladies. Several past American presidents, as well as prime ministers and monarchs have all been subjected to such temptations and traps, some of whom were lucky not to be caught 'with their pants down'. Poor Clinton got caught, but did lie under oath, which was very wrong. However, no state secrets or state security are known to have been leaked or compromised. Therefore, reprimand him, yes – impeach him, no. Incidentally, Gingrich is his own worst enemy. Unlike Newton the great scientist, he defied the consistent force of gravity as reflected in the polls and continued to attack and press for a full investigation. In the process, Newt nuked himself and his party lost some seats in the November 1998, Congress by-elections.

But, for the sake of humor alone, I shall take a little liberty again and offer a little advice to Clinton:

> "*Mr. President, I genuinely am glad that you were not impeached because you have been a good President (and are still a good musician). In any event, even the best President cannot stay in the Oval Office after two terms (eight years). You could go back to the legal profession, but that's not exciting enough for a young ex-president. But you do need to do something to pay your (legal) bills, Bill. I believe that your musical talent, combined with your charisma could make your concerts and discs and videos into big money-makers. (Your souvenirs are already earning top dollars, without earning any royalty or franchise fees for you.) While you're already good at playing the saxophone, don't confine yourself to this instrument. (Kenny G is sounding stale with his clarinet.) I suggest that you learn to play other instruments also, for variety sake, including the harmonica, AKA mouth-organ! - - - Also, Bill, you can create your own 'Bill'board'.*"

> *PS. Don't boxer me, just because I'm short and use conservative 'Y Front Jockey'.*

I'm also tempted to shoot my **trouble barrel gun** with some funny 'advice' for young women and aspiring First Ladies:

> *"If the young man at Little Rock or Hard Rock gains 'pole position' over your other suitors, make sure that his Rod-ham stays loyal and unrighteous!"*

I cannot help repeating the old adage: "Laugh, and the world laughs with you. Cry, and you cry alone." Doc Kapur, prescribes to himself and to others:

R_x daily doses of Bob Hope and/or Robin Williams, as frequently as possible. (Also, one dose after going to bed, and one dose before waking up. Come again?) Other similar brands or generic substitutes may also be administered.

Enough of prose - - - I now offer you some verses I have written on the benefits of a good laugh:

Daily Dose of Laughter

Try adding laughter and humour in your daily 'diet';
More nourishing and tasty than dining at the Hyatt!

Hearty laughs exercise lungs and abdomen,
Whether you're young or old, man or woman

Witty sayings reduce stress and tension;
Touches of humour improve the situation.

Jokes are more than matters of jest -
They're found a' plenty in Readers' Digest!

Be healthy and popular through a sense of humour;
Better than gossiping and just spreading rumour.

People with funny sayings are rich in friends,
And the great joy of life for them never ends!

Message:
With a sense of humour, managers and leaders can be healthier and
more popular and therefore more effective in the work place - - - and
at home.

33

CITIZEN OF THE PLANET

"Before I can walk in another man's shoes,
I must first remove my own."

(unknown)

Around the year 1960, when I was in my early teens, I enjoyed listening to what was meant to be a light-hearted song about a carefree hero in a popular Bollywood (Bombay/Mumbai) film. At that age, I too took the song in the same spirit. The opening lines of this Hindi song would translate as follows:

Don't ask my nationality,
Don't ask where I am from.
The whole world belongs to me
And I belong to the whole world.

It was only when I began to ponder over the concept of citizen of the planet, that the above lyrics came back to me with a much deeper meaning and feeling.

- No one can control his or her ethnic origin. Our ethnicity is given to us from the moment of conception.
- We learn languages, religion and culture from family, schooling and environment. Our eating habits and tastes are also influenced by these factors.

251

- At the end of the day, we all look different and think differently. This diversity is meant to be celebrated as a strength, as a relief from bland uniformity. On the other hand, we are all members of the human race and therefore, not all that different. Our planet would be poorer without this wealth of human diversity.
- The person who cherishes this human wealth, and who has moulded his or her attitudes in such a positive fashion, and is ready to befriend and help all types of people, regardless of apparent differences, is a Citizen of the Planet.
- A Citizen of the Planet is one whose heart has enthusiastically issued life-time, multiple entry visas of love to every member of the human race.
- Such citizenship is a state of mind, hopefully leading to states without borders.

Message:

To love mankind, to embrace humanity is a tremendous attribute. If senior executives, particularly of multinational corporations or global institutions, aspire to be successful leaders they will have to feel, think and behave in broad-minded and big-hearted ways, regardless of their origins and backgrounds. Such attitudes will also make them happier leaders of happier organizations or teams. This is a critical area where managers must lead by example and nurture a pro-human culture.

Leaders who care for humanity will always be more sensitive to the short and long-term consequences of their decisions on the community and environment. Irrespective of laws and regulations, good leadership and good citizenship mean much more than just or barely conforming with the rules.

Also, it is not possible to divorce true leadership from citizenship. An executive who sees himself/herself as a citizen of the entire planet, as a member of the family of man, has a far better chance of achieving leadership in a multinational arena.

34

CHARACTER COUNTS

"If I take care of my character,
my reputation will take care of itself"
Dwight L. Moody

Mr. K. Kuruvila Jacob, the headmaster of my high school in Madras, was one of the greatest educationists of his generation in India. He believed that education is not complete if the student does well in academics but falls short in discipline and moral values.

Once when I was in grade VII, he walked into our Moral Science class. With the tacit permission of the teacher, Mr. Jacob told us a story about one of the most successful headmasters in England in the early 1900s. Apparently, he was able to inspire students who later became respected leaders in government, military and business. We were told that this Englishman conveyed one of his most important lessons as follows: He would take one boy at a time and ask him to read and feel the message written at the back of the classroom door - **"Character is what you are in the dark."**

I must have forgotten many things I learnt in school, but those profound and valuable words are still with me. Therefore I say, "To Sir, with love ... and thanks."

Many of us do say that a boss has to have character <u>to qualify as a true leader</u>. It is also important that we do not confuse 'personality' with character.

Personality, I would say, is the more visible side of a person. A person may have a friendly approach or can stand confidently at the podium and make captivating speeches. A sense of humour is also an asset. The way in which one dresses and moves also makes a visual difference. Some people use a warm and modulated tone even in normal tête-à-têtes. All these traits or attributes are part of what some may call **'nice packaging'**. But is this the real person, the real character?

If I think of 'character', I automatically recall the English Headmaster's profound definition. So, character must be the inner person, the invisible qualities of a person - - - how a person thinks and behaves even when nobody is watching.

Some enlightened companies like McKinsey give a lot of attention to character issues in the selection process, once the candidate's technical/academic skills meet the standard. Isn't it interesting that character attributes do not appear in the CV or résumé of a candidate? They have to be 'found' in the person, not on a sheet of paper.

Admittedly, it is not an easy thing to assess character in a few interviews. On the other hand, most companies just focus on the job capabilities i.e. the CV or résumé items (and hope for the best).

Let us imagine two large companies - the first believes that even if the skills of the candidate are excellent, he/she should not be hired because the interviewing panel is not comfortable with the character aspects. On the other end of the scale, is the second company which just focuses on the skills, unless the candidate has a criminal history. Even though both companies may be in the same field of business, we shall observe, sooner or later that their corporate cultures will be very different. The values of the first company and the kind of people it hires will reflect its culture, the way it does business, the way it counsels and rewards its people and develops its leaders. This character and principle based culture is bound to achieve greater progress, other things being equal.

Let me attempt to list some of the key qualities of a fine character (I'm sure that you can add a few more):

Key Attributes

Trustworthiness	:	Says what he means and means what he says. Has no hidden agenda. He does not 'hog' the credit due to another, especially his junior.
Faith	:	Has faith in the divine. Has faith in his/her people.
Humaneness	:	Has a big heart. Feels for people, not just profit.
Humility	:	Does not fall in an ego trap or take his/her own position or power for granted. Willing to admit his/her mistake. This gains more respect. Also, others will feel less uncomfortable to own up their mistakes and take corrective action.
Vulnerability	:	Not self-righteous. Does not assume that he/she is infallible. Is open to constructive criticism to reach a better decision.
Love	:	Genuinely loves people. Believes that love is important at all times. Love can be a potent 'weapon' to improve relations, make peace and progress.
Care	:	Believes in the welfare of his/her people. Shows real interest in their aspirations and becomes a natural mentor.
Courage	:	Is willing to stand up for his/her beliefs; even willing to be on the minority side, when it comes to principles and values.

These are such important and much needed attributes that each deserves a full chapter. Unfortunately, I don't have the required 'depth' to do so. How much I would like to imbibe these highly desirable qualities. I must not give up trying. Just in writing and re-reading this chapter itself makes me pause and re-look at myself. I suppose there is hope for me too!

Mind you, I'm not at all suggesting that 'personality' is a negative feature. However, I wish to strongly state that personality alone is hollow - it is only the skin and only skin-deep. In fact, if a person does not have much of a personality, but has a solid character he/she may have a slower start, but will, over a slightly longer term, win respect and trust, which would eventually facilitate success. On the other hand, if a person can cultivate a good personality with a fine character, he/she has the ingredients to face the challenges of life and career so much better.

I now take the liberty to quickly **'x-ray'** a few famous people and how they ended their respective 'innings':

Person Position	Personality Score	Character Score	Outcome/Result
1 Ferdinand Marcos President of Philippines (1965-1985)*	High	low	Short-term success. Fled in disgrace.
2 Mahatma Gandhi Leader of India's 'bloodless' freedom movement (1906-1948)*	Low	very high	'Father of the Nation'. Respected and honored universally.
3 Gen. Dwight Eisenhower Allied Supreme Commander WW II, US President (1953-1961)*	High	high	Fine role model. Elected twice as US President. Popular, respected and successful.

* Denotes years in (high) office for each person.

| 4 | Gen. Colin Powel Chairman of US Joint Chiefs of Staff (1988-1992)* | high | high | Great role model. Was top choice of Republican Party to stand for President. Still very much admired and respected. |
| 5 | Bill Clinton US President (1993-)* | high | question-able | Won presidential election twice, mainly on the weight of personality and 'flexible' principles. Later, embarrassed and weakened. Lost credibility and popularity even when economic indicators were good. |

Some quick conclusions can be drawn from this simple table. The key points are:

i)   It is wonderful if one can have both personality and character.

ii) If a person 'lacks' personality but is endowed with character, he/she may have a slower start but can catch up in the long-run.

iii) One cannot make up for character deficiency by enhancing personality - the make-up will crack and peel-off in due course. Also, one is never at peace with one's conscience. There is an interesting old saying :

"You cannot make a crab walk straight."

35

MAN AND ENVIRONMENT

"He that follows nature, never loses his way"
(Proverb)

Man and environment cannot be separated. Therefore, although the book is essentially about people and leadership, I wish to talk about environmental implications - man's impact on the environment and the environment's impact on its inhabitants, including man. We desperately need people and leadership for improving the environment for our own benefit, our own sakes.

We have to admit that **man** is the **biggest polluter** on the face of the Earth (and beneath it, too). The combination of ignorance, poverty, greed and short-sightedness makes us the prime enemies of our own environment, our own **'home'**.

Just look at the sharp decline in forest cover in the so-called 'civilized' or 'advanced' countries in the last five decades. This was done primarily to build homes and make furniture, produce pulp for paper or clear land for large scale plantations and ranching. Many beautiful forests that provided us with oxygen have disappeared, taking precious wildlife with them. We are witnessing how deforestation and pollution of the atmosphere are affecting weather patterns to our detriment.

Chemical companies and 'smoke-stack' industries have been contaminating our air and water for big profits. We hear of more and more cases of respiratory and skin disorders because of foul air. We also note the rising incidence of cancer related to poisons in the air and water. Even fertilizers, that helped trigger **green revolutions** and save the world from starvation, have seeped into ground-water which in turn trickles into our drinking water resources. No wonder, there is such a tremendous rise in gastro-intestinal diseases on the one hand, and booming sales of **bottled water** all over the world. This is great business for 'EVIAN' and its clones in many countries.

Isn't it high time we arrested and reversed this dangerous trend in a united and comprehensive way?

I've got to say this, with your permission: The excrement of herbivorous animals like cows, buffaloes, elephants, et cetera (and even pigs) can be dried and converted into excellent manure. The benefit is double - no pollution and healthier crops, fruits and vegetables for mankind. Also, these excrements can be mixed with water and fermented, to make methane gas, which becomes an excellent low-cost fuel, with hardly any pollution. Can man boast about this capability of his own - - - you know what!

Fortunately, many enlightened governments and corporations have focused on pollution control and conservation of the environment. They have implemented several genuine eco-friendly policies.

On the subject, I would like to mention the example in which I was involved, although on the periphery. Henkel, the German chemical giant, is our joint-venture partner in Indonesia. Despite using hi-tech processes, filters and scrubbers, Henkel's plants (*inter alia*, in Germany) do release controlled volumes of effluents (within approved standards) into the air. Since the German government and Henkel have pledged to further reduce the negative impact of the (permissible) effluents, they are looking for creative solutions. One initial concept for Henkel to grow/finance planting of millions of trees in Germany was found unfeasible. Henkel is now looking to finance/adopt new tree plantations (industrial forests) in countries like Brazil and Indonesia. The principle is that Henkel is trying to ameliorate the problem by looking for oxygen replenishment resources on a global basis, regardless of the location of its own chemical plants.

Another fine example of a pro-environment company is ABB, the Swedish-Swiss engineering company. Similarly, we need to commend the enlightened government of Costa Rica, which has one of the most comprehensive and successful environmental conservation programmes in the world. Other countries would be well advised to learn from this small nation.

It is very heartening to see that the world's multilateral financial institutions like World Bank, International Finance Corporation, Asian Development Bank, etc., attach great importance to environment protection and bio-diversity in supporting development projects all over the world. The main problem is to prevent cheating by greedy violators.

I have to say that, regardless of our profession or corporate affiliation, we are part of the environment and its 'welfare' is our responsibility to ourselves, our co-inhabitants and to our future generations.

In order to convey my feelings on the subject, I am attaching two short stories that I wrote some time ago - "Dove's Eye View" and "Close Encounter with a Rain Drop and a Sunbeam".

DOVE'S EYE VIEW

I had been growing in peaceful darkness in what seemed like eternity. As I became more complete and my brain more developed, I began to wonder what it would be like outside the perfectly contoured, protective walls of my egg-shell.

Finally, I felt a piercing ray of light penetrate my delicate eyes through a sudden crack in my temporary dwelling. Immediately, I felt a strong urge to come out of my shell and to see the outside world. "I shall not be a frog in the well any longer", I chirped to myself. I pushed against the shell walls with my damp wings and beak. In no time Mom took me under her wing. It felt safe and warm. Soon I realized that I wasn't the only chick as I became part of a chorus shrieking for food.

The worms and nuts and fruits thrust into our eager mouths were refreshing, in fact exotic, after the boring diet of yolk and albumen while we were 'interns'. "Be patient", said Dad ...... "Learn to share", said Mom. "Remember, we doves are a sign of peace", said Grandpa. These were the first lessons we were taught. As we became stronger we learnt how to fly. Jump .... flap - flap ....crash! was the result of my first solo attempt. But Mom and Dad were always inspiring us by saying, "We know you can do it" and "Keep trying, don't give up". And what an exhilerating feeling it was when I mastered the technique and 'earned my wings' as a full-fledged flyer.

Soon I was allowed to make 'sorties' on my own. One day, I soared high in the sky and realized that the world wasn't just our forest. I noticed different kinds of feathered friends and four-legged creatures, big and small.

As I flew further South, I observed that the beautiful green trees began to thin-out and so did the sweet, fresh air that I had grown accustomed to. But my curiousity led me on. The smokey, foul air made me choke and cough and sneeze, but I maintained my bearing. Soon I saw great, big geometric nests which had over-sized pigeon-holes with two-legged, feather-less creatures going in and out of them.

None of them could fly. But they walked without stumbling. (I learnt later from Mom and Dad that they call themselves humans and their nests are made of strong concrete). Many humans in a hurry moved in contraptions with four rounded black legs that rolled. (I was told that these were automobiles.) Many humans also travelled in long mechanical centipedes that moved on tracks. I also saw huge, noisy, mechanical but feather-less birds that flew humans at high speeds without flapping their gigantic wings. On the whole, my first view of the human jungle was both exciting and frightening ...... an awesome experience.

I became eager to learn more about these humans whose nests were bigger and stronger than ours and who could fly higher and faster than us real birds with their screaming mechanical devices. On my return home, I started to ask a lot of questions. I was taught that in the process of evolution humans came last on earth, having evolved from monkeys. (I did not need a feather to tickle me!) Seriously, the Creator chose to make humans physically weaker than many creatures but also much superior in brain power. This brain power is meant to help improve humans' quality of life or 'civilization' as they arrogantly call it. I felt insulted when I heard that humans with less intelligence are called 'Bird Brains'. Some humans have rendered many birds and animals, flora and fauna extinct. They stuff some of us as trophies to boast about their hunting or 'Shikar' exploits. Many put us in cages to gape at us. What beak! I mean - cheek! What have we done to deserve this? Grandpa also told me that many humans have committed inhuman deeds abusing their brain power. They are human but not humane. They have the audacity to call themselves Mankind without being kind. They will do anything to satisfy their greed for wealth and power. They hurt and manipulated even their own kind for their selfish goals. They legitimize genocides by calling them Holy Wars. I shivered when I heard that covert wars are called Cold Wars. Some humans damage the environment in the name of industrial development and progress. Such humans have obviously disregarded the teachings of their wise ones and have stifled their own consciences. They don't realize that with their 'sophisticated' weapons of mass destruction and polluting practices (monkey business) they have put their own brainy race on the Endangered Species List! I wonder how the Creator will deal with them on Judgement Day.

Reflecting on the mis-deeds of those humans and after tasting their polluted rivers and breathing, or rather choking on their concrete jungle air I felt really down-hearted. I turned my beak up towards the Creator asking if there were any hope.

A few days later I descended on a beautiful park etched and landscaped between the concrete nests. I got a whiff of peanuts being scattered on the manicured grass by a kind old human with her grand-chick. At first, I hesitantly pecked and munched a few. The human kid called out to me in a friendly tone "eat, birdie, eat", and before long, my confidence grew and I was literally eating out of their hands. The two had warmed my little heart. I expressed my thanks with a tuneful whistle and a chuckle and by donating my most treasured feather to my new friends. Having satisfied my hunger, I performed a few loops and aerobatic tricks to entertain these kind souls and flew off to see if there are any more humane humans.

After a while, I landed on a fountain at the other end of the park to quench my thirst. As I was sipping the cool water I heard unusual sounds of musical harmony. I looked up and saw a large chorus of humans - black, white, brown and yellow - holding a huge banner that said:

"Peace For All

Save The Planet

Preserve Wildlife"
with a picture of my look-alike carrying an olive branch.

These two experiences at the end of the day filled my heart with inspiration and joy. With the sun about to depart to light-up another part of the earth I flew full throttle back to our cozy nest. I gathered the entire family and confidently announced, "Do not despair, there is hope for us all."

A CLOSE ENCOUNTER WITH
A RAIN DROP AND A SUNBEAM

One morning, just after it had rained and the sun peeped through a hole in the clouds, I stepped out into the garden. I treated my lungs to the clean fresh air while my eyes feasted on the bright green grass and vibrant colours of the bougainvillea and water lilies.

Then, all at once my eyes were attracted, in fact enchanted, by one pristine and glittering drop of rain that was smiling at me while it rested on a young and grateful leaf.

The next moment I wondered about the mission of this rain drop, this tiny 'piece' of water. The best way to get the answers was to smile back and start a dialogue. But even before my smile reached full bloom, the raindrop gave me a friendly wink and said, "Good morning! My name is Aardy, but you can also call me R.D." With some hesitation, I responded, "Hello, Aardy, welcome to my garden and thank you for bringing the cruel dry spell to an end. We have been praying and waiting for your return."

Aardy responded, "In recent years, we had brought too much water to your island causing floods, so El Niño asked us to shower over certain other places that were too dry for too long. Sorry for being late but we have to balance things and keep everybody happy."

"Yes, Aardy," I agreed, "You are quite right, natural resources are meant to be shared." Also, wanting to be cordial, I said, "Aardy, you look so clean and radiant this morning." Aardy replied, "Thank you, I did not want to descend on your garden as harmful acid rain so I had a good 'shower and scrub' before 'dropping' in..... ha, ha."

I joined in her laugh and said, "Aardy, you have a great attitude and I enjoy your wit." "Now, let me tell you why I am radiant," continued Aardy, "It's because my friend, the sunbeam is with me today." And with a twinkle the sunbeam said "Hi there, I'm Sunny. I know that you have missed Aardy but I'm your friend too." "Nice to meet you Sunny." I replied.

Then I addressed them both, "You two are both so different; what is your objective here?" Together they eagerly responded, "In unison we help seeds germinate and trees grow; flowers bloom and fruits ripen, etc, etc. Why, your very own body is almost 90% water and it cannot function without energy or heat. Can you imagine the world without water or sunlight? Depending on the need of the day, one of us is more active than the other. But whatever we do, we do in concert and for the general benefit of mankind and other species that share the planet."

"Tell me, Aardy" I inquired, "Why is it that you fall so much over the oceans when there are water shortages on land." Aardy said, "You should know but I'll give you a few quick answers: If I do not fall sufficiently over the oceans, they will become too salty and all marine life will perish, depriving you of vital proteins. Isn't one Dead Sea enough?" Then Sunny interjected, "Sometimes, I become more active in certain parts. As you know, heat and drought can help destroy certain harmful germs. In any event, certain phenomena that you call disasters are meant to restore ecological balance. When things are too damp, I get active and vaporize Aardy and she floats up to join a new cloud which moves to another area." And Aardy added, "When Sunny gets over-heated, I take over and cool him down --- the cycle goes on forever." "That's exactly right," Sunny concurred, "And we hope you humans realize our importance."

"Of course," I replied, "Both of you are important to the world and mankind has worshipped you both from the beginning of time."

Now, both Aardy and Sunny like a chorus of teachers said, "You people of the world know that you need us for your welfare, your survival. But too many people because of ignorance, selfishness, short-sightedness and poor planning abuse the resources gifted by God and now you have to pay the price. You pollute the atmosphere with sulphur and the like and invite acid rain; your CFCs dig big holes in the ozone layer which allow harmful ultra-violet rays to bombard earthlings."

"You have to mend your ways before it is too late. If you chop down your rainforests you'll be left with dust-bowls; if you fell too many trees in hilly areas you'll be deluged with floods and land-slides."

"You guys and your governments and businesses need to plan better with coordination. Build sensible dams and water catchments and distribution systems. At the same time, construct good drainage and re-cycling systems."

"There is no point in wasting water in one year and then complaining of monsoon failure in the next. You must have systems to control both flood and drought. You humans have the technology - - - you only need to improve your attitudes and priorities. Don't blame us for the greenhouse effect and global warming. Look at your own actions."

"Oh boy!" I said to myself: "What a lecture early in the morning! - - - and that too from a tiny droplet and a little sun-ray." I felt guilty and embarrassed. They could read my mind. I choked a bit and in a solemn tone said "I apologize on my own behalf and that of my kind for complaining about too much rain; too much sun... too little rain; too little sun and promised to be more sensible and caring for our precious resources and sharing them. Meanwhile, on our behalf, please implore El-Niño and his consort, La-Nina to look kindly on us."

Aardy and Sunny continued, "Remember, we are your friends, but you need us desperately and we don't need you. We have options, you don't. At the same time, we know that there are enough decent humans on earth to genuinely warrant our trust and support. From our side, we, Aardy and Sunny pledge to continue to work in harmony and team-spirit for all kinds of creatures that deserve our help."

As I smiled gratefully, Aardy and Sunny said, "Look up".... And my eyes beheld the most gorgeous twin rainbows decorating the morning sky. My whole being felt blessed as I continued to gaze adoringly at this true symbol of cooperation between a RAINDROP and a SUNBEAM for our benefit.

My mind echoed for a long time, "Thank you Aardy, thank you Sunny for your constant support. We shall not let you down... so help us God."

36

ENGULFED IN WAR

"He that will not have peace, God gives him war"
(Proverb)

In 1988, while I was working in Jeddah, affectionately known as 'the Bride of the Red Sea', with an affiliate of Chase Manhattan Bank, I received a phone call and the caller said that he wished to talk to me about a job. I politely told him that since there was a recession in the banking industry, we were not doing any recruitment at that time. However, I said that he was welcome to send me his CV, in case of future vacancies. At this point he laughed out and said, "Mr. Kapur, I don't want a job at your bank. In fact, I am calling you on behalf of a leading Saudi group, in Al Khobar for the top executive position next to the owner." I also burst out laughing and nearly fell out of my wobbly chair. I had never been to Al Khobar before, which was about 600 miles (1,000 km) away on the east cost of the Arabian peninsula. I had only heard that Jeddah was generally preferable to foreigners. I politely declined the offer, since both my wife and I were happy as things were. Anyway, to cut a long story short, the gentleman called me for a third time and eventually coaxed me to visit the Sheikh in Al Khobar which is a twin-city of Dhahran, the oil capital and fountain head of Saudi Arabia's wealth.

The Sheikh's business had expanded rapidly during the oil boom of the 1970s, especially since much of his business was in the form of oil field services to Aramco. Diversification in to a large hotel in 1981-

1982 coupled with the collapse in the petroleum prices in 1982 hurt the liquidity of this company. He was looking for someone to help him to turn around the business and improve his standing with the banks. I could see hope for this company. Also, I normally do not get 'hung-up' about religious beliefs of others, because of my own liberal upbringing, and because I had always worked for institutions with a secular orientation. However, I was a bit concerned about working for an Arab individual for the first time. Therefore, at the latter part of the interview, I asked the Sheikh about his position on religion (Islam) vis-à-vis business. He responded with these crisp words: "I leave my religion at home." This was a major 'plus' factor in my eventual decision to join him.

The Sheikh enticed me to join him even though my initial salary would be 20% lower than I was earning at the bank. But there was a profit sharing incentive which would be attractive if we achieved certain targets (after two years). Moreover, the bank job was becoming less challenging and routine in nature, and I had occasionally craved for an entrepreneurial experience. I saw this as a chance for this new adventure and decided to take the plunge. Convincing my wife wasn't easy. She was initially in a state of shock at my desire to make the drastic and risky change. In fact, all my banking colleagues, including Saudis, thought that I was crazy to join a pure Saudi single-owner enterprise. Some even bet that I would be looking for another job in five to six months. I just told them that I would try to be as adaptable as possible and that I could not resist the opportunity of feeling like a co-entrepreneur. I also reasoned that I was getting a bit stale being a banker for twenty-one years, still doing a lot of paper work and reporting to various committees. In my new job, I would only have one boss. This was no doubt a risk, but I had confidence that if things didn't work out with the Sheikh, I could always find another bank job. While I consider myself an adaptable person, I must mention two fine individuals who helped me make the transition. In fact, when I arrived for work, the Sheikh was already in Germany for emergency surgery, and his Senior Vice President, who was a kind and cultured Saudi, and his Chief Financial Officer, a dedicated Indian, went out of their way to make me feel welcome and comfortable.

It was an interesting experience for me to work for a Saudi entrepreneur. It is a very creditable achievement that a person who lost his father while he was still a toddler and went bare-foot to school till the age of twelve, grew up to become the founder and owner of this successful and wealthy group. The group's activities covered real estate/hotels, and providing oil-field services and equipment to **ARAMCO**, through joint ventures with leading American companies, including several partnerships with the respected **Dresser Industries**. I was able to learn more about the oil industry, its impact on the *well* being of the Saudi Kingdom, and its importance in geopolitics and economics, which was all very exciting. I was also involved in directing the real estate operations wherein we provided top quality housing to expatriates from leading MNCs, US Air Force, US Army and US Consulate.

I travelled a great deal with the Sheikh, particularly to London and the oil-patch cities of Houston and Dallas, for board meetings and business development. In general, I saw, first hand, the life style of a truly wealthy Arab. He loved fine clothes, enjoyed gourmet food and other good things in life. He was also a good family man. He did his best for his mother who had re-married; gave much more than moral support to his older sister, who had been abandoned by her husband since many years; treated his wife well; provided good education for his children – five attractive daughters and a handsome 'crown prince'.

It must have been my destiny to live and work in this very area during **Operation Desert Shield** which culminated in **Operation Desert Storm**. Readers would recall that Iraq invaded the tiny but oil rich Sheikdom of Kuwait in July, 1991. To say the least, there was great confusion and panic in our city because it was well within the range of Saddam Hussein's *Scuds*. Also, most people, including our staff, were afraid that these rockets would be used to deliver highly dangerous chemical/gas bombs. The use of these banned weapons by Iraq against Iran was still fresh in the minds of expatriates and Saudis. Most foreign companies evacuated expatriate families and all but most essential officers. As the tensions began to rise, many of our officers and workers wanted to leave. It was a major problem to make them stay voluntarily and work, especially when they were receiving emotionally charged phone-calls from their loved ones back home. It was my task to keep up the morale of our people in a sincere way.

By November, over 600,000 allied troops had been deployed in the 'theatre of war'. It was hoped that loud 'saber rattling' would make Saddam withdraw from Kuwait. On the contrary, this 'Servant of Allah' as he proudly called himself, boasted about his arsenal of lethal weapons and his elite Republican Guards. To make matters worse, Saddam proclaimed Kuwait as a new province of Iraq.

Each time that there were threatening noises from either side, the more nervous our people became. Many of our workers would come to me literally crying and begging to be allowed to return home. I tried to explain the difficulties of mass evacuation, as well as the importance of our group to remain fully operational since we were serving the war effort. I described the strategic nature of our business because we were serving Aramco, and providing housing and food to Air Force and Army personnel who would be 'active' in the likely event of war. I emphasized that it was these people who would protect us from the feared scuds. I also tried to convince our staff that I personally felt very safe and substantiated that feeling by the fact that my wife had not left the area even though she had a choice.

By December, the war clouds over the Gulf Region had grown darker and heavier and real action was only a matter of weeks. Consequently, staff morale had sunk even further. Workers in some other companies just abandoned their jobs and fled to Dubai or to remote parts of the Saudi Desert to get out of harm's way. The Desert escape only increased their suffering because they were soon short of food and water.

At this juncture, some foreign companies tried to make workers feel good by granting them a **'war/hardship allowances'**. My conscience told me that our company should do the same. I also felt the need to arrange special **war insurance** for our people, so that their families back home could at least feel financially secure, in the event that the 'worst' happened. I believed that this would demonstrate our concern for their welfare and this was, in fact, a good opportunity to win their continuing loyalty at this crucial time. I therefore, recommended to the Sheikh that we grant a 25% allowance to all our staff, regardless of seniority or nationality. The Sheikh's initial reaction was, "This allowance is not necessary - - - Do you realize that all this money will come out of my own pocket?", while pointing to the pocket in his elegant 'thobe' (full-length Arab shirt). Almost by reflex-action, I made a risky response in an appealing tone: "But, respectfully Sheikh, all the profit also goes straight into your pocket." (I now think that it was a case of 'foot in mouth' or rather 'tongue in <u>teeth</u>', because I bit my tongue hard, but too late.) I could readily tell from his facial expression that he did not like my choice of words. However, he did not react rudely. He said, "only foreign companies may be paying this allowance. Why should I spend this money when other Saudi companies aren't?" (He basically is a good hearted person. All that I needed to do was to make him feel good about giving.) As luck would have it, I responded, "that is exactly the point. Here is a great opportunity for you to be the first Saudi to grant the war allowance. You will be a hero, a star in this historic time." These words appealed to him and ours was probably the first Saudi company to grant this benefit.

While I was writing the chapter titled **"How to 'Manage' the Boss"**, I was thinking of various ways to sincerely achieve this objective, for the larger benefit. After writing about the more obvious items, I began to focus on the relatively sensitive issues of appealing to the boss' sense of humaneness or sense of ego. At that point, as I reflected back, I recalled how I had 'managed' the boss without being conscious of this concept at that time. The Sheikh basically wanted to be a good employer, but was reluctant to incur additional costs at that uncertain time. Fortunately, I had 'pressed the right button' on this occasion, with favourable results.

At that time, Saudis were probably even more insecure than expatriates. Their rich and comfortable feudalistic life style would be destroyed if Saddam over-ran Saudi Arabia. Saudi Arabia's own armed forces were tiny in number compared to Iraq's and they had no war experience. Saudis feared that their beautiful palaces and valuable business would be destroyed or taken away from them. Many businessmen moved with their families out of the Kingdom or at least to Jeddah on the West coast, which was safely outside the war arena. Some of these entrepreneurs would return periodically to the war zone in Eastern Province to check on their business and to show their staff that they had not run away in fear. At the same time, many top Saudis were in a mental state of denial. The extreme fear of the consequences of an invasion and Saddam's loud oratory that Americans would 'chicken-out' at the crucial moment *a la Vietnam,* was most disconcerting to the Saudis. Many Saudis, therefore, began to say and 'believe' that there would be no war eventually.

By October, I felt that I had to convince my Sheikh that the 'war of words' would culminate in the real thing, before too long. He somewhat angrily said, "I think you like war and, therefore you are saying that there will be war. Saddam is wrong but he is considered an **Arab brother**. Saddam should be punished, but how can we Saudis allow **foreigners** to launch a major war from our holy land against our own brothers." He became even more emotional while he added, "if we allow or join in this war, our future Arab generations will not forgive us - - - history will ridicule us." At that point, I got the feeling that he was quoting somebody from the Saudi royalty. "The only thing that we can permit," he continued, "is the presence of foreign troops and weapons on our soil to act as deterrents, but not for offensive purposes against Iraq." I sympathized with this sentiment and politely, but clearly said, "this time, there is such a huge international consensus for action, and many Arab and islamic countries have joined the US-led coalition. Moreover, especially because of the embarrassing Vietnam experience, US will not fight in a half-hearted way - - - America and its allies are totally committed this time. Also, Saddam is too stubborn to withdraw from Kuwait - - - there is no turning back by either side now - - - it is just too late to pull back - - - Believe me, I hate war, but my personal values have nothing to do with my simple prediction." The Sheikh got even more excited. He sprung out of his elegant chair and said, "Vipen, I bet you $50,000 that there will be no war." I was tempted to take him on, but I quickly felt that I should maintain some professional decorum vis-à-vis my boss. I, therefore, replied, "My opinion remains the same, but let's recall this interesting bet after the 'event'". That evening, I recounted to my wife, this highly 'charged' *tête-à-tête* at the office. (Since these were exciting and important discussions with the Sheikh, they remain implanted indelibly in my brain.)

Coming back to complete our Gulf War experience, the Air War was launched by the Allies in the early hours of January 16, 1992. Thanks to CNN, we got a 'blow-by-blow' live commentary, while in the comfort of our sofas. *'Sofa'* so good. (In a punny mood.) We enthusiastically watched the allied bombardment of Iraq's command and control centres as well as other strategic targets. There was jubilation and relief, among us, that things had started off so well. In fact, the 'kick-off' was far better than originally anticipated.

For the first few days after these successful assaults by the coalition, there was little retaliation from the Iraqi side. Then, as we were becoming more comfortable, even complacent, panic re-entered our hearts and minds. I remember watching a war update on television around 9 o'clock in the evening with my wife, when we were visibly shaken by a deafening bang. This was the first of Iraq's *Scuds*, as we discovered moments later. Strangely enough, the air-raid siren was sounded only two long minutes after this, the first scud had entered our area. Following the emergency instructions that were given to us, we hurriedly wore the gas masks that had been issued to us. However, we could barely breathe in these suffocating contraptions. If Saddam's nerve gas didn't kill us, these masks would certainly have done it on behalf of Saddam. Within a couple of minutes, we took off the masks to catch our breaths. For the next few moments, our hearts were still pounding with adrenaline gushing. We were uneasily wondering about the possible release of deadly gas. Fortunately, gas was not part of the payload.

In all, Iraq launched about seventy scuds at important cities and targets in Saudi Arabia and Israel. About twenty of these *Scuds* were directed towards our area. Overall, about fifteen of these rockets caused damage and took several lives in cities like Tel Aviv, Al Khobar, and Riyadh. Fortunately, several scuds were intercepted by the **Patriot missiles**, while some others 'disobeyed orders' of the Iraqi oppressor and fell far from strategic targets or populated areas.

However, it was ironic that the last scud, which came our way before Iraq surrendered, directly hit a warehouse in which many young American military personnel had been temporarily stationed. I had just come out of the shower, when I heard the loudest bang in my life. The mighty thundering explosion shattered some of our windows; our walls trembled and so did our knees! Both my wife and I said almost the same words simultaneously, "God, this is very big and very close." Nervous and excited, we quickly jumped into our car to witness what had happened. Many ambulances were racing to the spot and we later learnt about the extent of the tragedy – about thirty dead and many more severely wounded. How can we forget such a tragic event, which occurred only six hundred metres (as the crow flies) from our very home. On the other hand, we felt very lucky that we were safe, and that none of our colleagues, workers or friends had been hurt during the entire Operation Desert Storm. Perhaps, this is the reason why both of us do not feel so insecure in Indonesia during these turbulent times or 'year(s) of living dangerously'.

Some Royal Saudi Air Force and Army personnel did a good job during the campaign, but the scale of their brave contribution was like a pin drop in the thundering ocean of bombs and cruise missiles launched by the 'foreign' military might. Therefore, there was justification in the tongue-in-cheek quip - **'the Gulf War was won by Patriots and Expatriates'**. Alas, poor Saddam's much touted **'mother of all battles'** misfired or backfired - - - actually both!

By the way, the Sheikh and I never talked about the 'war'/'no war' bet again.

I left the Sheikh's company in February, 1993. I beat the skeptical bets taken against me by four years and five months! Since 'I was born under a wanderin' star', it was time to 'paint my (twenty foot) wagon' (container) and move along, before I really got the tax-free 'gold fever'. The gracious Sheikh and his charming wife hosted a sumptuous lunch for us and endowed us with generous gifts.

Why did I write this chapter?

1. I wanted to share this (hopefully) once in a lifetime experience with as many people as possible (not as a war correspondent, but as a resident in the theatre of war, who rubbed shoulders with some of the heroes of US military, who helped win the Gulf War).

2. To show how different human beings react to a crisis based on what is at stake for them; of conflicting personal feelings of what is right and wrong, and whether to punish an invader based on principles or racial considerations.

3. To demonstrate that bosses have a strong moral responsibility towards their people, especially in emergencies. In fact, this was a perfect and historic opportunity to demonstrate and practice real leadership, recognizing that every life is precious.

4. To remember what could have happened if the morally conscious world had ignored Saddam's invasion of Kuwait, which was in flagrant violation of all international convention and basic decency, as a localized Arab problem.

5.   To honour the great statesmen and leaders for building a multinational-cum-multiracial coalition. If the coalition was not formed at all, or fell apart because of conflicting ideologies or strategies, the Middle East and the world would have been very different after 1991.

6.   To record that, while people were overcome by fear from time to time, their faith in the Divine, and belief in the **'triumph of good over evil'** kept them going during this highly perilous period.

7.   The Gulf War Coalition of almost thirty countries is a shining and historic example of teamwork based on a very crucial and shared goal.

8.   To show the importance of appealing to the good sense, or even to the ego, of the boss to achieve a worthwhile objective.

9.   And if one is writing about power, people and principles, how can one ignore Saddam. He still has power, he still abuses his people, he still has no principles. It is a great pity that the common Iraqis and their children have to suffer because of the continuing UN sanctions. A new way must be found to help these helpless Iraqis. It is a matter of world conscience, that millions of innocent people have to suffer because the free world cannot come to terms with one powerful, unprincipled person.

10. As the old proverb goes "A just war is better than an unjust peace"

37

GO! FLY A KITE!

"Be aware when things are out of balance. Stay centred - - -"
"For Governing a country well
there is nothing better than moderation"
(From Chapters 53 and 59 respectively of Tao Te Ching)*

Sometimes when we are in a debate or an argument - with a friend or a colleague or subordinate - which is not going the way we want, we say aloud or mentally, "go take a walk!" or "go fly a kite!"

The other day, I lifted my tired eyes from my desk and turned to look out of the window. For a while, I refreshed my eyes by looking at the green trees and white puffs of clouds. Soon, I noticed several boys flying kites in the playground.

Within seconds, my thoughts shot back to my childhood when kite flying was quite a popular pastime. I then began to think of what goes into accomplished kite flying and its similarity with life in general. A good kite should be neither too heavy nor too light. If it is too heavy, it may not even lift-off. Likewise, if the organization is top heavy, its costs also become heavy. It becomes 'fat' and loses its nimbleness. It becomes sluggish and lacks agility. If a kite is too light, it would be weak and may capitulate in a strong wind. The same applies to humans and organizations. We have to be strong and agile - physically and mentally.

---

* As interpreted in 'Real Power' – Business lessons from the Tao Te Ching written by James A. Autry and Stephen Mitchell.

To fly properly, a kite should have balance. Otherwise, it would bank too much on one side. If the kite banks too much to the left, the flier will re-calibrate by adding a small 'weight' on the right side. Similarly, man needs balance to go through life successfully. Any extreme thought or behaviour will sooner or later be a cause of unhappiness and/or failure. On the same basis, a good manager will ensure that manpower, money and machines are in sync and are working in harmony on the foundation of sound values.

A good kite flier tries to select the right kite, based on the conditions of the area. The good executive selects his personnel by matching their skills with the organization's needs and objectives. The flier must also choose the right string to hold and guide the kite. If the string is too heavy, it creates a 'pot belly drag' on the kite; while if it is too light, it may not be tough enough against a strong wind. Such a string may break and the kite may be lost. Similarly, a manager should have the right kind of policies and controls that motivate people and yet pre-empt undue risk.

The kite flier maneuvers the kite with gentle tugs and measured releases of string. Similarly, the manager gives positive strokes and 'gives a long rope' to his people to encourage high performance. A good manager or leader will avoid jerking his people around unnecessarily. More importantly, a real leader has confidence in his people and gives them more empowerment, so that their performance may soar. When there is a slight tear in the kite, the kite flier repairs it quickly before the hole becomes too big and the kite becomes worthless. Likewise, a good supervisor tries to correct problems before they become too big or out of control or hurt morale.

Some countries have annual kite flying festivals which bring out creativity and the competitive spirit of people. They also bring entertainment and joy to those who come to watch. However, if the designers spend too much time on beauty, the kite may lose out on aerodynamics and not fly so well. Similarly, a good executive knows that while packaging is important, it is the quality of contents that is vital for winning the customer and beating the competition.

Isn't it amazing what one can learn from a small piece of stretched paper or cloth, that is being made to dance in the sky by enthusiastic youths on the ground?

38

SUCCESS AND MORALITY

"If you have a good reputation,
if you are right more often than you're wrong,
if your children respect you,
if your grandchildren are glad to see you,
if your friends can rely on you and
you can count on them in times of trouble,
if you can face your God and
say 'I have done my best',
then you are a success."

Ann Landers
(Advice Columnist)

On my father's 75th birthday, one of his best friends sent him a card which included the above definition of success.

You would note that power and money do not feature in this real principle based definition. This quote does not tell me that powerful and/or rich people cannot be successful. It tells me that for rich and powerful people to be truly successful, they cannot ignore Ms. Landers' advice which reminds us of good values.

Let us look at success from another angle, by quoting an enormously wealthy person – Warren Buffet[*], who clarifies very eloquently the difference between success and happiness.

---

[*] From a joint interview with Bill Gates, as reported in Fortune Magazine. Warren Buffet wins our respect as a highly successful investor with a human touch.

"Success is getting what you want;
Happiness is wanting what you get."

We can grasp his hint that both success and happiness are needed to be a more complete human being. Putting it in another way, happy people are successful people, at least by their own definition.

I would also like to quote Deepak Chopra, who has been highly successful in presenting ancient spiritual concepts to help modern society. His books have sold millions of copies and he has a tremendous following in many countries.

"Success in life could be defined as continued expansion of
happiness and progressive realization of worthy goals."

This tells us that financial wealth or power is not necessary for success. On the other hand, these attributes are not excluded from success.

On November 30th, 1966, the eve of starting my first job at Grindlay's Bank, my whole family was very excited. Having finished our customary swim at the century-old Madras Gymkhana Club, we were driving back home. My father said to me, "*Beta* (son), in the banking profession, there will be many temptations to make money the wrong way. Don't ever compromise your integrity. You will never be sorry for being honest."

In my school days, I once read a saying "*A touch of conscience is a glimpse of God.*" Being a firm believer in free enterprise, I wish we could find ways of profiting without harming or cheating people or violating laws and regulations. If a certain statute or rule is unfair or not in the general public interest, we should use democratic means to seek change instead of paying somebody to bend the rules for our selfish reasons. Otherwise, we are only perpetuating the disease.

I can also recall a few scenes from my younger days: A kid or adult has done something ethically wrong. The parent, teacher or superior officer reprimands the wrong-doer and sometimes adds, "Didn't you know that you could get caught for this?!" This line sends a wrong signal that the crime is in getting caught, rather than the actual incorrect/immoral behavior.

As I have grown older and, hopefully a little more experienced, I have come to believe that success has to be much more than position, power and money. Otherwise, people like Nelson Mandela, Mahatma Gandhi, Mother Teresa, Billy Graham, Hellen Keller and Swami Vivekananda, cannot be called successful people. Their true source of power is/was their moral authority. They pursue/pursued real ideals or principles. They 'fight'/'fought' for noble goals.

In this connection, let us consider two questions, when a 'successful' or popular CEO retires:

a) Is he fondly remembered for earning a multimillion dollar bonus, or for boosting stockholder value or down-sizing the company?

or

b) Is he cherished for 'non-financial' achievements like (i) his courage of conviction which helped to transform the culture of the company into a **caring and learning organization** or (ii) for (profitably) re-aligning the priorities of the institution whereby it became one of the great pillars of its community or (iii) dramatically improved industrial relations in a unionized industry on a durable basis, because he led by example, and built a great company which is widely respected?

I think that most people will agree that the outgoing CEO will be positively remembered for the second category of achievements, which reflect more character or spiritual issues rather than short-term gains. To illustrate corporate examples, I would choose Andrew Carnegie, the father of American steel industry and a genuine philanthropist and Thomas Watson, Jr. who made IBM the most admired corporation in the 1970s-1980s for many good reasons (including enviable profits).

I feel that a book on gaining power with the help of inspired people and time-honoured principles can hardly be complete without a chapter on morality which comes close to spirituality. I hasten to assure my readers that this chapter is not intended to preach any religion in particular.

While I was writing the chapter titled "The Importance of Stakeholders", I thought mainly about how to balance the conflicting needs and priorities of different kinds of people and institutions that have certain expectations or rights vis-à-vis the concerned organization.

Mark Twain once said: "*It is curious that physical courage should be so common in the world and moral courage so rare.*" I get the feeling that both forms of courage, especially the moral variety, have become even rarer in these times of self-centeredness.

As I observe developments at a personal level, corporate level or government level, I feel that we often fall into tempting traps for quick profits or shortcuts to achieve our goals or gain rewards, recognition, etc.

Bribery and corruption have two sides – the giver of the bribe who receives the favour and the receiver of the 'grease money' who grants the favour. Very often the briber complains that the government officer is very corrupt because he expects bribes. The briber does not realize that he could well be the corrupter because it is he who wants special privileges. In any event, it takes two to tango.

The Indian Civil Service (ICS followed by IAS) and Indian Police generally had high ethical standards up to the mid 1960s while Jawahalal Nehru was still the Prime Minister.

After Nehru, there was a visible moral decline in the country. Real incomes began to fall and income taxes started to rise to absurd levels. Salaries of Government officers became less and less attractive and the dignity of dedicated officials was diminished by corrupt politicians. In a period of just 15 years, the quality of the government officers had changed so that bribery became the rule rather than the exception. No longer did decent people choose a career in civil or public service for the noble cause or dignity of the position. Since the 1970s, these positions are deemed as 'tickets' or 'licenses' for unprincipled people to make 'hush-money'. Cynical as it may sound, so many taxes and surcharges and duties were increased or introduced so that such bureaucrats could find more areas to 'milk the public'. Similarly, investment rules were tightened so much that impatient businessmen would have to pay 'under-the-table' fees to smoothen or expedite the approval process.

On the other hand, it was sad to see how the minority of honest and sincere officers were frequently harassed or side-lined. Had there been an element of conscience or spirituality, things would not have been so bad.

So far, I have written about businesses that themselves are legitimate; the problem being how entrepreneurs or top executives (have to) compromise ethics to expedite a license or gain an unfair advantage.

Now, let's take a look at some blue chip and prestigious companies whose core business is questionable – tobacco products. These giants have done an outstanding job in developing and marketing brands like Marlboro, Benson & Hedges, Camel, Dunhill, etc. It was bad enough to make people think that their lifestyles and personalities were incomplete if they did not smoke. Not (yet) satisfied, they began to target teenagers through clever advertising. Worst of all, top honchos of cigarette companies strongly argued that smoking was not addictive, while they purposely added extra nicotine to make it even more difficult for 'addicted' smokers to give up the killer-habit.

Yes, the smoker is also to blame because he/she made the (unfortunate) choice; but the bulk of the blame falls squarely on the producers and marketers of this scourge of humanity. The cigarette lobbies promoted by huge companies like Phillip Morris, BAT, RJR, JTC and so on, are not helping the situation.

Some of these companies had seen the handwriting on the wall and tried to decrease their dependence on tobacco products by diversifying into foods, hotels, financial services, etc. However, they are still trying to push more cigarettes in less conscious markets like Russia and China. I believe that if smoking is not good for the American and British public, how can it be acceptable in these new 'growth markets'?

Perhaps, I am speaking like an idealist when I say that there should be a concrete time-bound plan for controlling and gradually phasing out this business – from plantation to manufacturing to marketing.

Naturally, incentives should be given to reduce the cost and pain to change to other crops and industries. There needs to be a holistic approach in which regulators, producers and consumers can help each other out of this industry which is causing more sickness and deaths than any other single economic activity. This has to be done in a way that does not boost illegal tobacco farming, smuggling and the like. These tobacco companies have big pockets and by now have sufficient experience in other consumer products so they can gradually modify their production and packing equipment to other healthy applications, which, in fact, are also growth areas because people are becoming more health conscious.

Again, this change requires a strong measure of conscience and morality. The top brass should be able to say: "We want to make more money for our shareholders, but we shall not include unethical or harmful products or practices to meet our goals."

Now, let's talk about the defense industry segment. It is said that, especially since the late 19th century, pioneers in modern weapons and high explosives would 'trigger' wars between countries in order to boost their own sales. At least Alfred Nobel sought atonement by instituting his Academy which, inter alia, awards the Nobel Peace Prize. We, with great delight, note that some defense equipment manufacturers apply defense technology and machinery for domestic appliances, cars, etc. in quite a few countries. It is hoped that this trend towards peaceful applications accelerates and widens.

There is no major shortage of entrepreneurs and executives who pray to God or believe in the Divine. The real problem is that many people pray on the off-business stage, but when they are back in their offices, profit and growth dominate their thoughts and actions. Again, there is nothing wrong in earning superior profits and growing market share. The question is whether such goals are achieved by clean and green products and processes, as well as clean means. In other words, our prayers, if any, regarding our corporate or career goals, should ask Him for inspiration and guidance to be successful in the proper, ethical way. We should not have to pray just to overcome guilt.

I believe that it is very worthwhile quoting the concluding paragraph of Pope John Paul II's speech titled **"The Moral Structure of Freedom"** to the United Nation General Assembly in October 1995:

"We must not be afraid of the future. We must not be afraid of man. It is no accident that we are here. Each and every human person has been created in the 'image and likeness' of the One who is the origin of all that is. We have within us the capacities for wisdom and virtue. With these gifts, and with the help of God's grace, we can build in the next century and the next millennium a civilization worthy of the human person, a true culture of freedom. We can and must do so! And in doing so, we shall see that the tears of this century have prepared the ground for a new springtime of the human spirit."

At this stage I would like to add a very meaningful analysis made by **Juan Mascaró** in the Introduction to his translation of the **Bhagvad Gita**. Mascaró tells us that the **essence of our 'Being', our 'Self' is joy, ANANDA**. He quotes **Benedict de Spinoza** (1632-1677) on virtue: "*Blessedness is not a reward of virtue; it is virtue in itself. We do not find joy in virtue because we control our lusts: but, contrariwise, because we find joy in virtue, we are able to control our lusts.*" (I must admit that I read these lines a few times to fully grasp their meaning.)

Conclusion:

My humble advice to people in power and future leaders, who would wield power: Please count your blessings and be grateful to the **PEOPLE** who helped you gain your **POWER**; use this power with good **PRINCIPLES**. Otherwise, the people will take back the power they gave you.

39

LEARNING FROM FLOWERS

"Flowers set a fine example for mankind"

I frequently do a few stretching exercises in the morning in our back garden, which has beautiful orchids, bougainvillea, wild roses and a pond with gold fish resting or darting between water lilies and lotuses. The other morning, when I returned inside the house and began to shave (my second and final shave with that, otherwise, nice **Gillette Sensor Excel**), my mind suddenly flashed back to my childhood, remembering my infatuation with flowers, and (now) feeling grateful for flowers in our lives.

From my very early days, I enjoyed flowers in a very special way. I was intrigued by their different and radiant colours, and their delicate, but unique fragrances. In my early botany classes (called Nature Study in those days), I enjoyed bringing home seeds, sowing them, nurturing them and patiently observing the phenomena of germination to flowering. I learnt that the flower's pistil (frequently red-tipped) was 'designed' to be somewhat aloof from the yellow pollen carrying stamens, to avoid self-pollination, because self-pollination lowered the quality of the next generation of seeds. I was taught about the process of fertilization, starting from the contact of the pollen with the head of the pistil. The curious little *cat* in me (before my upper lip had even a hint of whiskers) would also bring home caterpillars and tadpoles to observe and document the miracle of metamorphosis to beautiful butterflies and Kermit's cousins, respectively. But my curiosity must have stopped at the 'eighth' experiment, otherwise somebody else would be writing this book! (Please pardon this writer's digression. I don't want to reach the stage of 'readers don't digest', and had better return to the floral theme.)

I also observed that virtually people of every race, religion or income level appreciated flowers. I noticed flowers being used for such a variety of occasions, literally from birth to burial or cremation.

We realize that other than providing beauty and pleasant smells, flowers have many other functions. The extracts of flowers have tremendous medicinal qualities. There is a great revival of aromatherapy, based on floral essential oils (of which I too am a user). I'm sure that there are many useful attributes of so many flowers in our homes, parks, nurseries and forests that our scientists have yet to discover.

By now, you're probably wondering what this chapter has to do with the main theme of this book.

There is great significance attached to the lotus, the holy flower of the Hindus and Buddhists. The lotus has its roots in muddy waters but the flower is clean and softly radiant, untainted by the murky water that sustains it. The lotus is the sign of wisdom, purity and dignity.

Roses and violets are flowers given by men to their sweethearts. Carnations often adorn the lapels of men's jackets during weddings.

Flowers are really special. No wonder, girls are often christened after noble flowers like: Rose, Lily, Violet, Jasmine, Padma (Lotus in Hindi/Sanskrit).

A couple of decades ago, my mother in her usual modest and subtle way, said to me that an INSAN's (Hindi for human's) life should be like the flower. The flower, she said, represents beauty and purity. The flower gives us fragrance to lift our spirits when we are feeling down, or to calm us down when tempers are high.

Coming back to my floral thoughts, while lathering my stubble-filled face, in front of the bathroom mirror, I began to think further about learning from flowers and I began to see and sniff more and more about what could be learned from these gifts from God. By the time, I finished my shave (and blunted my Sensor Excel), I got the following answers:

- Like flowers, we should add beauty to our families and relationships.
- Like flowers, we should be pure in our hearts.
- Like flowers open their bosoms to all insects, we should open ours to all beings.
- Like flowers, we should find happiness in making others happy.
- Like flowers give us sweet nectar and fragrance, we should sweeten the lives of others, particularly the less fortunate.
- Like flowers, we should not complain or offend others.
- Like flowers, we should develop and nurture better 'seedlings'. (In fact, when flowers wither, they help to form compost to provide excellent natural nutrients to the following generations.)
- Like flowers, when our missions have been accomplished, we should learn to retire gracefully, without looking back and craving for our bygone youthful beauty and power.

Therefore, we have to admit that flowers set a fine example for mankind.

I would again like to switch from prose to poetry by:

A TRIBUTE TO FLOWERS

Have you thought, 'why are there flowers?'
They are God's creations with varied powers.
The flower is a stage between seed and fruit.
That's often as important as the plants tap root.

The flower is flora's crucial reproductive organ,
Its nectar and scent makes bees transfer pollen.
The pollen kiss to the pistil starts fertilization.
This love affair keeps up our plant population.

Flowers, indeed have quite short lives,
Flowers, still touch all facets of our lives.
Flowers are presented for the newborn's glory,
Flowers are offered in every love story.

Flowers become bouquets for your dear girl friend,
Flowers keep you company till your very end.
Flowers become garlands to honour the lion-hearted,
Flowers become wreaths for the soul that's departed.

Flowers are squeezed for their exciting fragrance,
Flowers are crushed for their medicinal essence.
Flowers are given to show true friendship,
Flowers are offered in places of worship.

Flowers enrich our lives very selflessly,
Flowers kill our sorrow and increase our glee.
Flowers! Oh Flowers! You earned a great repute,
Flowers! Oh Flowers! Please accept my tribute.

40

PATIENCE,
BUT NOT COMPLACENCE

"Patience surpasses learning"
(Proverb)
vs
"Procrastination is the thief of time"
Edward Young

From the very earliest days, mankind's ancestors or forerunners - Homo-Erectus, Neanderthal, Cro-Magnon or whatever - have looked enviously at birds in the sky and wished that they too could fly. There have been several romantic and tragic sagas of brave inventors and pioneers who have tried to fly. It was not until 1903 that this dream was actually realized through the first successful **'heavier than air, motorized flying machine'** created by the Wright brothers. Just imagine, it took thousands upon thousands of years before man could develop the first successful airplane.

Then, in a span of a mere 63 years from that biplane, NASA developed the rocket to carry Neil Armstrong to the moon for his first *"small step for man and gigantic step for mankind"*.

This is only one of innumerable examples of how, after the first invention, which takes many, many generations of patience and endurance, the subsequent advancements take place in a dramatically compressed time frame. We have reached a stage when many things have become **'instant'**, including our expectations.

295

We have unwittingly entered the era of **'instant gratification'** because of the relative ease with which we can get things, especially in the economically prosperous countries. In the early 1950s, very few homes had TVs, which were considered a luxury in those days. Today, nearly every kid wants and gets a personal TV, in those societies. I got my first Philips compact cassette tape recorder at the age of twenty-three, while our daughter got her first (and better model) at the age of five. I made my first overseas trip in my twenty-third year, while our son had his first in his sixth month!

Whichever way we look at it, things are happening, changing and often improving at a tremendous clip. Similarly, things can also deteriorate equally quickly. We are participants and sometimes victims of the 'instant syndrome'.

People's expectations are getting higher and higher:

- Many of us are hooked on instant tea and coffee. Instant foods are becoming more and more popular.
- Some expectant mothers wish "the baby would just hurry and come out!" Fortunately, they also know the risk associated with premature babies, and do not act on the wish.
- The boss expects **'instant results'** from his subordinates. This can cause under-preparedness and stress, leading to quality problems, assigning blame … more stress and drop in employee morale.
- The bright up-start who is already on a fast-track, wants an 'extra' **instant reward** because he/she did something good. Excess or premature rewards can actually spoil the high potential candidates and hurt staff morale.
- The shareholder, especially if he/she is of the Wall Street mentality, wishes for **instant returns**. This makes the executives focus on quarterly performance and give little attention to long-term progress and vitality.

- As the stakes are getting higher and higher in the world of sports, many athletes are tempted to use harmful performance enhancement steroids and drugs. Doctors on the opposing side are rightfully warning us of the danger of this abuse, which is triggered by the desire of **instant glory**, and often, **instant wealth**.
- When I was a kid, we used to, in a tentative tone say, "Mummy, please may I have this?" Today's kids demand, "Mom, I want this **now!**"

In many aspects, we are fortunate to be alive during this age of ever increasing conveniences. Thanks to the global reach of television through satellite systems, and the more recent Internet phenomenon, the pace of change (good or bad) will only accelerate.

How do we people, who want to share in the benefit of rapid change, and yet not get victimized by the pressures that high speeds bring along, behave? I believe that some 'old' values are still valid here. We should be patient in a positive way, whether we are boss or high potential employee or shareholder. My advice to myself and especially new members of the company, is that while we wish to improve the culture of the enterprise, we have to be patient but not complacent. We have to keep pushing softly with encouragement and flexibility, based on each situation. There are no ready-made quick fixes and shortcuts.

I keep reminding myself that patience must not be confused with complacence. We have to 'blend' our patience with persistence and perseverance. If a door is shut on our change idea, we should analyze "why". If we need to refine it, to make it more palatable or applicable, we have to do so, and go back again. We learn to thank people for their positive criticism and avoid confrontations.

Positive patience gives us more staying power and more endurance, which are vital in a long-term game, especially managing or participating in culture change. We cannot force change, but we cannot afford to lose heart and give up. We have to be the catalysts and help usher change. If we thrust it down their throats, they will choke and vomit it back at us and we get dirty all over! (Ugh!!)

Whatever the plan, be sure that after proper analysis, your goals and strategies are aligned. Involve a good and broad representation of the organization in finalizing the plan to ensure applicability and 'buy-in'. Then implement with enthusiasm, but be prepared for hurdles, and even, roadblocks. If we have a healthy dose of patience we have more scope to understand, creatively fine tune or seek help. We have to give the other party the opportunity to be understood. On the other hand, if we show frustration, tempers will rise and a 'professional issue' needlessly becomes a 'personal issue' – everybody, including the organization, loses. Therefore, let us aim for win-win and rejoice together, and enjoy that cordial feeling.

On the other side of the coin, the smart leader will inject a 'measured dose' of impatience from time-to-time to preempt complacency. At the same time, he/she will pro-actively show understanding regarding difficulties and offer tangible support.

It is equally important for the subordinate not to automatically see the supervisor's patience as a sign of weakness.

Some people may think that I am giving too much importance to patience in this age of discontinuity where quick innovations are key to wealth creation. No doubt, speed is becoming more and more important with surging competition. We may have a great new product but *time to market* is also an important success factor. Compressing the time taken from concept to consumer saves development costs and takes the opposition by surprise. Again, if the boss gives over-emphasis to speed, his projects will lose coordination or not get timely input from auxiliary units - resulting in frustration, blaming each other, and consequent delays. So, if we are not careful to moderate our speed to get the necessary 'buy-in' of all the key players, progress will stop intermittently and the speed objectives will be undermined.

Here's a railroad analogy: A railroad company wishes to introduce a train that can zoom at 300 MPH in order to win back regional business from airlines. If there is too much pressure on speedy implementation, there may not be enough time to check or upgrade all the tracks, signals and fail-safe systems. This could result in disaster.

Let's take a real and recent example: The inauguration date of the huge, new Hong Kong Airport was set to coincide with the first anniversary of the **'handing over'** to China and the related Clinton visit. Ceremonial and prestige factors were forced over operational issues. Result: Delayed flights, lost baggage and cargo, angry passengers, and loss of face, and more expense. (Things are fine now.)

Message:
There is a burning need for real co-operation with a strong but realistic sense of urgency.

41

CORPORATE PRAYER

"Prayer works when followed by sincere thought and work"

I had started the Introduction with a little prayer that I may have fun and learn while writing this book.

Now, I can see the finish line of this journey. I cannot think of a better way to than to reach the end by encapsulating the essence of this effort in the form of a short corporate prayer.

Dear God:

Help us cherish the right business principles and values.

Help us grow profitability, with adequate policies and systems to protect our assets and gains.

Help us develop excellent human resource policies and practices so that we are able to attract the best people and keep them happily motivated, which would build spontaneous mutual loyalty.

Help us beat our competition through excellence and fair play, and earn their respect.

Help us to be alert and adaptable to meet emerging opportunities and challenges, without compromising our principles and values.

Help us say 'no' if a tempting opportunity violates our beliefs or the laws of the land.

Help us reward our shareholders for trusting us with their money.

Help us protect and improve our environment for the welfare of all inhabitants and future generations.

Help us genuinely support the weaker sections of our societies, not just indulge in superficial public relations.

Help us use our economic power for the benefit of <u>all</u> stakeholders.

We realize, dear God, that prayer works only when it is followed by sincere thought and work.

In other words, dear God, help us become the kind of company that would make You smile with pride.

Individuals Mentioned/Quoted

Aquino, Benigno 'Ninoy'

Aquino, Cory

Artko, David

Autry, James A.

Bhutto, Benazir

Branson, Richard

Bucham, John

Buffet, Warren

Caesar, Augustus

Carnegie, Andrew

Castle, Barbara

Castro, Fidel

Chopra, Deepak

Churchill, Winston

Clinton, Bill

Copperfield, David

Covey, Stephen

Cromwell, Oliver

Cunningham, George

Dell, Michael

Dev, Kapil

Drucker, Peter

Dunlap, Al

Eisenhower, Dwight

Emerson, Ralph W.

Ford, Henry

Franklin, Benjamin

Fulghum, Robert

Gandhi, Indira

Gandhi, MK (Mahatma)

Gandhi, Priyanka

Gandhi, Sonia

Gates, Bill

Gianini, AP

Gianini, Mario

Gopal, TS

Groove, Andy

Gupta, Rajat

Habibie, BJ

Handy, Charles

Heraclitus

Hingis, Martina

Hope, Bob

Hussein, Saddam

Ibrahim, Anwar

Jacob, K. Kuruvila

Jayalalitha

John-Paul II, Pope

Jones, Reginald

Karunanidhi

Kilam, Suresh

Koo, Bon-Moo

Kumaratunga, Chandrika

Landers, Ann

Leonidas

Mascaró, Juan

Mahathir

Mandela, Nelson

Marcos, Ferdinand

Marcos, Imelda

McGinnis, Mack

McGregor, Douglas

Menezes, Victor

Mitchell, Stephen

Moody, Dwight L.

Murthy, Narayan

Nadar, Shiv

Nehru, Jawaharlal

Nelson, Admiral

Nilo, Gus

Njoto, Sukrisno

Pawitra, Teddy

Peron, Eva

Pitt, William

Pitt, The Younger

Powell, Colin

Ramachandran, M.G.

Ramos, Fidel

Reagan, Ronald

Reed, John

Rockefeller, John D.

Sarwal, Tej

Shakespeare, William

Simpson, Alan

Sitaram, K. V.

Smith, Charles F.

Soeharto

Spinoza, Benedict de

Swift, Jonathan

Talwar, Rana

Tan, Siauw Liang

Teresa, Mother

Tee, Hendrik

Thatcher, Margaret

Titze, Michael

Twain, Mark

Vajpayee, Atal Behari

Vivekananda, (Swami)

Watson, Thomas, Jr.

Welch, Jack

Widjaja, Eka Cipta

Widjaja, Franky

Widjaja, Indra

Widjaja, Muktar

Widjaja, Sukmawati

Wijaya, Teguh Ganda

Williams, Robin

Companies Mentioned

ABB - Asea Brown Boveri

Acer Computer

American Home Products

Aramco

Au Bon Pain

Bank of America

Birlas

Body Shop

Burger King

Caltex

Canon

Carrefour

Channel

Daimler-Chrysler

Danone

Delice de France

Dell Computer

Dresser Industries

EDS - Electronic Data Systems

Exxon/Esso/MOBIL

General Electric (GE)

GIL

Grindlays Bank, ANZ

HCL/NIIT

HDFC Bank

Henkel

Hermés

Infosys

Intel

Kentucky Fried Chicken

Levi Strauss

LG Group

L'oreal

Marubeni

Matsushita

McDonalds

McKinsey & Co.

Microsoft

Mitsubishi

Mitsui

Modis

Monsanto

Motorola

Nirulas

Nissho Iwai

Nordstrom

Novartis

Online America

Pinault Printemps Redoute

Procter & Gamble

Promodés

Reader's Digest

Shell

Sinar Mas Group

Singapore Airlines

Singapore Technologies

Singhanias

Southwest Airlines

Standard Chartered Bank

Standard Oil Co.

Sumitomo

Thapars

Toyota Motor Co.

Travellers

Unilever

Virgin Group

Walt Disney

Yahoo